THE BEST OF OUR BESTSELLERS

THE ESSENTIAL

Company's Coming

Volume 2

CHICKEN

Jean Paré

www.companyscoming.com

visit our website

The Essential Company's Coming Volume 2: Chicken

First Printing January 2014

Library and Archives Canada Cataloguing in Publication
Paré, Jean, author
The essential Company's Coming chicken / Jean Paré.

(Essential series)
Includes index.
ISBN 978-1-927126-62-2 (bound)

1. Cooking (Chicken). 2. Cookbooks. I. Title. II. Series:
Paré, Jean, date. Essential series.

TX750.5.C45P367 2014   641.6'65   C2013-904153-2

Published by
Company's Coming Publishing Limited
2311 – 96 Street
Edmonton, Alberta, Canada T6N 1G3
Tel: 780-450-6223   Fax: 780-450-1857
www.companyscoming.com

Company's Coming is a registered trademark owned by Company's Coming Publishing Limited

We acknowledge the financial support of the Government of Canada through the Canada Book Fund for our publishing activities.

Printed in China

PC: 21

Table of Contents

Appetizers

Salads

Soups & Stews

Sandwiches

Grilled Greats

Stovetop Stunners

Oven Ovations

Slow Cooker
Sensations

The Company's Coming Story

Jean Paré (pronounced "jeen PAIR-ee") grew up understanding that the combination of family, friends and home cooking is the best recipe for a good life. From her mother, she learned to appreciate good cooking, while her father praised even her earliest attempts in the kitchen. When Jean left home, she took with her a love of cooking, many family recipes and an intriguing desire to read cookbooks as if they were novels!

When her four children had all reached school age, Jean volunteered to cater the 50th anniversary celebration of the Vermilion School of Agriculture, now Lakeland College, in Alberta, Canada. Working out of her home, Jean prepared a dinner for more than 1,000 people, launching a flourishing catering operation that continued for over 18 years. During that time, she had countless opportunities to test new ideas with immediate feedback—resulting in empty plates and contented customers! Whether preparing cocktail sandwiches for a house party or serving a hot meal for 1,500 people, Jean Paré earned a reputation for great food, courteous service and reasonable prices.

> *"Never share a recipe you wouldn't use yourself."*

As requests for her recipes increased, Jean was often asked the question, "Why don't you write a cookbook?" Jean responded by teaming up with her son, Grant Lovig, in the fall of 1980 to form Company's Coming Publishing Limited. The publication of *150 Delicious Squares* on April 14, 1981 marked the debut of what would soon become one of the world's most popular cookbook series.

The company has grown since those early days when Jean worked from a spare bedroom in her home. Nowadays every Company's Coming recipe is *kitchen-tested* before it is approved for publication.

Company's Coming cookbooks are distributed in Canada, the United States, Australia and other world markets. Bestsellers many times over in English, Company's Coming cookbooks have also been published in French and Spanish.

Familiar and trusted in home kitchens around the world, Company's Coming cookbooks are offered in a variety of formats. Highly regarded as kitchen workbooks, the softcover Original Series, with its lay-flat plastic comb binding, is still a favourite among readers.

Jean Paré's approach to cooking has always called for *quick and easy recipes* using *everyday ingredients*. That view has served her well. The recipient of many awards, including the Queen Elizabeth Golden Jubilee Medal, Jean was appointed Member of the Order of Canada, her country's highest lifetime achievement honour.

Jean continues to share what she calls The Golden Rule of Cooking: *Never share a recipe you wouldn't use yourself.* It's an approach that has worked—*millions of times over!*

Foreword

It seems we can't get enough chicken. In the last 30 years, chicken consumption in Canada has almost doubled. Chicken entrees now take up a great deal of real estate on restaurant and fast-food menus that were once dominated by beef, and there seems to be an endless assortment of chicken options available in the freezer section of supermarkets. It's easy to see why this humble little bird has become so popular.

For one, chicken is versatile. You can dress it up for company or dress it down for fast family meals. You can choose between dark or white meat, or cook it whole, ground or in separate pieces—and it's equally delicious served hot or cold.

It is also economical. Whole birds and breasts may a little more costly, but chicken thighs are one of the most inexpensive meats you can buy.

Perhaps the most significant reason for the rising popularity of chicken, however, is the health benefits that come with choosing chicken over red meat. Chicken is a low fat meat, and almost half of the fat it contains is the heart healthy mono unsaturated variety. It is low in saturated fat and does not contain any of the unhealthy trans fats that can be found in beef and lamb. It is also a good source of iron, B vitamins, selenium and zinc.

The environmentally conscious consumer chooses chicken because it has less of a carbon footprint than the other popular meats—chickens produce no methane, a known greenhouse gas, and less manure that can seep into the groundwater and streams. They also require less feed and smaller tracts of land than cows, sheep or pigs.

In honour of chicken's rise in popularity, we've scoured our extensive recipe library for our favourite chicken recipes, and we've assembled them in this handy book just for you.

We've included updates of old favourites, such as Chicken Sloppy Joes and Sunday Fried Chicken as well as more contemporary flavour combinations such as our fragrant Coconut Curry Rice Casserole or savoury Chicken Aztec (you've gotta love a recipe that sneaks in a little dark chocolate!).

Whatever type of chicken recipe you are looking for, whether an appetizer, soup, salad, sandwich or entree, from the barbecue to the slow cooker, we've got you covered. Peruse these pages to see the best of the best chicken recipes we've created!

Jean Paré

Nutrition Information Guidelines

Each recipe is analyzed using the most current versions of the Canadian Nutrient File from Health Canada, and the United States Department of Agriculture (USDA) Nutrient Database for Standard Reference.

- If more than one ingredient is listed (such as "butter or hard margarine"), or if a range is given (1 – 2 tsp., 5 – 10 mL), only the first ingredient or first amount is analyzed.
- For meat, poultry and fish, the recommended serving size per person is 4 oz. (113 g) uncooked weight (without bone), which is 2 – 3 oz. (57 – 85 g) cooked weight (without bone)—approximately the size of a deck of playing cards.
- Milk used is 1% M.F. (milk fat), unless otherwise stated.
- Cooking oil used is canola oil, unless otherwise stated.
- Ingredients indicating "sprinkle," "optional" or "for garnish" are not included in the nutrition information.
- The fat in recipes and combination foods can vary greatly depending upon the sources and types of fats used in each specific ingredient. For these reasons, the amount of saturated, monounsaturated and polyunsaturated fats may not add up to the total fat content.

Introduction

Chicken is a versatile, healthy and nutritious meal option that can be incorporated into everything from snacks and soups to formal dinners for entertaining. It is easy to cook with and can be used in a large variety of dishes that can be sweet and sour, savoury or simple in flavour. It is also reasonably priced and widely available.

Buying Chicken

These days you can buy organic chicken, free-range chicken or factory-raised chicken. Go for organic, whenever possible. Not only are they tastier, they also do not have the levels of antibiotics or hormones that have been found in factory-raised chicken. Also, chemical fertilizers and pesticides are not used in the production of organic chicken, so by choosing organic, you'll be helping to keep some of those nasty contaminants out of our rivers and groundwater. Plus, you'll have the added peace of mind knowing that the birds were raised humanely.

All organic chicken is free-range, but not all free-range chicken is organic. Free-range simply means that the chickens have access to the outdoors; the label does not dictate what type of feed the birds are given or whether or not antibiotics, fertilizers or pesticides are used.

Whole chickens are sold based on their size. A broiler or fryer is a young chicken weighing 1.5 to 3.86 lbs (700 g to 1.75 g). A roaster weighs more than 3.86 lbs (1.75 g). A stewing hen is an older hen of about 5.5 lbs (2.5 kg) and is best suited for moist cooking methods such as braising and stewing.

Whether you buy the whole bird or pieces, make sure the package is cold, tightly wrapped and has no holes or tears in the covering plastic. Check the best-before date on the label. Pick up the chicken as the last item before going through the check-out, and get it home within two hours (one hour if it is hot outside). Leave the packages of chicken in the supermarket bags so they don't leak onto your other groceries.

Chicken Storage

Once home, put the chicken in the fridge or freeze immediately. If you refrigerate it, use whole chicken and parts within two days; cook ground chicken within 24 hours.

Never defrost frozen chicken at room temperature. Place it in the refrigerator on a tray (allow 5 hours per pound; 10 hours per kg) or in cold water, changing the water every 30 minutes (allow 1 hour per pound; 2 hours per kg). Frozen chicken pieces can also be defrosted in the microwave.

Cutting up a Whole Chicken

You can buy a whole chicken, or you can buy the chicken already cut into breasts, thighs, wings, etc. A whole bird is more economical, and it is not difficult to cut it up into eight pieces (two wings, two thighs, two drumsticks and two breasts). Videos showing the procedure are available on the Internet, but basically you start by making sure your hands and work surface are clean and your knife is sharp.

Cooking with Chicken

As with any foods, exercise caution when cooking with chicken. Don't wash it before cooking—you run the risk of spreading bacteria all over your sink and the surrounding area. Use paper towels not cloth when wiping up spills, and make sure your hands, work surfaces and utensils are washed with soap and hot water. Use a separate cutting board for chicken and for veggies, and never put cooked chicken back onto a plate that held the meat when it was raw.

Marinate chicken in the fridge, not at room temperature. Boil leftover marinade 5 to 7 minutes before basting. Do not re-use marinades. Baste cooked surfaces only, and don't use a brush that has touched raw meat.

If you are stuffing the bird, make sure stuffing is completely cool before inserting into the cavity, and stuff the bird just before cooking. Remember that the stuffing will expand while cooking, so stuff no more than 2/3 full. Leftover stuffing should be stored in a separate container than the chicken and should be refrigerated promptly.

Always cook poultry until done. Use an instant-read thermometer and insert into the thickest part of the meat, or, if the chicken is whole, into the thickest end of the breast near the wing. Cooking times vary depending on the type of chicken you are cooking (ground, chicken pieces or whole) and can range from 165°F (74°C) to 185°F (85°C), depending on the recipe.

If your recipe calls for chicken breast and you have chicken thighs, just remember that if it calls for bone-in (or boneless), use a bone-in (or boneless) substitute of the same weight. White meat cooks quicker than dark meat; adjust the cooking times accordingly.

Chicken is a considered a healthy, low fat meat but how healthy it is depends on how you prepare it. Removing the skin before you cook the meat can reduce the fat content of your recipe. Grilled, roasted or baked dishes are best, as long as you don't add loads of fats or unhealthy ingredients; fried chicken is perhaps not the healthiest option and should be eaten in moderation.

Leftovers

Refrigerate leftovers within two hours (one hour if the room is very warm). Remove meat from the carcass immediately after the first meal and store in shallow containers so it cools quickly. Boil the carcass within three days for stock, or freeze it for up to three months.

Asian Chicken Salad Rolls

Fresh-tasting salad rolls are made even better when they're stuffed with bean sprouts and cilantro. Served up with sweet chili sauce, these will disappear fast!

Rice vermicelli, broken up	2 1/2 oz.	70 g
Finely chopped cooked chicken (see Tip, page 58)	3/4 cup	175 mL
Shredded romaine lettuce, lightly packed	1/2 cup	125 mL
Grated carrot	1/3 cup	75 mL
Chopped fresh bean sprouts	2 tbsp.	30 mL
Chopped fresh cilantro (or parsley)	2 tbsp.	30 mL
Sesame oil (for flavour)	1 tsp.	5 mL
Salt	1/8 tsp.	0.5 mL
Rice paper rounds (6 inch, 15 cm, diameter)	16	16
Sweet chili sauce	1/2 cup	125 mL

Place vermicelli in small heatproof bowl. Cover with boiling water. Let stand for about 5 minutes until tender. Drain. Rinse with cold water. Drain well. Transfer to medium bowl.

Add next 7 ingredients. Toss.

Place 1 rice paper round in shallow bowl of hot water until just softened. Place on work surface. Spoon about 1/4 cup (60 mL) chicken mixture across centre. Fold sides over filling. Roll up tightly from bottom to enclose filling. Transfer to serving plate. Cover with damp towel to prevent drying. Repeat with remaining rice paper rounds and chicken mixture.

Serve with chili sauce. Makes 16 rolls.

1 roll with 1 1/2 tsp. (7 mL) chili sauce: 292 Calories; 4.0 g Total Fat (0.2 g Mono, 0.1 g Poly, 0.2 g Sat); 6 mg Cholesterol; 63 g Carbohydrate; trace Fibre; 5 g Protein; 787 mg Sodium

Chicken Spinach Spirals

Let the good times roll! These pretty white and green spirals are a terrific choice for a dinner party. For even more colour, use tomato or spinach tortillas. Serve hot or cold.

Cooking oil	1 tsp.	5 mL
Lean ground chicken	1/2 lb.	225 g
Finely chopped onion	2 tbsp.	30 mL
Salt	1/4 tsp.	1 mL
Pepper	1/8 tsp.	0.5 mL
Ground nutmeg	1/8 tsp.	0.5 mL
Box of frozen chopped spinach (10 oz., 300 g), thawed and squeezed dry	1	1
Cream cheese, softened and cut up	4 oz.	113 g
Finely chopped dried cranberries	1/4 cup	60 mL
Finely chopped pecans	2 tbsp.	30 mL
Flour tortillas (9 inch, 23 cm, diameter)	4	4

Heat cooking oil in medium frying pan on medium. Add next 5 ingredients. Scramble-fry for about 5 minutes until chicken is no longer pink and any liquid has evaporated.

Add spinach. Heat and stir until just combined. Transfer to medium bowl.

Add next 3 ingredients. Stir well.

Spread chicken mixture evenly on each tortilla, almost to edge. Roll up tightly, jelly-roll style. Trim ends. Cut each roll diagonally into 8 slices. Makes 32 slices.

1 slice: 64 Calories; 3.4 g Total Fat (0.6 g Mono, 0.3 g Poly, 1.0 g Sat); 4 mg Cholesterol; 6 g Carbohydrate; 1 g Fibre; 3 g Protein; 100 mg Sodium

Onion Apple Phyllo Rolls

These appies are chic and dashing, tantalizing and tempting.

Butter (or hard margarine)	2 tbsp.	30 mL
Chopped onion	2 cups	500 mL
Grated peeled cooking apple (such as McIntosh)	1 cup	250 mL
Lean ground chicken	1/2 lb.	225 g
Grated Gruyère cheese	2/3 cup	150 mL
Chopped fresh thyme (or 1/2 tsp., 2 mL, dried)	2 tsp.	10 mL
Salt	1/2 tsp.	2 mL
Pepper	1/4 tsp.	1 mL
Phyllo pastry sheets, thawed according to package directions	6	6
Butter (or hard margarine), melted	1/3 cup	75 mL

Melt first amount of butter in large frying pan on medium. Add onion. Cook for 5 to 10 minutes, stirring often, until softened.

Add apple. Stir. Reduce heat to medium-low. Cook for about 20 minutes, stirring occasionally, until onion is very soft and golden. Transfer to medium bowl. Cool for 10 minutes.

Add next 5 ingredients. Mix well.

Lay pastry sheets on top of each other. Cut sheets in half crosswise, making 12 sheets. Place 1 sheet on work surface with long side closest to you. Cover remaining sheets with damp towel to prevent drying.

Brush sheet with melted butter. Cut sheet in half crosswise. Place about 1 tbsp. (15 mL) chicken mixture on lowest end of 1 half of sheet, about 1 inch (2.5 cm) from edge. Fold bottom edge of sheet over chicken mixture. Fold in sides. Roll up from bottom to enclose filling. Place seam side down on greased baking sheet with sides. Cover with separate damp towel. Repeat with remaining pastry sheets and chicken mixture. Brush tops of rolls with any remaining butter. Bake in 400°F (200°C) oven for about 15 minutes until pastry is golden, chicken is no longer pink and internal temperature reaches 175°F (80°C). Makes 24 rolls.

1 roll: 82 Calories; 5.9 g Total Fat (1.3 g Mono, 0.2 g Poly, 2.7 g Sat); 12 mg Cholesterol; 4 g Carbohydrate; trace Fibre; 3 g Protein; 111 mg Sodium

Pictured on page 17.

Spicy Sausage Rolls

After they are baked, the rolls can be frozen for up to one month. Reheat from frozen in a 375°F (190°C) oven for about 12 minutes until heated through.

Canola oil	2 tsp.	10 mL
Chopped onion	2 cups	500 mL
Finely chopped fennel bulb (white part only)	2 cups	500 mL
Dried crushed chilies	2 tsp.	10 mL
Dried oregano	1 tsp.	5 mL
Dried thyme	1 tsp.	5 mL
Finely chopped peeled tart apple (such as Granny Smith)	1 1/2 cups	375 mL
Large flake rolled oats	1/3 cup	75 mL
Salt	1/2 tsp.	2 mL
Pepper	1/4 tsp.	1 mL
Lean ground chicken	1/2 lb.	225 g
Phyllo pastry sheets, thawed according to package directions	4	4

Heat canola oil in large frying pan on medium. Add next 5 ingredients. Cook for about 12 minutes, stirring often, until onion and fennel are softened.

Add apple. Stir. Cook for about 8 minutes until fennel is very soft. Remove from heat. Let stand for 20 minutes, stirring occasionally.

Combine next 3 ingredients in large bowl. Add apple mixture. Stir. Add chicken. Mix well.

Spray 1 pastry sheet with cooking spray. Place another one over top. Spray with cooking spray. Repeat, layering remaining pastry sheets and spraying with cooking spray. Cut pastry stack crosswise into 4 rectangles. Divide chicken mixture into 4 portions. Shape 1 portion on sheet of waxed paper into 13 inch (33 cm) long log. Transfer to long side of 1 pastry rectangle. Brush opposite long edge with water. Roll to enclose filling. Press seam against roll to seal. Repeat with remaining chicken mixture and pastry rectangles for a total of 4 rolls. Spray rolls with cooking spray. Cut each roll into 12 pieces. Using sharp knife, cut small slash across top of each piece. Arrange, seam side down, on greased baking sheet with sides. Bake in 400°F (200°C) oven for about 20 minutes until pastry is golden and chicken is no longer pink inside. Makes 48 rolls.

1 roll: 20 Calories; <1 Total Fat (trace Mono, trace Poly, trace Sat); <3 mg Cholesterol; 3 g Carbohydrate; trace Fibre; 1 g Protein; 40 mg Sodium

Spring Rolls

Loaded with chicken and vegetables, these spring rolls are surprisingly easy to make. Serve with your favourite peanut or chili sauce for dipping.

Sesame (or cooking) oil	2 tsp.	10 mL
Chopped fresh white mushrooms	1 1/2 cups	375 mL
Lean ground chicken	1/2 lb.	225 g
Granulated sugar	1 tsp.	5 mL
Ground ginger	1 tsp.	5 mL
Salt	1 tsp.	5 mL
Garlic powder	1/4 tsp.	1 mL
Chopped fresh bean sprouts	3 cups	750 mL
Grated carrots	1/2 cup	125 mL
Green onions, thinly sliced	4	4
Oyster sauce	2 tbsp.	30 mL
Dry sherry	1 tbsp.	15 mL
Spring roll wrappers	25	25

Cooking oil, for deep-frying

Heat sesame oil in large frying pan on medium. Add mushrooms and chicken. Scramble-fry for 5 to 10 minutes until chicken is no longer pink and liquid is evaporated.

Add next 4 ingredients.

Add next 3 ingredients. Stir-fry on medium-high for about 5 minutes until liquid is evaporated. Add oyster sauce and sherry. Stir-fry for 1 minute.

Spoon about 2 tbsp. (30 mL) chicken mixture near bottom right corner of each wrapper. Fold corner up and over filling. Fold in sides. Dampen edges with water. Roll to opposite corner and press to seal.

Deep-fry in batches, in hot (375°F, 190°C) cooking oil (see Tip, page 112) for about 5 minutes until golden. Transfer to paper towels to drain. Makes 25 spring rolls.

1 spring roll: 85 Calories; 1.9 g Total Fat (0.9 g Mono, 0.5 g Poly, 0.2 g Sat); 8 mg Cholesterol; 12 g Carbohydrate; 1 g Fibre; 4 g Protein; 336 mg Sodium

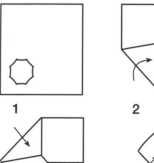

1

2

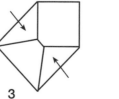

3

4

Crispy Jerk Chicken Rolls

Indulge your guests with the crisp, fried fare that is so enjoyed at get-togethers—just make yours a cut above the rest with the Jamaican flair of spicy jerk chicken.

Cooking oil	1 tsp.	5 mL
Chopped onion	1 cup	250 mL
Grated carrot	1 cup	250 mL
Chopped pickled jalapeño pepper	1 tbsp.	15 mL
Jerk paste	1 1/4 tsp.	6 mL
Garlic clove, minced	1	1
Ground allspice	1/8 tsp.	0.5 mL
Chopped cooked chicken	1 cup	250 mL
Plain yogurt	2 tbsp.	30 mL
Spring roll wrappers (6 inch, 15 cm, square)	8	8
Egg white (large)	1	1
Water	1 tbsp.	15 mL
Cooking oil	3 cups	750 mL

Heat cooking oil in frying pan on medium. Add next 6 ingredients and cook for about 10 minutes until onion is softened.

Stir in chicken and yogurt.

Arrange wrappers on work surface. Place about 1/4 cup (60 mL) chicken mixture near bottom right corner. Fold corners up and over filling, folding in sides. Dampen edges with a mixture of egg white and water. Roll to opposite corner and press to seal. Repeat.

Heat cooking oil in large frying pan on medium-high (see Tip, page 112). Shallow-fry 2 or 3 rolls at a time, turning often, until golden. Transfer to a plate lined with paper towel. Makes 8 rolls.

1 roll: 150 Calories; 5.1 g Total Fat (2.6 g Mono, 1.3 g Poly, 0.6 g Sat); 16 mg Cholesterol; 18 g Carbohydrate; 1 g Fibre; 9 g Protein; 227 mg Sodium

Potstickers

Do you fancy chicken and dumplings? How about chicken in dumplings?
As fun to make as they are to eat.

DIPPING SAUCE

Water	1/2 cup	125 mL
Rice vinegar	2 tbsp.	30 mL
Soy sauce	2 tbsp.	30 mL
Sweet chili sauce	2 tbsp.	30 mL
Sesame oil	1 tbsp.	15 mL

POTSTICKERS

Dried shiitake mushrooms	6	6
Boiling water	1 cup	250 mL
Lean ground chicken	1/2 lb.	225 g
Finely chopped green onion	1/3 cup	75 mL
Soy sauce	2 tbsp.	30 mL
Finely chopped fresh cilantro or parsley (or 1 1/2 tsp., 7 mL, dried)	2 tbsp.	30 mL
Finely grated ginger root (or 3/4 tsp., 4 mL, ground ginger)	1 tbsp.	15 mL
Garlic cloves, minced (or 1/2 tsp., 2 mL, powder)	2	2
Sesame oil	1 tsp.	5 mL
Dried crushed chilies	1/4 tsp.	1 mL
Water	1/4 cup	60 mL
Cornstarch	1 tbsp.	15 mL
Round dumpling wrappers	24	24
Cooking oil	3 tbsp.	45 mL
Water	3 tbsp.	45 mL

Dipping Sauce: Combine all 5 ingredients in small bowl. Stir. Makes about 1 cup (250 mL) sauce.

Potstickers: Put mushrooms into small heatproof bowl. Add boiling water. Stir. Let stand for about 20 minutes until softened. Drain. Remove and discard stems. Finely chop caps. Set aside.

Combine next 8 ingredients in medium bowl.

(continued on next page)

Stir first amount of water into cornstarch in small cup. Place 1 wrapper on work surface. Cover remaining wrappers with damp towel to prevent drying. Place about 1 tbsp. (15 mL) chicken mixture in centre of wrapper. Dampen edges of wrapper with cornstarch mixture. Fold in half over filling. Crimp edges to seal. Cover filled dumplings with separate damp towel to prevent drying. Repeat with remaining wrappers, chicken mixture and cornstarch mixture.

Heat cooking oil in large frying pan on medium until very hot. Arrange dumplings in single layer in pan. Cook for 3 to 5 minutes until bottoms of dumplings are golden. Turn. Add second amount of water. Cook, covered, for about 5 minutes until internal temperature reaches 175°F (80°C), water is evaporated and bottoms of dumplings are crisp. Transfer to plate. Serve immediately with dipping sauce. Makes 24 potstickers.

1 potsticker with 2 tsp. (10 mL) sauce: 72 Calories; 3.9 g Total Fat (1.3 g Mono, 0.9 g Poly, 0.3 g Sat); 1 mg Cholesterol; 6 g Carbohydrate; trace Fibre; 3 g Protein; 291 mg Sodium

Chicken Salad Shells

Almost too cute for words, these tiny chicken salad servings are all dolled up in crunchy, edible shells. Delicious!

Mayonnaise	2 tbsp.	30 mL
Lime juice	1 tbsp.	15 mL
Sweet chili sauce	1 tbsp.	15 mL
Soy sauce	2 tsp.	10 mL
Diced cooked chicken (see Tip, page 58)	1 1/4 cups	300 mL
Finely chopped celery	1/4 cup	60 mL
Finely chopped red pepper	1/4 cup	60 mL
Finely sliced green onion	3 tbsp.	45 mL
Pepper	1/4 tsp.	1 mL
Packages of Siljan mini croustade shells (24 per package), see Note	2	2
Sesame seeds, toasted (see Tip, page 22)	2 tsp.	10 mL

Combine first 4 ingredients in medium bowl.

Add next 5 ingredients. Stir.

Spoon chicken mixture into croustade shells.

Sprinkle with sesame seeds. Serve immediately. Makes 48 salad shells.

1 salad shell: 19 Calories; 1.1 g Total Fat (0.4 g Mono, 0.2 g Poly, 0.2 g Sat); 4 mg Cholesterol; 1 g Carbohydrate; trace Fibre; 1 g Protein; 48 mg Sodium

Note: Croustade shells can generally be found in the deli, cracker or imported section of your grocery store.

Pictured on page 17.

Pesto Chicken Tarts

Which came first, the chicken or the egg? In this recipe they come together. Pesto and cheese make these tasty mini quiches hard to beat.

Large eggs	4	4
Milk	1/2 cup	125 mL
Basil pesto	1/4 cup	60 mL
Grated Parmesan cheese	1/4 cup	60 mL
Pepper	1/4 tsp.	1 mL
Finely chopped cooked chicken (see Tip, page 58)	1 cup	250 mL
Unbaked tart shells (unsweetened)	16	16
Grated Parmesan cheese	4 tsp.	20 mL

Beat first 5 ingredients in medium bowl until frothy.

Add chicken. Stir.

Place tart shells on ungreased baking sheet with sides. Spoon about 2 tbsp. (30 mL) of egg mixture into each tart shell. Sprinkle tarts with second amount of cheese. Bake in 375°F (190°C) oven for about 25 minutes until pastry is golden and wooden pick inserted in centre comes out clean. Makes 16 tarts.

1 tart: 206 Calories; 11.5 g Total Fat (3.5 g Mono, 0.3 g Poly, 2.8 g Sat); 56 mg Cholesterol; 18 g Carbohydrate; trace Fibre; 7 g Protein; 177 mg Sodium

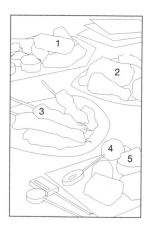

1. Onion Apple Phyllo Rolls, page 10
2. Salt and Pepper Wings, page 26
3. Lemon Grass Chicken Skewers, page 120
4. Corn Chicks, page 19
5. Chicken Salad Shells, page 15

Corn Chicks

Ordinary chicken meatballs are transformed into golden nuggets with a crispy coating of corn chips. Serve with your favourite dipping sauce.

Large egg, fork-beaten	1	1
Fine dry bread crumbs	1/2 cup	125 mL
Seasoned salt	1/2 tsp.	2 mL
Poultry seasoning	1/4 tsp.	1 mL
Pepper	1/8 tsp.	0.5 mL
Lean ground chicken	1 lb.	454 g
Finely crushed corn chips	1 cup	250 mL

Combine first 5 ingredients in large bowl. Add chicken. Mix well. Roll into 1 inch (2.5 cm) balls.

Put chips into small shallow dish. Roll each meatball in corn chips until coated. Discard any remaining chips. Arrange meatballs on greased baking sheet with sides. Bake in 350°F (175°C) oven for about 25 minutes until fully cooked and internal temperature reaches 175°F (80°C). Makes about 28 meatballs.

1 meatball: 57 Calories; 3.0 g Total Fat (0.1 g Mono, trace Poly, 0.1 g Sat); 6.7 mg Cholesterol; 3 g Carbohydrate; trace Fibre; 3 g Protein; 84 mg Sodium

Pictured on page 17.

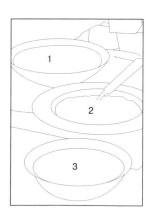

1. Black Bean Chicken Soup, page 60
2. Chicken Corn Chowder, page 62
3. Garden Noodle Soup, page 65

Appetizers

Stuffed Grape Leaves

In Greece, they're commonly called dolmades *but you can just call them delicious. Everyone will agree that these chicken-and-rice-stuffed grape leaves are simply de-vine! Serve with lemon wedges and our delicious Cucumber Dill Dip, which also goes great with cut-up veggies.*

Long grain white rice	1/2 cup	125 mL
Boiling water	1 cup	250 mL
Chopped pine nuts, toasted (see Tip, page 50), optional	3 tbsp.	45 mL
Parsley flakes	2 tsp.	10 mL
Dried oregano	1 tsp.	5 mL
Garlic powder	1/2 tsp.	2 mL
Dried rosemary, crushed	1/4 tsp.	1 mL
Salt	1/4 tsp.	1 mL
Pepper	1/8 tsp	0.5 mL
Lean ground chicken	1/2 lb.	225 g
Grape leaves, rinsed and drained, tough stems removed (see Note)	24	24
Prepared chicken broth	1 cup	250 mL

CUCUMBER DILL DIP		
Sour cream	1 cup	250 mL
Grated English cucumber (with peel), squeezed dry	1/2 cup	125 mL
White vinegar	1 tsp.	5 mL
Garlic clove, minced (or 1/4 tsp., 1 mL, powder)	1	1
Chopped fresh dill	1 tsp.	5 mL
Salt	1/4 tsp.	1 mL
Pepper	1/8 tsp.	0.5 mL

Put rice into small bowl. Add water. Stir. Let stand for 15 minutes. Drain. Rinse with cold water. Drain well.

Combine next 7 ingredients in medium bowl. Add chicken and rice. Mix well.

Place 1 leaf on work surface, vein side up, stem side (bottom of leaf) closest to you. Place about 1 tbsp. (15 mL) of chicken mixture about 1/2 inch (12 mm) from bottom of leaf. Fold bottom of leaf over chicken mixture. Fold in sides. Roll up from bottom to enclose filling. Place seam side down in large saucepan. Repeat with remaining leaves and filling.

(continued on next page)

Appetizers

Pour broth over stuffed leaves. Bring to a boil. Reduce heat to medium-low. Simmer, covered, for 35 minutes. Remove from heat. Let stand, covered, for 15 to 20 minutes until internal temperature reaches 175°F (80°C) and liquid is almost all absorbed.

Cucumber Dill Dip: Combine all 7 ingredients in small bowl. Makes about 1 cup (250 mL) dip. Serve with stuffed leaves. Makes 24 stuffed leaves.

1 stuffed leaf with 2 tsp. (10 mL) dip: 65 Calories; 3.8 g Total Fat (0.3 g Mono, 0.3 g Poly, 1.3 g Sat); 7 mg Cholesterol; 4 g Carbohydrate; trace Fibre; 3 g Protein; 205 mg Sodium

Note: Grape leaves can generally be found in the import section of your grocery store.

Chicken Little Tarts

Delicious warm or cool, these tarts really add to a tray of appetizers.

CHEESE PASTRY

Butter (or hard margarine), softened	1/2 cup	125 mL
Cream cheese, softened	4 oz.	125 g
All-purpose flour	1 cup	250 mL

FILLING

Finely chopped cooked chicken	1/2 cup	125 mL
Large egg	1	1
Milk	1/2 cup	125 mL
Grated Swiss cheese or medium or sharp Cheddar cheese	1/2 cup	125 mL
Salt	1/4 tsp.	1 mL
Onion powder	1/4 tsp.	1 mL
Ground thyme	1/8 tsp.	0.5 mL
Cayenne pepper, sprinkle		

Cheese Pastry: Cream butter and cream cheese until smooth and light. Add flour. Mix until smooth. Shape into long roll. Mark off into 24 pieces. Cut. Press into small tart tins forming pastry shells.

Filling: Divide chicken among shells, about 1 tsp. (5 mL) each.

Put remaining ingredients into blender. Process until smooth, or beat in mixing bowl. Pour into shells. Bake on bottom rack in 350°F (175°C) oven for 20 to 25 minutes until set. Makes 24 quiche tarts.

1 tart: 90 Calories; 7 g Total Fat (1.5 g Mono, 0 g Poly, 4 g Sat); 30 mg Cholesterol; 5 g Carbohydrate; 0 g Fibre; 3 g Protein; 80 mg Sodium

Empanadas

Allow extra time to make these little finger foods—they're well worth it.

Butter (or hard margarine)	1 tbsp.	15 mL
Chopped onion	1/2 cup	125 mL
Ground raw chicken	1/2 lb.	250 g
All-purpose flour	2 tbsp.	30 mL
Milk	1/2 cup	125 mL
Chopped ripe olives	3 tbsp.	45 mL
Raisins, coarsely chopped	1/4 cup	60 mL
Worcestershire sauce	1 tsp.	5 mL
Chicken bouillon powder	1 tsp.	5 mL
Hot pepper sauce	1/8 tsp.	0.5 mL
Salt	1/8 tsp.	0.5 mL

Pastry for 3 or 4 double crust pies

Heat butter in frying pan. Add onion. Sauté until partially cooked.

Add chicken. Scramble-fry until no pink remains.

Stir in flour. Stir in milk until mixture boils and thickens. Remove from heat.

Add next 6 ingredients. Stir.

Roll pastry. Cut into 3 inch (7.5 cm) rounds. Place 1 tsp. (5 mL) chicken mixture in centre of each. Moisten half of outside edge with water. Fold over. Press with fork to seal. Cut slits in top. Arrange on ungreased baking sheet. Bake in 400°F (200°C) oven for 15 to 20 minutes until browned. Serve hot. Makes 4 1/2 to 5 dozen empanadas.

1 empanada: 130 Calories; 8 g Total Fat (3.5 g Mono, 2 g Poly, 2 g Sat); <3 mg Cholesterol; 12 g Carbohydrate; <1 g Fibre; 2 g Protein; 150 mg Sodium

Pictured on page 288.

 When toasting nuts, seeds or coconut, cooking times will vary for each different ingredient—so never toast them together. For small amounts, place the ingredient in an ungreased shallow frying pan. Heat on medium for 3 to 5 minutes, stirring often, until golden. For larger amounts, spread the ingredient evenly in an ungreased shallow pan. Bake in a 350°F (175°C) oven for 5 to 10 minutes, stirring or shaking often, until golden.

Curried Chicken Samosa Strudel

The crisp, delicate, flaky texture of phyllo pastry heightens the sensation of biting into these mildly spiced strudels.

Cooking oil	2 tsp.	10 mL
Minced onion	1 1/2 cups	375 mL
Madras curry paste	2 tbsp.	30 mL
Garlic cloves, minced	2	2
Canned chickpeas (garbanzo beans), rinsed and drained, mashed	1 cup	250 mL
Chopped chicken breast	1 cup	250 mL
Frozen peas	1/2 cup	125 mL
Grated carrot	1/2 cup	250 mL
Phyllo pastry sheets, thawed according to package directions	8	8
Unsalted butter, melted	1/4 cup	60 mL

Heat cooking oil in frying pan on medium. Add next 3 ingredients and cook until onion starts to soften. Let stand until cool.

Stir in next 4 ingredients.

Layer 4 sheets of phyllo pastry, lightly brushing each layer with melted butter. Keep remaining phyllo covered with damp towel to prevent drying. Spread half of chicken mixture along bottom of sheet, leaving 1 1/2 inch (3.8 cm) edge on each side. Fold in sides and roll up from bottom to enclose. Place, seam side down, on ungreased baking sheet. Brush with butter. Cut several small vents on top to allow steam to escape. Repeat. Bake in 400°F (200°C) oven for about 20 minutes until golden. With serrated knife, cut strudels diagonally into 7 slices each. Makes 14 slices.

1 slice: 155 Calories; 6.2 g Total Fat (1.9 g Mono, 0.9 g Poly, 2.6 g Sat); 17 mg Cholesterol; 18 g Carbohydrate; 2 g Fibre; 7 g Protein; 148 mg Sodium

Bourbon Chicken Bites

Enjoy the flavour of popular Buffalo chicken wings without the sticky fingers! These fiery chicken bites have a bold blue cheese sauce that can also be served with crisp vegetable sticks.

Bourbon whiskey	1/4 cup	60 mL
Chili powder	1 tsp.	5 mL
Dried oregano	1 tsp.	5 mL
Pepper	1/8 tsp.	0.5 mL
Boneless, skinless chicken thighs, cut into twenty-seven 1 inch (2.5 cm) pieces	1 lb.	454 g
Louisiana hot sauce	2 tbsp.	30 mL
Butter (or hard margarine), melted	2 tsp.	10 mL
Ranch dressing	1/4 cup	60 mL
Crumbled blue cheese	2 tbsp.	30 mL
Cocktail picks	27	27

Combine first 4 ingredients in small bowl. Put chicken into large resealable freezer bag. Pour whiskey mixture over top. Seal bag. Turn until coated. Marinate in refrigerator for 6 hours or overnight, turning occasionally. Remove chicken. Discard any remaining marinade. Arrange in single layer on greased baking sheet with sides. Cook in 450°F (230°C) oven for about 10 minutes until no longer pink inside.

Combine hot sauce and butter in large bowl. Add chicken. Stir until coated. Arrange on serving platter.

Whisk dressing and cheese in small bowl until combined. Insert cocktail picks into chicken. Serve with dressing mixture. Makes 27 chicken bites.

1 chicken bite with 1/2 tsp. (2 mL) dressing mixture: 42 Calories; 2.8 g Total Fat (0.6 g Mono, 0.3 g Poly, 0.8 g Sat); 13 mg Cholesterol; trace Carbohydrate; trace Fibre; 3 g Protein; 70 mg Sodium

Parmesan Wings

Crunchy and cheesy. Delicious.

Plain yogurt	1/2 cup	125 mL
Lemon juice	3 tbsp.	45 mL
Prepared mustard	2 tsp.	10 mL
Prepared horseradish	1/4 tsp.	1 mL
Garlic powder	1/4 tsp.	1 mL
Ground thyme	1/4 tsp.	1 mL
Dry fine bread crumbs	1/3 cup	75 mL
Grated Parmesan cheese	2/3 cup	150 mL
Salt	1 tsp.	5 mL
Chicken drumettes (or whole wings)	2 lbs.	900 g

Mix first 6 ingredients in bowl.

Mix bread crumbs, cheese and salt in second bowl.

Add drumettes to yogurt mixture (if using whole wings, first discard tips and cut wings apart at joint). Stir to coat. Marinate in refrigerator for 2 to 3 hours or longer. Remove from marinade. Drain. Roll in cheese mixture and place on greased foil-lined tray. Bake in 350°F (175°C) oven for about 45 minutes until tender. Serve hot. Makes about 16 drumettes or 24 pieces of whole wings.

1 wing: 70 Calories; 2.5 g Total Fat (0.5 g Mono, 0 g Poly, 1 g Sat); 25 mg Cholesterol; 2 g Carbohydrate; 0 g Fibre; 10 g Protein; 190 mg Sodium

Glazed Wings

The glaze has a tasty, mild zip that will have you reaching for more.

Chicken drumettes (or whole wings)	3 lbs.	1.36 kg
Apricot jam	1 cup	250 mL
Cider vinegar	3 tbsp.	45 mL
Soy sauce	2 tsp.	10 mL
Onion powder	1/4 tsp.	1 mL
Ground ginger	1/4 tsp.	1 mL

Arrange drumettes on greased or greased foil-lined baking tray. If using whole wings, discard tips and cut wings apart at joint. Bake in 350°F (175°C) oven for 30 minutes.

Stir remaining ingredients together in small saucepan. Heat until quite warm so it will spread easier. Brush over drumettes. Continue to cook for 15 to 20 minutes, turning and brushing with sauce 2 or 3 times until tender. Makes about 24 drumettes or 36 pieces of whole wings.

1 wing: 70 Calories; 1.5 g Total Fat (0 g Mono, 0 g Poly, 0 g Sat); 20 mg Cholesterol; 6 g Carbohydrate; 0 g Fibre; 8 g Protein; 50 mg Sodium

Nutty Crunch Drumettes

Everyone will go nuts for these crisp, spicy drumettes.

Finely crushed nacho chips	1/2 cup	125 mL
Finely chopped almonds	1/4 cup	60 mL
Chicken drumettes (or split chicken wings, tips discarded)	2 lbs.	900 g
PEACHY LIME SALSA		
Peach jam	1/2 cup	125 mL
Salsa	1/2 cup	125 mL
Chopped fresh basil	2 tbsp.	30 mL
Lime juice	2 tbsp.	30 mL
Orange juice	2 tbsp.	30 mL

Combine chips and almonds in large resealable freezer bag. Add drumettes. Toss until coated. Arrange drumettes in single layer on greased wire rack set in foil-lined baking sheet with sides. Discard any remaining chip mixture. Spray drumettes with cooking spray. Bake in 400°F (200°C) oven for about 45 minutes until fully cooked and internal temperature reaches 170°F (77°C).

Peachy Lime Salsa: Combine all 5 ingredients in small bowl. Makes about 1 1/3 cups (325 mL) salsa. Serve with drumettes. Makes about 16 drumettes (or 24 wing pieces).

1 drumette with 1 tbsp. (15 mL) salsa: 187 Calories; 11.1 g Total Fat (1.3 g Mono, 0.4 g Poly, 2.6 g Sat); 43 mg Cholesterol; 10 g Carbohydrate; trace Fibre; 11 g Protein; 99 mg Sodium

Salt and Pepper Wings

Forget wing night at the local pub. No pub can top these simple and tasty tidbits.

Split chicken wings, tips discarded (or chicken drumettes)	2 lbs.	900 g
Soy sauce	2 tbsp.	30 mL
Montreal steak spice	2 tsp.	10 mL
Coarsely ground pepper	1/2 tsp.	2 mL
Lemon pepper	1/2 tsp.	2 mL

Arrange wing pieces in single layer on greased wire rack set in foil-lined baking sheet with sides.

Brush soy sauce on both sides of wing pieces. Sprinkle remaining 3 ingredients on both sides of wing pieces. Bake in 425°F (220°C) oven for about 40 minutes, turning at halftime, until crisp golden brown and fully cooked. Makes about 24 wing pieces (or 16 drumettes).

1 wing: 86 Calories; 6.0 g Total Fat (0 g Mono, 0 g Poly, 1.6 g Sat); 28 mg Cholesterol; trace Carbohydrate; trace Fibre; 7 g Protein; 190 mg Sodium

Pictured on page 17.

Blue Chicken Wings

Way better for you than the deep-fried restaurant variety! Chicken drumettes are the meatiest part of the chicken wing, so you get a better meat-to-fat ratio. This recipe also gives you a delicious homemade chicken stock. Simply chill the cooking liquid overnight, then remove and discard any fat before using.

Water	6 cups	1.5 L
Chicken drumettes	3 lbs.	1.4 kg
Medium carrots, quartered	2	2
Medium onion, quartered	1	1
Bay leaf	1	1
Apricot jam	1/4 cup	60 mL
Louisiana hot sauce	2 tbsp.	30 mL
Salt	1/4 tsp.	1 mL
LIGHT BLUE DIP		
95% fat-free spreadable cream cheese	1/4 cup	60 mL
Crumbled blue cheese	1/4 cup	60 mL
Light sour cream	1/4 cup	60 mL
Chopped chives (or green onion)	3 tbsp.	45 mL

Combine first 5 ingredients in Dutch oven or large pot. Bring to a boil. Reduce heat to medium. Simmer, uncovered, for about 20 minutes until drumettes are no longer pink inside. Strain cooking liquid into medium bowl. Reserve for another use. Remove and discard carrot, onion and bay leaf.

Stir next 3 ingredients in large bowl. Add hot drumettes. Toss until jam is melted and drumettes are coated. Transfer to greased foil-lined baking sheet with sides, reserving apricot mixture in bowl. Bake in 450°F (230°C) oven for about 20 minutes, turning occasionally, until browned. Toss drumettes in remaining apricot mixture. Makes about 28 chicken wings.

Light Blue Dip: Combine all 4 ingredients in small bowl. Makes about 2/3 cup (150 mL) dip. Serve with wings.

1 drumette and 1 tsp. (5 mL) dip: 120 Calories; 8 g Total Fat (3 g Mono, 1.5 g Poly, 2.5 g Sat); 39 mg Cholesterol; 2 g Carbohydrate; 0 g Fibre; 10 g Protein; 114 mg Sodium

Bali Wings

The sauce on these scrumptious wings is reminiscent of a sweet and sour sauce.
A real crowd-pleaser!

Chicken drumettes (or whole wings)	4 lbs.	1.8 kg
BALI SAUCE		
Brown sugar, packed	1/2 cup	125 mL
Granulated sugar	1/4 cup	60 mL
Cornstarch	1/4 cup	60 mL
Ground ginger	1/2 tsp.	2 mL
Salt	1/2 tsp.	2 mL
Pepper	1/4 tsp.	1 mL
Water	1 cup	250 mL
White vinegar	1/2 cup	125 mL
Soy sauce	1/3 cup	75 mL

Arrange drumettes on greased or greased foil-lined baking tray. If using whole wings, discard tips and cut wings apart at joint. Bake in 350°F (175°C) oven for 30 minutes.

Bali Sauce: Stir first 6 ingredients together in small saucepan.

Stir in water, vinegar and soy sauce. Heat and stir until it boils and thickens. Brush over drumettes. Continue to bake for 15 to 20 minutes until tender, turning and brushing with sauce at least 2 more times. Makes about 32 drumettes or 48 pieces of whole wings.

1 wing: 60 Calories; 1.5 g Total Fat (0 g Mono, 0 g Poly, 0 g Sat); 20 mg Cholesterol; 4 g Carbohydrate; 0 g Fibre; 9 g Protein; 160 mg Sodium

Fiery Wings

Crispy grilled Buffalo wings get an extra chili kick from sambal oelek. Starting with a spice
rub adds great depth of flavour.

Cooking oil	2 tbsp.	30 mL
Chili powder	1 tsp.	5 mL
Coarse salt	1 tsp.	5 mL
Paprika	1 tsp.	5 mL
Pepper	1 tsp.	5 mL
Celery seed	1/2 tsp.	2 mL
Split chicken wings, tips discarded (or chicken drumettes)	2 lbs.	900 g
Butter (or hard margarine), melted	2 tbsp.	30 mL
Chili paste (sambal oelek)	2 tbsp.	30 mL
Louisiana hot sauce	2 tbsp.	30 mL

(continued on next page)

Combine first 6 ingredients in large bowl. Add chicken wings. Toss until coated. Preheat barbecue to medium-low. Place wings on greased grill. Close lid. Cook for about 15 minutes per side until no longer pink inside

Combine remaining 3 ingredients in small bowl. Brush over wings. Close lid. Cook for about 3 minutes per side until crisp and golden (see Note). Transfer to serving platter. Makes about 24 wing pieces (or 16 drumettes).

1 wing: 62 Calories; 4.0 g Total Fat (1.5 g Mono, 0.8 g Poly, 1.2 g Sat); 19 mg Cholesterol; trace Carbohydrate; trace Fibre; 6 g Protein; 184 mg Sodium

Note: If a barbecue flare-up occurs, move the wings to one side of the grill until flames die down. If necessary, a light spritz from a water bottle can control small flames. Serious flare-ups should be doused with baking soda.

Stuffed Mushrooms

These tasty little tidbits can be made a few hours ahead, then broiled when you need them.

Medium mushrooms	24	24
Butter (or hard margarine)	3 tbsp.	45 mL
Finely chopped onion	1/2 cup	125 mL
Finely chopped celery	3 tbsp.	45 mL
Ground cooked chicken	1/2 cup	125 mL
Dry bread crumbs	1/4 cup	60 mL
Sour cream	1/4 cup	60 mL
Poultry seasoning	1/4 tsp.	1 mL
Chicken bouillon powder	1/2 tsp.	2 mL
Salt	1/4 tsp.	1 mL
Pepper	1/8 tsp.	0.5 mL
Grated Parmesan cheese	2 tbsp.	30 mL

Gently twist stems from mushrooms. Chop stems and set aside.

Melt butter in frying pan. Add onion, celery and mushroom stems. Sauté until soft.

Add next 7 ingredients. Stir well. Stuff mushrooms.

Dip tops in cheese. Arrange on baking sheet. Broil on second rack from top for 3 to 5 minutes or bake in 350°F (175°C) oven for 10 to 15 minutes until crusty. Makes 24 stuffed mushrooms.

1 stuffed mushroom: 40 Calories; 2.5 g Total Fat (0.5 g Mono, 0 g Poly, 1.5 g Sat); 10 mg Cholesterol; 2 g Carbohydrate; 0 g Fibre; 2 g Protein; 75 mg Sodium

Spiced Panko Chicken with Tropical Rum Dip

These refined chicken fingers are paired with an adult coconut rum dip. Delicious!

Olive oil	1/4 cup	60 mL
Dijon mustard	3 tbsp.	45 mL
Montreal steak spice	1 tsp.	5 mL
Boneless, skinless chicken breasts, cut into ten 1 inch (2.5 cm) wide strips, about 3 inches (7.5 cm) long	3/4 lb.	340 g
Panko crumbs	1 1/2 cups	375 mL
Paprika	1/2 tsp.	2 mL

TROPICAL RUM DIP

Pineapple orange juice	1 1/2 cups	375 mL
Brown sugar, packed	1/4 cup	60 mL
Coconut rum	2 tbsp.	30 mL
Dijon mustard	2 tsp.	10 mL

Combine first 3 ingredients in a large resealable freezer bag. Add chicken and marinate in refrigerator for 4 hours. Drain, discarding marinade.

Combine panko crumbs and paprika. Press chicken into panko mixture until coated. Arrange on greased wire rack set in baking sheet. Spray with cooking spray. Bake in 450°F (230°C) oven for about 15 minutes until crisp and no longer pink inside.

Tropical Rum Dip: Combine juice and brown sugar in saucepan. Boil gently on medium for about 25 minutes until thickened to syrup consistency.

Stir in rum and mustard. Serve with chicken. Serves 10.

1 serving: 148 Calories; 4.6 g Total Fat (3.1 g Mono, 0.5 g Poly, 0.7 g Sat); 20 mg Cholesterol; 16 g Carbohydrate; trace Fibre; 9 g Protein; 141 mg Sodium

Grilled Chicken and Artichoke Salad

A colourful, tangy salad that's perfect for company.

BALSAMIC MARINADE

Olive (or cooking) oil	1/3 cup	75 mL
Balsamic vinegar	1/4 cup	60 mL
Liquid honey	2 tbsp.	30 mL
Chopped fresh basil (or 3/4 tsp., 4 mL, dried)	1 tbsp.	15 mL
Garlic cloves, minced (or 1/2 tsp., 2 mL, powder)	2	2
Lemon pepper	1 tsp.	5 mL
Boneless, skinless chicken breast halves	3/4 lb.	340 g
Large red onion, cut into 8 wedges	1	1
Bag of fresh spinach (6 oz., 170 g), stems removed	1	1
Can of artichoke hearts (14 oz., 398 mL), drained and coarsely chopped	1	1
Halved cherry tomatoes	1 cup	250 mL
Chopped walnuts, toasted (see Tip, page 22)	1 cup	250 mL
Crumbled feta cheese (about 4 oz., 113 g)	3/4 cup	175 mL

Balsamic Marinade: Combine first 6 ingredients in jar with tight-fitting lid. Shake well. Makes about 3/4 cup (175 mL) marinade.

Place chicken in large resealable freezer bag. Pour 1/2 of marinade over top. Seal bag. Turn until coated. Marinate in refrigerator for 3 hours. Drain and discard marinade. Preheat barbecue to medium. Cook chicken on greased grill for about 5 minutes per side until no longer pink inside. Chop coarsely. Transfer to large bowl.

Cook onion on greased grill for about 10 minutes, turning once, until softened and grill marks appear. Add to chicken.

Add remaining 5 ingredients. Toss. Drizzle with remaining marinade. Toss. Makes about 11 cups (2.75 L) salad. Serves 6.

1 serving: 369 Calories; 24.4 g Total Fat (8.7 g Mono, 9.3 g Poly, 4.9 g Sat); 58 mg Cholesterol; 15 g Carbohydrate; 4 g Fibre; 26 g Protein; 459 mg Sodium

Peach and Chicken Salad

A delightfully sweet and refreshing summer salad.

Boneless, skinless chicken breast halves	1 lb.	454 g
Seasoned salt	1 tsp.	5 mL
Pepper	1/2 tsp.	2 mL
Cut or torn romaine lettuce, lightly packed	6 cups	1.5 L
Chopped red pepper	2 cups	500 mL
Can of sliced peaches (14 oz., 398 mL), drained and chopped	1	1
Pecan pieces, toasted (see Tip, page 22)	1/2 cup	125 mL
Thinly sliced green onion	1/2 cup	125 mL
Chopped fresh parsley	1/4 cup	60 mL
PEACH VINAIGRETTE		
White vinegar	3 tbsp.	45 mL
Peach jam	2 tbsp.	30 mL
Cooking oil	1 tbsp.	15 mL
Garlic clove, minced (or 1/4 tsp., 1 mL, powder)	1	1
Red wine vinegar	1 tsp.	5 mL
Salt	1/4 tsp.	1 mL
Pepper	1/8 tsp.	0.5 mL

Sprinkle chicken with seasoned salt and pepper. Preheat gas barbecue to medium-high. Cook chicken on greased grill for about 6 to 8 minutes per side until fully cooked and internal temperature reaches 170°F (77°C). Remove to cutting board. Let stand for 5 minutes. Cut crosswise into 1/2 inch (12 mm) strips. Cool slightly.

Put next 6 ingredients into extra-large bowl. Toss gently. Add chicken.

Peach Vinaigrette: Combine all 7 ingredients in jar with tight-fitting lid. Shake well. Makes about 1/3 cup (75 mL) dressing. Drizzle over salad. Toss gently. Makes about 10 cups (2.5 L).

1 cup (250 mL): 156 Calories; 6.5 g Total Fat (3.4 g Mono, 1.9 g Poly, 0.7 g Sat); 26 mg Cholesterol; 14 g Carbohydrate; 3 g Fibre; 12 g Protein; 231 mg Sodium

Pictured on page 35.

Vermicelli Chicken Salads

Want to get fresh? There's nothing fresher than this cool treat. Doubles easily.

TERIYAKI LIME DRESSING

Lime juice	1/2 cup	125 mL
Sweet chili sauce	1/2 cup	125 mL
Thick teriyaki basting sauce	1/2 cup	125 mL
Boneless, skinless chicken breast halves	1 lb.	454 g
Prepared chicken broth	4 cups	1 L
Thick teriyaki basting sauce	2 tbsp.	30 mL
Finely grated ginger root	2 tsp.	10 mL
Boiling water	6 cups	1.5 L
Rice vermicelli	8 1/2 oz.	250 g
Shredded suey choy (Chinese cabbage)	4 cups	1 L
Sliced English cucumber (with peel)	1 1/2 cups	375 mL
Grated carrot	1 cup	250 mL
Chopped fresh mint	1/3 cup	75 mL
Fresh bean sprouts	2 cups	500 mL
Chopped green onion	1/4 cup	60 mL
Chopped salted peanuts	1/4 cup	60 mL

Teriyaki Lime Dressing: Combine all 3 ingredients in small bowl. Makes about 1 1/2 cups (375 mL) dressing.

Combine chicken, broth, teriyaki sauce and ginger in large saucepan. Bring to a boil. Reduce heat to medium-low. Simmer, uncovered, for about 15 minutes until chicken is fully cooked and internal temperature reaches 170°F (77°C). Remove from heat. Transfer chicken with slotted spoon to small bowl. Cool. Reserve broth mixture.

Add boiling water and vermicelli to reserved broth mixture. Let stand for 5 to 10 minutes until vermicelli is softened. Drain. Rinse with cold water. Drain well. Return to same saucepan. Add 1 cup (250 mL) Teriyaki Lime Dressing. Toss.

Arrange next 4 ingredients on 4 individual serving plates. Spoon noodles over top. Cut chicken crosswise into 1/8 inch (3 mm) strips. Arrange over noodles.

Sprinkle remaining 3 ingredients over chicken. Drizzle remaining dressing over salads. Makes 4 salads.

1 salad: 602 Calories; 8.3 g Total Fat (3.3 g Mono, 2.3 g Poly, 1.6 g Sat); 66 mg Cholesterol; 83 g Carbohydrate; 8 g Fibre; 43 g Protein; 2414 mg Sodium

Pictured on page 35.

Chicken Greens Salad

A piquant oil and vinegar dressing makes this salad really stand out.

Chicken breasts, halved, skin and bones removed	4	4
Cooking oil	1 tbsp.	15 mL
Romaine lettuce, torn or cut bite size	6 cups	1.35 L
Medium tomatoes, diced	3	3
Green onions, chopped	4	4
Medium zucchini, slivered	2	2

HOUSE DRESSING		
Cooking oil	1/4 cup	60 mL
White vinegar	2 tbsp.	30 mL
Granulated sugar	1/2 tsp.	2 mL
Salt	1/4 tsp.	1 mL
Prepared mustard	1/2 tsp.	2 mL
Garlic powder	1/8 tsp.	0.5 mL
Pepper, light sprinkle		
Grated Parmesan cheese	1 tbsp.	15 mL

Brown chicken on both sides in cooking oil in frying pan. Continue to cook until no pink remains. Remove from heat and cut into 1/2 inch (12 mm) slices.

Toss next 4 ingredients together in large bowl.

House Dressing: Stir all ingredients together in small bowl. Pour over salad. Toss to coat. Divide among 8 salad plates. Top with warm chicken. Serves 8.

1 serving: 250 Calories; 12 g Total Fat (5 g Mono, 2.5 g Poly, 2 g Sat); 80 mg Cholesterol; 7 g Carbohydrate; 2 g Fibre; 31 g Protein; 890 mg Sodium

1. Hawaiian Chicken Salads, page 38
2. Vermicelli Chicken Salads, page 33
3. Peach and Chicken Salad, page 32

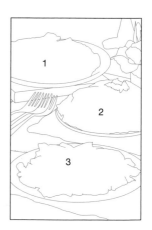

Sweet Chicken Salad

An attractive salad full of sweet, tangy goodness! This won't last long.

Chopped or torn romaine lettuce, lightly packed	7 cups	1.75 L
Chopped cooked chicken	3 cups	750 mL
Cherry tomatoes, haved	5 oz.	140 g
Dried cranberries	1/2 cup	125 mL
Crumbled feta cheese (about 2 1/2 oz., 70 g)	1/2 cup	125 mL
Thinly sliced red onion	1/4 cup	60 mL
Toasted sliced natural almonds (see Tip, page 22)	3 tbsp.	45 mL
POPPY SEED DRESSING		
Cooking oil	3 tbsp.	45 mL
Balsamic vinegar	2 tbsp.	30 mL
Granulated sugar	1 tbsp.	15 mL
Poppy seeds	2 tsp.	10 mL
Worchestershire sauce	1/2 tsp.	2 mL
Pepper, sprinkle		

Put first 7 ingredients into large bowl. Toss.

Poppy Seed Dressing: Combine all 6 ingredients in jar with tight-fitting lid. Shake well. Makes about 1/3 cup (75 mL) dressing. Drizzle over salad. Toss well. Serves 6.

1 serving: 308 Calories; 17.8 g Total Fat (7.9 g Mono, 4.2 g Poly, 4.3 g Sat); 79 mg Cholesterol; 11 g Carbohydrate; 3 g Fibre; 26 g Protein; 231 mg Sodium

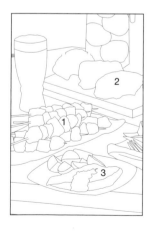

1. Pineapple Rum Kabobs, page 117
2. Cedar Plank Chicken, page 133
3. Chicken Aztec, page 132

Cherry Chicken Salad

Rich and colourful, this cheery cherry salad makes a delicious lunch or an attractive supper side. Feel free to be creative and use other dried fruit such as cranberries, chopped figs or apricots.

Mixed salad greens, lightly packed	8 cups	2 L
Dried cherries	1 cup	250 mL
Sliced natural almonds, toasted (see Tip, page 22)	3/4 cup	175 mL
Cooking oil	1 tsp.	5 mL
Boneless, skinless chicken breast halves, cut crosswise into 1/2 inch (12 mm) slices	1/2 lb.	225 g
Salt, sprinkle		
Pepper, sprinkle		
PESTO DRESSING		
Red wine vinegar	1/4 cup	60 mL
Basil pesto	3 tbsp.	45 mL
Olive (or cooking) oil	1 tbsp.	15 mL

Put first 3 ingredients into large bowl. Toss.

Heat cooking oil in small frying pan on medium-high. Add chicken. Sprinkle with salt and pepper. Cook for about 5 minutes, stirring occasionally, until chicken is no longer pink inside. Remove from heat. Cool. Add to salad mixture. Toss.

Pesto Dressing: Whisk all 3 ingredients in small bowl until combined. Makes about 1/3 cup (75 mL) dressing. Drizzle over salad. Toss. Makes about 8 cups (2 L).

1 cup (250 mL): 204 Calories; 10.3 g Total Fat (4.5 g Mono, 1.6 g Poly, 1.2 g Sat); 18 mg Cholesterol; 16 g Carbohydrate; 4 g Fibre; 11 g Protein; 82 mg Sodium

Hawaiian Chicken Salads

The fresh, fruity flavours of the islands will have you hanging 10 in no time.

Thick teriyaki basting sauce	1/3 cup	75 mL
Boneless, skinless chicken breast halves (about 4 oz., 113 g, each)	4	4
Spring mix lettuce, lightly packed	8 cups	2 L
Frozen mango pieces, thawed, drained and chopped	1 1/2 cups	375 mL
Frozen pineapple pieces, thawed and drained	1 1/2 cups	375 mL
Chopped raw macadamia nuts, toasted (see Tip, page 22)	1/2 cup	125 mL

(continued on next page)

Shredded coconut, toasted (see Tip, page 22)	2 tbsp.	30 mL
Raspberry vinaigrette	1/2 cup	125 mL

Brush teriyaki sauce on both sides of chicken. Preheat gas barbecue to medium-high (see Tip, page 84). Cook chicken on greased grill for 6 to 8 minutes per side, basting with remaining teriyaki sauce, until chicken is fully cooked and internal temperature reaches 170°F (77°C). Remove to cutting board. Cut chicken diagonally into 1/2 inch (12 mm) strips. Cool slightly.

Arrange lettuce on 4 individual serving plates. Arrange one sliced breast over lettuce on each plate. Arrange mango and pineapple over chicken.

Sprinkle macadamia nuts and coconut over top. Drizzle vinaigrette over salads. Makes 4 salads.

1 salad: 461 Calories; 16.6 g Total Fat (10.5 g Mono, 0.9 g Poly, 3.9 g Sat); 66 mg Cholesterol; 51 g Carbohydrate; 6 g Fibre; 30 g Protein; 929 mg Sodium

Pictured on page 35.

Chicken Waldorf Salad

Crunchy, fruity and nutty—what more could you ask for?

Salad dressing (or mayonnaise)	1/2 cup	125 mL
Milk	2 tbsp.	30 mL
Granulated sugar	1 tsp.	5 mL
Diced apple, with peel	2 cups	500 mL
Diced cooked chicken	2 cups	500 mL
Diced celery	1 cup	250 mL
Chopped pecans or walnuts	1/2 cup	125 mL
Raisins	1/2 cup	125 mL
Salt	1/4 tsp.	1 mL
Shredded lettuce (or leaves)	2 cups	500 mL

Mix first 3 ingredients in bowl. Add apple Immediately to keep it from turning brown.

Add next 5 ingredients. Stir.

Spread lettuce over large plate or individual plates. Spoon salad over top. Makes 4 cups (1 L).

1/2 cup (125 mL): 190 Calories; 9 g Total Fat (3.5 g Mono, 2 g Poly, 1 g Sat); 30 mg Cholesterol; 18 g Carbohydrate; 2 g Fibre; 10 g Protein; 260 mg Sodium

Creamy Curry Chicken Salad

Never bland, never boring—you'll find that a little spice is extra nice in this chicken salad.
Serve with warm garlic bread.

Boneless, skinless chicken breast halves, cut crosswise into thin strips (see Tip, page 47)	1/2 lb.	225 g
Italian dressing	1/3 cup	75 mL
Olive (or cooking) oil	1 tsp.	5 mL
Cut or torn romaine lettuce, lightly packed	3 cups	750 mL
Cherry (or grape) tomatoes, halved	2 cups	500 mL
Can of artichoke hearts (14 oz., 398 mL), drained and halved	1	1
Kalamata (or black) olives, halved	16	16
CREAMY CURRY DRESSING		
Mayonnaise	1/3 cup	75 mL
Finely chopped fresh basil	2 tbsp.	30 mL
Lemon juice	2 tbsp.	30 mL
Liquid honey	1 tbsp.	15 mL
Chili paste (sambal oelek)	1 tsp.	5 mL
Curry powder	1 tsp.	5 mL

Stir chicken and Italian dressing in medium bowl until coated. Let stand, covered, in refrigerator for 1 hour, stirring occasionally. Drain and discard dressing.

Heat olive oil in small frying pan on medium-high. Add chicken. Cook for about 5 minutes, stirring occasionally, until no longer pink inside. Transfer to large bowl. Chill.

Add next 4 ingredients. Toss.

Creamy Curry Dressing: Combine all 6 ingredients in small bowl. Makes about 1/2 cup (125 mL) of dressing. Drizzle over salad. Toss. Makes about 8 cups (2 L).

1 cup (250 mL): 196 Calories; 13.5 g Total Fat (7.8 g Mono, 3.9 g Poly, 1.4 g Sat); 25 mg Cholesterol; 11 g Carbohydrate; 4 g Fibre; 9 g Protein; 308 mg Sodium

Asian Chicken Salad

A colourful and crunchy combination of fresh ingredients, with tender pieces of marinated chicken and a gingery soy dressing. A nice, light meal for a warm evening.

Soy sauce	3 tbsp.	45 mL
Brown sugar, packed	2 tsp.	10 mL
Ground ginger	1/8 tsp.	0.5 mL
Boneless, skinless chicken breast halves (4 oz., 113 g, each)	2	2
Rice vinegar	1/3 cup	75 mL
Sesame oil (for flavour)	3 tbsp.	45 mL
Smooth peanut butter	2 tbsp.	30 mL
Soy sauce	2 tbsp.	30 mL
Brown sugar, packed	1 tbsp.	15 mL
Chili paste (sambal oelek)	1/2 tsp.	2 mL
Garlic powder	1/4 tsp.	1 mL
Ground ginger	1/4 tsp.	1 mL
Shredded savoy cabbage, lightly packed	4 cups	1 L
Fresh bean sprouts	2 cups	500 mL
Fresh spinach leaves, lightly packed	1 cup	250 mL
Thinly sliced bok choy	1 cup	250 mL
Julienned carrot (see Tip, page 86)	1/2 cup	125 mL
Roasted sesame seeds	2 tbsp.	30 mL

Combine first 3 ingredients in shallow bowl. Add chicken. Turn until coated. Marinate, covered, in refrigerator for 1 hour. Transfer chicken to greased baking sheet with sides. Discard any remaining soy sauce mixture. Broil on centre rack in oven for about 8 minutes per side until internal temperature reaches 170°F (77°C). Transfer to cutting board. Let stand until cool enough to handle. Slice thinly.

Whisk next 8 ingredients in extra-large bowl until smooth.

Add next 5 ingredients and chicken. Toss until coated.

Sprinkle with sesame seeds. Makes about 10 cups (2.5 L). Serves 6.

1 serving: 180 Calories; 10 g Total Fat (3 g Mono, 3 g Poly, 2 g Sat); 20 mg Cholesterol; 10 g Carbohydrate; 2 g Fibre; 13 g Protein; 780 mg Sodium

Grilled Chicken and Squash on Spinach Salad

Turning leaves can signal the perfect time to barbecue garden offerings. It's never too late in the year to take advantage of the natural sweetness elicited from grilled butternut squash. Enjoy this rich harvest of colourful, flavourful delights!

Boneless, skinless chicken thighs, (about 6)	1 1/4 lbs.	560 g
Butternut squash, cut into 1/2 inch (12 mm) slices	1 lb.	454 g
Cooking oil	2 tbsp.	30 mL
Granulated sugar	1 tbsp.	15 mL
Ground cinnamon	1 tbsp.	15 mL
Salt	1 tsp.	5 mL
Pepper	1/4 tsp.	1 mL
Baby spinach leaves, lightly packed	8 cups	2 L
Coarsely chopped walnuts, toasted (see Tip, page 22)	1/2 cup	125 mL
Thinly sliced red onion	1/2 cup	125 mL
Goat (chèvre) cheese, cut up	2 oz.	57 g
Orange juice	2/3 cup	150 mL
Cooking oil	2 tbsp.	30 mL
Dijon mustard (with whole seeds)	2 tbsp.	30 mL
Brown sugar, packed	1 tbsp.	15 mL

Brush chicken and squash with cooking oil.

Combine next 4 ingredients and sprinkle over top. Grill on direct medium heat for about 5 minutes per side until chicken is no longer pink inside and squash is tender. Let stand until cool enough to handle. Slice chicken into thin strips and cut squash into cubes. Transfer to a large bowl.

Add next 4 ingredients and toss.

Whisk remaining 4 ingredients together until sugar is dissolved. Drizzle over salad and toss. Makes about 10 cups (2.5 L). Serves 4.

1 serving: 571 Calories; 37.1 g Total Fat (13.8 g Mono, 13.6 g Poly, 6.7 g Sat); 90 mg Cholesterol; 33 g Carbohydrate; 6 g Fibre; 32 g Protein; 923 mg Sodium

Grilled Greek Chicken Salad

Warm grilled chicken, vegetables and toasted pita make a vibrant, rich-tasting taverna-style Greek salad—perfect for a summer lunch or light dinner.

Diced Roma (plum) tomato	1 1/2 cups	375 mL
Chopped English cucumber (with peel), 1/2 inch (12 mm) pieces	1 cup	250 mL
Crumbled feta cheese	1/2 cup	125 mL
Sliced pitted kalamata olives	1/3 cup	75 mL
Balsamic vinegar	1 tbsp.	15 mL
Olive (or cooking) oil	1 tbsp.	15 mL
Slices of medium red onion, 1/2 inch (12 mm) thick	2	2
Small yellow peppers, halved	2	2
Pita bread (7 inch, 18 cm, diameter)	1	1
Olive (or cooking) oil	2 tsp.	10 mL
Greek seasoning	2 tsp.	10 mL
Boneless, skinless chicken breast halves	3/4 lb.	340 g
Olive (or cooking) oil	1 tsp.	5 mL
Greek seasoning	1 tsp.	5 mL
Cut or torn romaine lettuce, lightly packed	4 cups	1 L

Combine first 6 ingredients in large bowl.

Brush next 3 ingredients with second amount of olive oil. Sprinkle with Greek seasoning. Preheat barbecue to medium-high. Place onion, pepper and pita on greased grill. Close lid. Cook for about 4 minutes per side until grill marks appear and pita is crisp and browned. Transfer to cutting board. Let stand until cool enough to handle. Slice pepper. Chop onion. Add to tomato mixture. Stir. Break pita into bite-sized pieces.

Brush chicken with third amount of olive oil. Sprinkle with second amount of Greek seasoning. Place chicken on greased grill. Close lid. Cook for about 8 minutes per side until internal temperature reaches 170°F (77°C). Transfer to cutting board. Let stand until cool enough to handle. Chop. Add chicken, pita and lettuce to tomato mixture. Toss. Makes about 10 cups (2.5 L).

1 cup (250 mL): 118 Calories; 5.5 g Total Fat (2.8 g Mono, 0.7 g Poly, 1.7 g Sat); 26 mg Cholesterol; 7 g Carbohydrate; 1 g Fibre; 10 g Protein; 181 mg Sodium

Variation: Make individual salads by arranging tomato and lettuce mixture on serving plates and topping with sliced chicken.

Chicken Avocado Salad

Extra fruity with raisins and banana. A good addition to a salad luncheon.

Salad dressing (or mayonnaise)	1/2 cup	125 mL
Granulated sugar	1 tsp.	5 mL
Milk	2 tbsp.	30 mL
Diced cooked chicken	2 cups	500 mL
Diced celery	1/2 cup	125 mL
Chopped pecans or walnuts	1/4 cup	60 mL
Raisins	1/3 cup	75 mL
Salt	1/4 tsp.	1 mL
Pepper	1/8 tsp.	0.5 mL
Banana, sliced	1	1
Avocado, sliced	1	1
Bite-sized lettuce	2 cups	500 mL

In medium bowl mix first 3 ingredients.

Add chicken, celery, pecans, raisins, salt and pepper. Stir together well.

Fold in banana and avocado.

Line serving bowl or platter with lettuce. Pile salad on top. Individual plates may be lined with lettuce with salad divided among them. Makes 3 1/3 cups (775 mL). Serves 4.

1 serving: 440 Calories; 27 g Total Fat (12 g Mono, 9 g Poly, 4.5 g Sat); 60 mg Cholesterol; 32 g Carbohydrate; 6 g Fibre; 21 g Protein; 430 mg Sodium

Chicken Taco Salad

A great meal salad that's low in calories, fat and sodium. Serve with homemade or store-bought baked tortilla chips if desired.

Canola oil	1 tsp.	5 mL
Extra-lean ground chicken breast	3/4 lb.	340 g
Chili powder	2 tsp.	10 mL
Ground cumin	1/2 tsp.	2 mL
Garlic powder	1/4 tsp.	1 mL
Salsa	1/4 cup	60 mL
Cut or torn romaine lettuce, lightly packed	8 cups	2 L
Canned black beans, drained and rinsed	1 cup	250 mL
Slivered red pepper	1 cup	250 mL
Thinly sliced red onion	1/2 cup	125 mL

(continued on next page)

Light sour cream	1/4 cup	60 mL
Salsa	1/4 cup	60 mL
Lime juice	2 tbsp.	30 mL
Granulated sugar	1/2 tsp.	2 mL
Diced avocado	1 cup	250 mL
Diced tomato	1 cup	250 mL
Chopped fresh cilantro (or parsley)	2 tbsp.	30 mL

Heat canola oil in large frying pan on medium. Add next 4 ingredients. Scramble-fry for about 8 minutes until chicken is no longer pink. Add first amount of salsa. Stir. Remove from heat. Let stand for 10 minutes.

Toss next 4 ingredients in large bowl.

Stir next 4 ingredients in small bowl until smooth. Add to lettuce mixture. Toss. Add remaining 3 ingredients and chicken mixture. Toss. Makes about 13 cups (3.25 L)

1 cup (250 mL): 80 Calories; 3 g Total Fat (1.5 g Mono, 0 g Poly, 0.5 g Sat); 20 mg Cholesterol; 8 g Carbohydrate; 3 g Fibre; 8 g Protein; 139 mg Sodium

Polynesian Chicken Salad

A wonderful meaty sauce spooned hot over lettuce. Different and so good.

Cooking oil	2 tbsp.	30 mL
Chicken breast, halved, skin and bones removed, cut bite size	1	1
Chicken thighs, skin and bones removed, cut bite size	4	4
Thinly sliced celery	1 cup	250 mL
Green onions, sliced	6	6
Can of bamboo shoots (10 oz., 284 mL), drained	1	1
Can of sliced mushrooms (10 oz., 284 mL), drained	1	1
Medium tomatoes, cubed	2	2
Soy sauce	3 tbsp.	45 mL
Ground ginger	1/8 tsp.	0.5 mL
Garlic powder	1/8 tsp.	0.5 mL
Salt	1/4 tsp.	1 mL
Cut or torn head lettuce	6 cups	1.35 L

Heat cooking oil in wok or frying pan. Add chicken and celery. Sauté until no pink remains in meat.

Add next 8 ingredients. Stir-fry about 2 minutes.

Divide lettuce among 6 plates. Spoon hot mixture over top. Makes 6 servings.

1 serving: 180 Calories; 8 g Total Fat (3.5 g Mono, 2 g Poly, 1 g Sat); 60 mg Cholesterol; 7 g Carbohydrate; 3 g Fibre; 21 g Protein; 880 mg Sodium

Chicken Salad Amandine

*pants? Who cares? When you have the perfect picnic salad, nothing can ruin
...ting. Doubles easily for larger crowds. If you're making the salad in advance, wait until
just before serving to add the dressing.*

Water	4 cups	1 L
Salt	1/2 tsp.	2 mL
Elbow macaroni	1 cup	250 mL
Chopped cooked chicken (see Tip, page 58)	2 cups	500 mL
Diced medium Cheddar cheese	1/2 cup	125 mL
Sliced celery	1/2 cup	125 mL
Sliced natural almonds, toasted (see Tip, page 22)	1/2 cup	125 mL
Jar of sliced pimento (2 oz., 57 mL), well drained and chopped	1	1
Sliced green onion	3 tbsp.	45 mL
Salt	1/4 tsp.	1 mL
Pepper	1/8 tsp.	0.5 mL
Salad dressing (or mayonnaise)	1/2 cup	125 mL
Sweet pickle relish	1 tbsp.	15 mL
White vinegar	1 tbsp.	15 mL
Granulated sugar	1 1/2 tsp.	7 mL

Combine water and salt in large saucepan. Bring to a boil. Add macaroni. Boil, uncovered,
for 6 to 8 minutes, stirring occasionally, until tender but firm. Drain. Rinse with cold water.
Drain. Transfer to large bowl.

Add next 8 ingredients. Toss.

For the dressing, combine last 4 ingredients in small bowl. Makes about 3/4 cup (175 mL)
dressing. Pour over chicken mixture. Toss. Makes about 6 cups (1.5 L).

*1 cup (250 mL): 405 Calories; 25.4 g Total Fat (12.9 g Mono, 6.9 g Poly, 4.6 g Sat); 56 mg Cholesterol;
26 g Carbohydrate; 2 g Fibre; 18 g Protein; 507 mg Sodium*

Spinach Orzo Salad

The complaints about eating leftover chicken will soon cease when your family tastes this light and fresh salad. This colourful spinach creation contains orzo, a tiny pasta similar in shape to rice.

Water	2 cups	500 mL
Salt	1/4 tsp.	1 mL
Orzo	1/2 cup	125 mL
Fresh spinach leaves, lightly packed	4 cups	1 L
Chopped cooked chicken (see Tip, page 58)	2 cups	500 mL
Diced fresh tomato	1 1/2 cups	375 mL
Kalamata olives, chopped	1/2 cup	125 mL
FETA DRESSING		
Crumbled feta cheese	1/3 cup	75 mL
Olive (or cooking) oil	1/4 cup	60 mL
Balsamic vinegar	2 tbsp.	30 mL
Lemon juice	1 tbsp.	15 mL
Chopped fresh oregano (or 1/4 tsp., 1 mL, dried)	1 tsp.	5 mL
Salt	1/4 tsp.	1 mL
Pepper	1 tsp.	5 mL

Combine water and salt in small saucepan. Bring to a boil. Add orzo. Boil, uncovered, for about 8 minutes, stirring occasionally, until tender but firm. Drain. Rinse with cold water. Drain well. Transfer to large bowl.

Add next 4 ingredients. Toss.

Feta Dressing: Process all 7 ingredients in blender until smooth. Makes about 1/2 cup (125 mL) dressing. Drizzle over salad. Toss. Makes about 8 1/2 cups (2.1 L).

1 cup (250 mL): 210 Calories; 11.4 g Total Fat (7.2 g Mono, 1.2 g Poly, 2.4 g Sat); 37 mg Cholesterol; 14 g Carbohydrate; 1 g Fibre; 13 g Protein; 333 mg Sodium

Pictured on page 144.

 To slice meat easily, place it in the freezer for about 30 minutes before you cut it. It should be just starting to freeze. If using meat from frozen a state, partially thaw it before cutting.

Mulligatawny Soup

Although carrot and celery aren't in the authentic recipe, they make a colourful addition.

Butter (or hard margarine)	2 tbsp.	30 mL
Sliced onion	1 cup	250 mL
All-purpose flour	1/3 cup	75 mL
Curry powder	2 tsp.	10 mL
Chicken broth	6 cups	1.35 L
Cooking apple, (McIntosh is good) peeled and diced	1	1
Ground cloves, sprinkle		
Diced cooked chicken	2 cups	500 mL
Cream	1/3 cup	75 mL
Leftover cooked rice	3/4 cup	175 mL

Melt butter in large pot. Add onion. Sauté until soft.

Mix in flour and curry powder. Stir in broth until it boils and thickens.

Add apple and cloves. Cover. Simmer for 30 minutes.

Add chicken and cream. Simmer 5 minutes.

Divide rice among 6 soup dishes. Pour soup over top and serve. Makes 6 3/4 cups (1.5 L) of soup not including rice. Serves 6.

1 serving: 230 Calories; 8 g Total Fat (2.5 g Mono, 1 g Poly, 4.5 g Sat); 55 mg Cholesterol; 22 g Carbohydrate; 2 g Fibre; 15 g Protein; 620 mg Sodium

Cabbage and Chicken Soup

Quite thick. Tasty and filling.

Prepared chicken broth	6 cups	1.35 L
Long grain rice, uncooked	1/3 cup	75 mL
Chopped onion	1/2 cup	125 mL
Ketchup	1 tbsp.	15 mL
Grated cabbage, packed	3 cups	750 mL
Diced cooked chicken	1 cup	250 mL
Salt	1/4 tsp.	1 mL
Pepper, sprinkle		
Grated medium or sharp Cheddar cheese	6 tbsp.	90 mL

(continued on next page)

In large saucepan combine chicken broth, rice, onion and ketchup. Cover. Cook for about 15 minutes until rice is tender.

Add cabbage, chicken, salt and pepper. Return to a boil. Cook for about 5 minutes to cook cabbage.

Sprinkle each serving with cheese. Makes 6 1/3 cups (1.4 L). Serves 6.

1 serving: 220 Calories; 9 g Total Fat (3 g Mono, 1.5 g Poly, 3 g Sat); 60 mg Cholesterol; 13 g Carbohydrate; 1 g Fibre; 19 g Protein; 770 mg Sodium

Only Chicken Soup

It's not a lie—everything but the chicken is blended smooth! This creamy, golden soup has a wonderful medley of vegetable and chicken flavours.

Chopped onion	1 cup	250 mL
Chopped celery	1 cup	250 mL
Garlic clove, minced (or 1/4 tsp., 1 mL, powder)	1	1
Cooking oil	1 tbsp.	15 mL
Water	6 cups	1.5 L
Chopped carrot (about 2 medium)	1 cup	250 mL
Medium potatoes, peeled and cut into 8 chunks	2	2
Peeled diced zucchini	1 1/2 cups	375 mL
Boneless, skinless chicken breast halves (about 2)	8 oz.	225 g
Chicken bouillon powder	3 tbsp.	45 mL
Parsley flakes	2 tsp.	10 mL
Bay leaf	1	1
Alphabet pasta, uncooked (optional)	1/2 cup	125 mL

Sauté onion, celery and garlic in cooking oil in large uncovered pot or Dutch oven until onion is soft and clear.

Stir in remaining 10 ingredients. Cover. Simmer for 1 hour. Remove chicken to cutting board. Remove and discard bay leaf. Purée soup, in 2 batches, in blender or with hand blender until smooth (see Safety Tip). Return to pot. Cut chicken into bite-sized pieces. Return to soup. Makes 10 2/3 cups (2.7 L).

1 cup (250 mL): 77 Calories; 1.9 g Total Fat (0.9 g Mono, 0.5 g Poly, 0.2 g Sat); 13 mg Cholesterol; 10 g Carbohydrate; 1 g Fibre; 6 g Protein; 961 mg Sodium

Safety Tip: Follow manufacturer's instructions for processing hot liquids.

Creamy Chicken Soup

Creamy good with a taste of cheese.

Peeled, diced potato	2 1/2 cups	625 mL
Chopped onion	1/2 cup	125 mL
Chopped carrot	1/2 cup	125 mL
Chopped celery	1/2 cup	125 mL
Condensed cream of mushroom soup (10 oz., 284 mL)	1	1
Milk	2 1/2 cups	625 mL
Diced cooked chicken	1 cup	250 mL
Worcestershire sauce	1/4 tsp.	1 mL
Parsley flakes	1/4 tsp.	1 mL
Salt	1/4 tsp.	1 mL
Pepper	1/8 tsp.	0.5 mL
Ground thyme	1/8 tsp.	0.5 mL
Grated medium or sharp Cheddar cheese	1 cup	250 mL

Cook potato, onion, carrot and celery in some boiling water until tender. Drain. Mash together.

Add next 8 ingredients. Stir. Heat to a simmer.

Stir in cheese until it melts. Makes 6 2/3 cups (1.6 L). Serves 6.

1 serving: 270 Calories; 12 g Total Fat (3 g Mono, 1.5 g Poly, 6 g Sat); 45 mg Cholesterol; 23 g Carbohydrate; 2 g Fibre; 18 g Protein; 650 mg Sodium

 tip Pine nuts have a relatively high oil content and burn easily, so take care when toasting them.

Comfort Chicken Noodle Soup

There's nothing like a comforting bowl of chicken noodle soup to cure what ails you! This long-simmered, made-from-scratch soup is well worth the effort. Use whichever cuts of chicken you prefer, as long as the weight used is equal to that listed.

CHICKEN STOCK

Bone-in chicken parts	4 lbs.	1.8 kg
Water	10 cups	2.5 L
Celery ribs, with leaves, halved	2	2
Large onion, quartered	1	1
Large carrot, halved	1	1
Sprigs of fresh thyme	3	3
Sprig of fresh parsley	1	1
Bay leaves	2	2
Garlic clove	1	1
Whole black peppercorns	12	12
Cooking oil	2 tsp.	10 mL
Chopped onion	1/2 cup	125 mL
Chopped carrot	1/2 cup	125 mL
Chopped celery	1/2 cup	125 mL
Spaghetti, broken into about 3 inch (7.5 cm) pieces	3 oz.	85 g
Chopped fresh parsley	1/4 cup	60 mL
Salt	3/4 tsp.	4 mL
Pepper	1/4 tsp.	1 mL

Chicken Stock: Put chicken and water into Dutch oven or large pot. Bring to a boil. Boil, uncovered, for 5 minutes without stirring. Skim and discard foam from side of pot.

Add next 8 ingredients. Stir. Bring to a boil. Reduce heat to medium-low. Simmer, uncovered, for about 3 hours, stirring occasionally, until chicken is tender and starts to fall off bones. Remove from heat. Remove chicken and bones to cutting board using slotted spoon. Remove chicken from bones. Discard bones and skin. Chop enough chicken to make 2 cups (500 mL). Reserve remaining chicken for another use. Strain stock through sieve into large bowl. Discard solids. Skim fat from stock. Makes about 6 1/2 cups (1.6 L) stock.

For the soup, heat cooking oil in large saucepan on medium. Add next 3 ingredients. Cook for 5 to 10 minutes, stirring often, until onion is softened. Add stock. Bring to a boil.

Add spaghetti. Cook, uncovered, for about 10 minutes, stirring occasionally, until spaghetti and vegetables are tender.

Add chicken and remaining 3 ingredients. Heat and stir until chicken is heated through. Makes about 7 1/2 cups (1.9 L).

1 cup (250 mL): 137 Calories; 4.3 g Total Fat (1.8 g Mono, 1.1 g Poly, 0.9 g Sat); 34 mg Cholesterol; 11 g Carbohydrate; 1 g Fibre; 13 g Protein; 287 mg Sodium

Asian Chicken Soup

Clear broth with fine egg threads and vegetables.

Cans of condensed chicken broth (10 oz., 284 mL)	2	2
Water	2 1/2 cups	575 mL
Sliced fresh mushrooms	1/2 cup	125 mL
Thinly sliced bok choy	1 cup	250 mL
Finely chopped celery	1/3 cup	75 mL
Diced cooked chicken	1/2 cup	125 mL
Chopped water chestnuts	2 tbsp.	30 mL
Salt	1/2 tsp.	2 mL
Pepper	1/8 tsp.	0.5 mL
Large egg, beaten frothy	1	1

Combine first 9 ingredients in large saucepan. Bring to a boil. Simmer for 15 minutes.

Add beaten egg slowly in a thin stream to boiling liquid as you whisk with a fork. It will cook in fine threads. Makes 5 generous cups (1.2 L).

Variation: To make soup thicker, mix 2 tsp. (10 mL) cornstarch with 1 tbsp. (15 mL) water. Stir into boiling liquid.

1 cup (250 mL): 80 Calories; 3 g Total Fat (1 g Mono, 0.5 g Poly, 1 g Sat); 55 mg Cholesterol; 3 g Carbohydrate; <1 g Fibre; 11 g Protein; 1030 mg Sodium

1. Sunday Fried Chicken, page 259
2. Grilled Hoisin Drumsticks, page 129
3. Italian Burgers, page 104

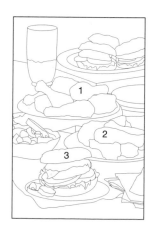

Cock-a-leekie Soup

A chicken and leek soup that was served in Scotland as early as the 16th century—it's sure to bring out the Scot in anyone! This version includes the traditional ingredient of dried prunes, which adds a rich flavour.

Prepared chicken broth	10 cups	2.5 L
Leeks, white part only, chopped	8	8
Long-grain rice, uncooked	1/4 cup	60 mL
Quartered pitted dried prunes	1 1/2 cups	375 mL
Parsley flakes	1/2 tsp.	2 mL
Ground thyme	1/8 tsp.	0.5 mL
Salt	1/2 tsp.	2 mL
Pepper	1/4 tsp.	1 mL
Diced cooked chicken (see Tip, page 58)	3 cups	750 mL

Combine first 8 ingredients in large pot. Bring to a boil. Cook slowly for about 30 minutes.

Add chicken. Cover. Cook for another 10 minutes. Makes about 14 cups (3.5 L).

1 cup (250 mL): 125 Calories; 2.4 g Total Fat (0.9 g Mono, 0.5 g Poly, 0.7 g Sat); 27 mg Cholesterol; 15 g Carbohydrate; 1 g Fibre; 10 g Protein; 935 mg Sodium

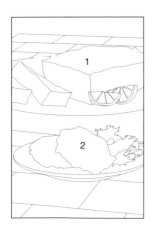

1. Chipotle Chicken Loaf, page 257
2. Chili-rubbed Chicken, page 268

Hot and Sour Chicken Pot Soup

Familiar and comforting with just the right blend of spicy and sour ingredients, this soup will have you on your feet in no time.

Chinese dried mushrooms	6	6
Boiling water	1 cup	250 mL
Prepared chicken broth	4 cups	1 L
Diced cooked chicken (see Tip, page 58)	2 cups	500 mL
Sliced carrot	2 cups	500 mL
Cubed firm tofu	1 cup	250 mL
Sliced celery	1 cup	250 mL
Soy sauce	1/4 cup	60 mL
Rice vinegar	2 tbsp.	30 mL
Chili paste (sambal oelek)	1 tsp.	5 mL
Prepared chicken broth	1/4 cup	60 mL
Cornstarch	2 tbsp.	30 mL
Sesame oil (optional)	1 tsp.	5 mL
Chopped baby bok choy	2 cups	500 mL
Thinly sliced green onion	1/4 cup	60 mL
Rice vinegar	1 tbsp.	15 mL

Put mushrooms into small heatproof bowl. Add boiling water. Stir. Let stand for about 20 minutes until softened. Drain. Remove and discard stems. Slice caps into thin strips. Transfer to 3 1/2 to 4 quart (3.5 to 4 L) slow cooker.

Add next 8 ingredients. Stir well. Cook, covered, on Low for 4 to 6 hours or High for 2 to 3 hours until carrot is tender.

Combine next 3 ingredients in small bowl. Add to slow cooker. Stir. Add bok choy and green onion. Stir well. Cook, covered, on High for about 5 minutes until slightly thickened.

Stir in second amount of vinegar. Makes about 8 cups (2 L).

1 cup (250 mL): 118 Calories; 2.1 g Total Fat (0.6 g Mono, 0.6 g Poly, 0.6 g Sat); 34 mg Cholesterol; 9 g Carbohydrate; 2 g Fibre; 15 g Protein; 1142 mg Sodium

Chicken and Bacon Pea Soup

The combination of chicken and bacon really adds depth to this delicious, creamy soup.

Cooking oil	2 tsp.	10 mL
Chopped red pepper	1 cup	250 mL
Chopped green onion	1 cup	250 mL
Boneless, skinless chicken thighs, cut into 1/2 inch (12 mm) pieces	6 oz.	170 g
Chopped lean back bacon	1/3 cup	75 mL
Paprika	1/2 tsp.	2 mL
Pepper	1/2 tsp.	2 mL
All-purpose flour	2 tbsp.	30 mL
Milk	2 cups	500 mL
Low-sodium prepared chicken broth	2 cups	500 mL
Frozen peas	1 cup	250 mL
Light sour cream	2 tbsp.	30 mL

Heat cooking oil in large saucepan on medium. Add next 6 ingredients. Cook for 5 to 10 minutes, stirring occasionally, until chicken is no longer pink inside.

Add flour. Heat and stir for 1 minute.

Slowly add milk and broth, stirring constantly. Heat and stir until boiling and thickened. Reduce heat to medium-low. Simmer, uncovered, for 10 minutes, stirring occasionally.

Add peas and sour cream. Stir. Cover. Simmer for about 5 minutes, stirring occasionally, until peas are heated through. Makes 5 1/2 cups (1.4 L). Serves 6.

1 serving: 149 Calories; 5 g Total Fat (2.1 g Mono, 1.0 g Poly, 1.7 g Sat); 33 mg Cholesterol; 13 g Carbohydrate; 2 g Fibre; 13 g Protein; 361 mg Sodium

Chicken Borscht

A full-bodied, beautifully coloured soup.

Prepared chicken broth	8 cups	1.8 L
Medium carrot, slivered	1	1
Medium parsnip, slivered	1	1
Medium beet, peeled and slivered	1	1
Chopped onion	1 cup	250 mL
Grated raw potato, packed	2 cups	500 mL
Tomato sauce	7 1/2 oz.	213 mL
White vinegar	1 tbsp.	15 mL
Parsley flakes	1/2 tsp.	2 mL
Dill weed	1/4 tsp.	1 mL
Salt	1/2 tsp.	2 mL
Pepper	1/8 tsp.	0.5 mL
Diced cooked chicken (see Tip, below)	1 cup	250 mL
Diced cooked ham	1 cup	250 mL
Grated cabbage, packed	3 cups	750 mL
Sour cream	2/3 cup	150 mL

Put first 12 ingredients into large pot. Cover and cook slowly for about 20 minutes.

Add chicken, ham and cabbage. Cook, covered, for 10 minutes more.

To each serving, add 1 tbsp. (15 mL) sour cream in centre. Makes 12 cups (3 L). Serves 10.

1 serving: 130 Calories; 4.5 g Total Fat (1.5 g Mono, 0 g Poly, 2 g Sat); 20 mg Cholesterol; 13 g Carbohydrate; 2 g Fibre; 7 g Protein; 750 mg Sodium

 Don't have any leftover chicken? Start with 2 boneless, skinless chicken breast halves (about 4 oz., 113 g, each). Place them in a large frying pan with 1 cup (250 mL) water or chicken broth. Simmer, covered, for 12 to 14 minutes until no longer pink inside. Drain. Chop. Makes about 2 cups (500 mL) of cooked chicken.

Chicken Corn Soup

Your standard chicken soup just went south of the border and came back with the exciting flavours of chipotle, lime and cilantro.

Canola oil	1 tsp.	5 mL
Frozen kernel corn	2 cups	500 mL
Chopped onion	1 cup	250 mL
Garlic cloves, minced	2	2
(or 1/2 tsp., 2 mL, powder)		
Finely chopped chipotle pepper in adobo sauce (see Tip, page 78)	1/2 tsp.	2 mL
Low-sodium prepared chicken broth	3 cups	750 mL
Can of diced tomatoes (14 oz., 398 mL), with juice		
Pepper	1/4 tsp.	1 mL
Chopped cooked chicken (see Tip, page 58)	2 cups	500 mL
Chopped fresh cilantro	1 tbsp.	15 mL
Lime juice	1 tbsp.	15 mL

Heat canola oil in large saucepan on medium-high. Add next 4 ingredients. Cook, uncovered, for about 4 minutes, stirring often, until onion is softened.

Add next 3 ingredients. Stir. Bring to a boil. Reduce heat to medium. Boil gently, covered, for 6 minutes to blend flavours.

Add chicken. Cook and stir for about 3 minutes until heated through.

Add cilantro and lime juice. Stir. Makes about 7 cups (1.75 L). Serves 6.

1 serving: 201 Calories; 5.6 g Total Fat (1.8 g Mono, 1.1 g Poly, 1.1 g Sat); 58 mg Cholesterol; 16 g Carbohydrate; 1 g Fibre; 22 g Protein; 699 mg Sodium

Black Bean Chicken Soup

This salsa-spiced bean soup will get you shaking your maracas in no time! Garnish with a dollop of sour cream and serve with a slice of cornbread.

Cooking oil	1 tbsp.	15 mL
Chopped onion	2 cups	500 mL
Boneless, skinless chicken thighs, chopped	1/2 lb.	225 g
Chopped fresh jalapeño pepper (see Tip, page 166)	2 tbsp.	30 mL
Garlic cloves, minced (or 3/4 tsp., 4 mL, powder)	3	3
Dried oregano	1 tsp.	5 mL
Ground coriander	1/2 tsp.	2 mL
Ground cumin	1/2 tsp.	2 mL
Prepared chicken broth	4 cups	1 L
Bay leaves	2	2
Can of diced tomatoes (28 oz., 796 mL), with juice	1	1
Can of black beans (19 oz., 540 mL), rinsed and drained	1	1
Barbecue sauce	1/3 cup	75 mL
Salsa	1/4 cup	60 mL
Chopped fresh cilantro or parsley	1/4 cup	60 mL
Lime juice	3 tbsp.	45 mL
Pepper	1/4 tsp.	1 mL

Heat cooking oil in Dutch oven or large pot on medium. Add next 7 ingredients. Cook, uncovered, for about 10 minutes, stirring occasionally, until onion is softened and chicken is no longer pink.

Add broth and bay leaves. Stir. Bring to a boil. Reduce heat to medium-low. Simmer, covered, for 10 minutes to blend flavours.

Process next 4 ingredients in blender or food processor until almost smooth. Add to soup. Stir. Bring to a boil. Reduce heat to medium-low. Simmer for 5 minutes to blend flavours. Discard bay leaves.

Add remaining 3 ingredients. Stir. Makes about 10 1/2 cups (2.6 L).

1 cup (250 mL): 162 Calories; 3.9 g Total Fat (1.7 g Mono, 1.0 g Poly, 0.8 g Sat); 14 mg Cholesterol; 21 g Carbohydrate; 4 g Fibre; 12 g Protein; 723 mg Sodium

Pictured on page 18.

Shredded Chicken Soup

Turn notions of classic chicken soup upside down with this shredded version studded with pimientoes.

Water	10 cups	2.5 L
Chicken legs, back attached, skin removed	2 lbs.	900 g
Bone-in chicken breast halves, skin removed	1 lb.	454 g
Chopped carrot	1 cup	250 mL
Chopped celery	1 cup	250 mL
Chopped onion	1 cup	250 mL
Chicken bouillon powder	2 tbsp.	30 mL
Bay leaf	1	1
Dried thyme	1/2 tsp.	2 mL
Salt	1/4 tsp.	1 mL
Pepper	1/4 tsp.	1 mL
Cayenne pepper	1/8 tsp.	0.5 mL
Jar of sliced pimiento (2 oz., 57 mL), well drained	1	1
Water	1/2 cup	125 mL
All-purpose flour	2 tbsp.	30 mL

Combine first 12 ingredients in Dutch oven or large pot. Bring to a boil. Reduce heat to medium-low. Simmer, uncovered, for about 1 1/2 hours, stirring occasionally, until chicken is tender and starts to fall off bones. Remove from heat. Transfer chicken and bones to cutting board using slotted spoon. Remove chicken from bones. Discard bones. Shred chicken. Set aside. Discard bay leaf. Skim and discard fat from broth.

Add pimiento. Carefully process with hand blender or in blender until smooth (see Safety Tip). Add chicken. Bring to a boil. Reduce heat to medium.

Stir second amount of water into flour in small bowl until smooth. Add to soup. Stir. Cook for about 5 minutes, stirring occasionally, until thickened. Makes about 10 cups (2.5 L).

1 cup (250 mL): 190 Calories; 4.5 g Total Fat (1.5 g Mono, 1.5 g Poly, 1.5 g Sat); 105 mg Cholesterol; 5 g Carbohydrate; <1 g Fibre; 29 g Protein; 730 mg Sodium

Safety Tip: Follow blender manufacturer's instructions for processing hot liquids.

Chicken Corn Chowder

Consider this to be the food version of a warm, comforting hug.

Cooking oil	1 tbsp.	15 mL
Boneless, skinless chicken breast halves, chopped	1 lb.	454 g
Chopped onion	1 cup	250 mL
Chopped deli ham	3/4 cup	175 mL
Chopped celery	1/2 cup	125 mL
Dried crushed chilies	1/2 tsp.	2 mL
Prepared chicken broth	4 cups	1 L
Frozen kernel corn	2 1/2 cups	625 mL
Chopped peeled potato	2 cups	500 mL
Diced red pepper	1 cup	250 mL
Sliced green onion	1/2 cup	125 mL
Sprigs of fresh thyme	2	2
Bay leaf	1	1
Salt	1/4 tsp.	1 mL
Can of evaporated milk (13 1/2 oz., 385 mL)	1	1
All-purpose flour	3 tbsp.	45 mL

Heat cooking oil in Dutch oven or large pot on medium. Add next 5 ingredients. Stir. Cook, uncovered, for about 10 minutes, stirring occasionally, until chicken is no longer pink and vegetables are softened.

Add next 8 ingredients. Stir. Bring to a boil. Reduce heat to medium-low. Simmer, covered, for about 15 minutes until potato is tender.

Whisk evaporated milk and flour in small bowl until smooth. Stir into soup. Increase heat to medium. Heat and stir for about 5 minutes until boiling and thickened. Discard thyme sprigs and bay leaf. Makes about 10 cups (2.5 L).

1 cup (250 mL): 225 Calories; 6.2 g Total Fat (2.2 g Mono, 1.0 g Poly, 2.3 g Sat); 42 mg Cholesterol; 25 g Carbohydrate; 2 g Fibre; 9 g Protein; 580 mg Sodium

Pictured on page 18.

Chicken Pumpkin Soup

Pumpkins abound in October—put them to good use in this elegant soup.

Butter (or hard margarine)	2 tbsp.	30 mL
Boneless, skinless chicken breast halves, cut in 1/2 inch (12 mm) cubes	6 oz.	170 g
Finely chopped onion	2 1/2 cups	625 mL
Garlic cloves, minced	3	3
Bay leaves	2	2
Salt	1/4 tsp.	1 mL
Pepper	1/4 tsp.	1 mL
Prepared chicken broth	3 cups	750 mL
Can of pure pumpkin (no spices) (14 oz., 398 mL)	1	1
Chopped fresh dill (or 1 1/2 tsp., 7 mL, dried)	2 tbsp.	30 mL
Sour cream	1/2 cup	125 mL
Chopped salted, roasted shelled pumpkin seeds	1/4 cup	60 mL
Chopped fresh dill (or 1/4 tsp., 1 mL, dried)	1 tsp.	5 mL

Melt butter in large saucepan on medium. Add next 6 ingredients. Cook, uncovered, for about 10 minutes, stirring occasionally, until onionis very soft and chicken is no longer pink.

Add next 3 ingredients. Stir. Bring to a boil. Reduce heat to medium-low. Simmer, covered, for 5 minutes to blend flavours. Discard bay leaves. Remove from heat.

Stir sour cream into soup. Sprinkle pumpkin seeds and dill over individual servings. Makes about 7 cups (1.75 L) soup. Serves 4.

1 serving: 341 Calories; 18.8 g Total Fat (4.0 g Mono, 3.4 g Poly, 8.9 g Sat); 60 mg Cholesterol; 23 g Carbohydrate; 5 g Fibre; 21 g Protein; 892 mq Sodium

Chicken Gumbo

This southern favourite is sure to pique the hot-sauce lover's interest.

Cooking oil	1 tbsp.	15 mL
Boneless, skinless chicken breast halves, cut into 1 inch (2.5 cm) cubes	1/2 lb.	225 g
Cooking oil	3 tbsp.	45 mL
All-purpose flour	3 tbsp.	45 mL
Can of stewed tomatoes (14 oz., 398 mL)	1	1
Tomato paste (see Tip, page 136)	2 tbsp.	30 mL
Paprika	1 tsp.	5 mL
Prepared chicken broth	4 cups	1 L
Fresh (or frozen, thawed) okra, cut into 1/2 inch (12 mm) slices	2 cups	500 mL
Diced celery	1 cup	250 mL
Diced green pepper	1 cup	250 mL
Diced onion	1 cup	250 mL
Sliced smoked ham sausage	1 cup	250 mL
Garlic cloves, minced (or 1/2 tsp., 2 mL, powder)	2	2
Bay leaf	1	1
Louisiana hot sauce	1 tsp.	5 mL
Dried thyme	1 tsp.	5 mL
Long grain white rice	1/2 cup	125 mL
Frozen, uncooked medium shrimp (peeled and deveined), thawed (optional)	1/2 lb.	225 g

Heat first amount of cooking oil in Dutch oven or large pot on medium-high. Add chicken. Cook, uncovered, for about 3 minutes, stirring occasionally, until lightly browned. Transfer to small bowl. Set aside.

Heat second amount of cooking oil in same pot on medium. Add flour. Heat and stir for about 3 minutes until deep golden brown.

Slowly add next 3 ingredients, stirring constantly and breaking up tomatoes with spoon, until combined. Heat and stir for 1 minute.

Add next 11 ingredients and chicken. Stir. Bring to a boil. Reduce heat to medium-low. Simmer, covered, for 45 to 60 minutes, stirring occasionally, until rice and chicken are tender. Discard bay leaf.

Add shrimp. Stir. Cook, covered, for about 3 minutes until shrimp turn pink. Makes about 10 cups (2.5 L).

1 cup (250 mL): 220 Calories; 11.3 g Total Fat (5.8 g Mono, 2.4 g Poly, 2.4 g Sat); 23 mg Cholesterol; 17 g Carbohydrate; 2 g Fibre; 13 g Protein; 667 mg Sodium

Garden Noodle Soup

All the long hours spent toiling in your garden finally pay off! Fantastically fresh!

Cooking oil	2 tsp.	10 mL
Boneless, skinless chicken breast halves, chopped	1 lb.	454 g
Chopped zucchini (with peel)	1 cup	250 mL
Chopped onion	1/2 cup	125 mL
Chopped carrot	1/3 cup	75 mL
Prepared chicken broth	4 cups	1 L
Chopped tomato	1 1/2 cups	375 mL
Medium egg noodles	3/4 cup	175 mL
Chopped fresh asparagus	1/2 cup	125 mL
Sprig of fresh thyme (or 1/8 tsp., 0.5 mL dried)	1	1
Salt	1/4 tsp.	1 mL
Pepper	1/8 tsp.	0.5 mL
Chopped fresh spinach leaves, lightly packed	1 cup	250 mL
Chopped fresh basil	1 tbsp.	15 mL

Heat cooking oil in large saucepan or Dutch oven on medium-high. Add chicken. Stir. Cook, uncovered, for about 5 minutes, stirring occasionally, until no longer pink.

Add next 3 ingredients. Reduce heat to medium. Cook for about 5 minutes, stirring often, until onion is softened.

Add next 7 ingredients. Stir. Bring to a boil. Reduce heat to medium-low. Simmer, partially covered, for about 8 minutes until noodles are tender but firm. Discard thyme sprig.

Add spinach and basil. Heat and stir for 2 to 3 minutes until spinach is wilted. Makes about 7 cups (1.75 L).

1 cup (250 mL): 143 Calories; 3.5 g Total Fat (1.4 g Mono, 0.9 g Poly, 0.7 g Sat); 41 mg Cholesterol; 8 g Carbohydrate; 2 g Fibre; 19 g Protein; 578 mg Sodium

Pictured on page 18.

Quick Chicken Quinoa Stew

Does waiting around for hours for stew to simmer get you stewing mad? Well, if patience is not your virtue, this is the stew for you. Serve with crusty bread.

Olive (or cooking) oil	2 tsp.	10 mL
Boneless, skinless chicken thighs (about 3 oz., 85 g, each)	6	6
Chopped celery	1 cup	250 mL
Chopped onion	1 cup	250 mL
Chopped red pepper	1 cup	250 mL
Garlic cloves, minced (or 1/2 tsp., 2 mL, powder)	2	2
Can of plum tomatoes (28 oz., 796 mL), with juice	1	1
Prepared chicken broth	2 cups	500 mL
Chopped sun-dried tomatoes in oil, blotted dry	1/4 cup	60 mL
Tomato paste (see Tip, page 136)	3 tbsp.	45 mL
Dried basil	1 tsp.	5 mL
Dried crushed chilies	1/2 tsp.	2 mL
Dried oregano	1/2 tsp.	2 mL
Salt	1 tsp.	5 mL
Pepper	1/4 tsp.	1 mL
Dried rosemary, crushed	1/8 tsp.	0.5 mL
Quinoa, rinsed and drained	2/3 cup	150 mL

Heat olive oil in Dutch oven on medium-high. Add chicken. Cook, uncovered, for 2 to 3 minutes per side until browned. Remove to plate. Set aside. Reduce heat to medium.

Add celery and onion to same pot. Cook for about 5 minutes, stirring often, until onion starts to soften. Add red pepper and garlic. Cook for 1 minute, stirring occasionally.

Add next 10 ingredients. Stir. Cook for about 5 minutes, stirring occasionally and breaking up tomatoes, until boiling.

Add quinoa and chicken. Reduce heat to medium-low. Simmer, covered, for about 30 minutes until chicken is fully cooked and quinoa is tender. Serves 6.

1 serving: 298 Calories; 10.4 g Total Fat (4.4 g Mono, 2.3 g Poly, 2.4 g Sat); 57 mg Cholesterol; 29 g Carbohydrate; 5 g Fibre; 22 g Protein; 1089 mg Sodium

Souper Chicken Stew

This recipe is hearty like a stew, and rich and creamy like a soup—if you can't decide which comfort food you're in the mood for, this gives you both!

Cooking oil	2 tsp.	10 mL
Bone-in chicken thighs, skin removed (about 5 oz., 140 g, each)	8	8
Chopped carrot	2 cups	500 mL
Chopped celery	2 cups	500 mL
Chopped fresh white mushrooms	1 cup	250 mL
Chopped onion	1/2 cup	125 mL
Dried thyme	1/2 tsp.	2 mL
Paprika	1/2 tsp.	2 mL
Pepper	1/2 tsp.	2 mL
Ground allspice	1/4 tsp.	1 mL
Water	1 1/2 cups	375 mL
Can of condensed cream of chicken soup (10 oz., 284 mL)	1	1
Can of condensed tomato soup (10 oz., 284 mL)	1	1
Dry sherry	1/2 cup	125 mL
Balsamic vinegar	2 tbsp.	30 mL
Bay leaf	1	1
Fresh (or frozen) whole green beans, quartered	2 cups	500 mL

Heat cooking oil in Dutch oven or large pot on medium-high. Add chicken. Cook for about 3 minutes per side until browned. Transfer to plate.

Add next 8 ingredients to same pot. Cook for about 8 minutes, stirring often, until onion is softened.

Stir next 5 ingredients in medium bowl until smooth. Add to carrot mixture.

Add bay leaf and chicken. Stir. Bring to a boil. Reduce heat to medium-low. Simmer, covered, for about 45 minutes, stirring occasionally, until chicken is tender and no longer pink inside.

Add green beans. Stir. Cook, uncovered, for about 10 minutes until green beans are tender-crisp. Remove and discard bay leaf. Makes about 9 cups (2.25 L).

1 cup (250 mL): 248 Calories; 9.9 g Total Fat (3.6 g Mono, 2.6 g Poly, 2.4 g Sat); 68 mg Cholesterol; 18 g Carbohydrate; 3 g Fibre; 20 g Protein; 617 mg Sodium

Pictured on page 197.

Nutty Chicken Stew

This flavourful offering puts all your leftover chicken to good use—and it's healthy too! Serve over couscous to make a complete meal.

Cooking oil	1 tsp.	5 mL
Chopped carrot	1 cup	250 mL
Chopped onion	1 cup	250 mL
Ground cumin	2 tsp.	10 mL
Garlic cloves, minced	2	2
Ground cinnamon	1/4 tsp.	1 mL
Salt	1/2 tsp.	2 mL
Pepper	1/8 tsp.	0.5 mL
Can of diced tomatoes (with juice) (28 oz., 796 mL)	1	1
Can of lentils, rinsed and drained (19 oz., 540 mL)	1	1
Chopped cooked chicken (see Tip, page 58)	2 cups	500 mL
Small cauliflower florets	2 cups	500 mL
Chopped dried apricot	1/2 cup	125 mL
Peanut butter	1/4 cup	60 mL
Coarsely chopped unsalted peanuts	1/4 cup	60 mL
Chopped fresh parsley	2 tbsp.	30 mL

Heat cooking oil in Dutch oven on medium. Add next 7 ingredients. Cook for about 8 minutes, stirring often, until onion is softened.

Add next 6 ingredients. Stir. Bring to a boil. Reduce heat to medium-low. Simmer, covered, for about 30 minutes until cauliflower and carrot are tender-crisp.

Scatter peanuts and parsley over top. Makes about 7 1/2 cups (1.9 L). Serves 6.

1 serving: 340 Calories; 12 g Total Fat (2.5 g Mono, 1.5 g Poly, 2 g Sat); 33 mg Cholesterol; 39 g Carbohydrate; 7 g Fibre; 25 g Protein; 850 mg Sodium

Pictured on page 161.

Chicken Stew and Dumplings

This down-home favourite has been given an uptown makeover.

Bone-in chicken thighs, skin removed	1 1/2 lbs.	680 g
Chicken drumsticks, skin removed (see Tip, page 188)	1 1/2 lbs.	680 g
Salt, sprinkle		
Pepper, sprinkle		

(continued on next page)

Butter (or hard margarine)	1 tbsp.	15 mL
Chopped onion	2 cups	500 mL
Paprika	2 tsp.	10 mL
Garlic clove, minced (or 1/4 tsp., 1 mL, powder)	1	1
Caraway seed, crushed (see Tip, page 204)	1/2 tsp.	2 mL
Chopped fresh marjoram (or 1/8 tsp., 0.5 mL, dried)	1/2 tsp.	2 mL
All-purpose flour	1 tbsp.	15 mL
Chicken bouillon powder	1 tbsp.	15 mL
Water	3 cups	750 mL
DUMPLINGS		
All-purpose flour	2 1/4 cups	550 mL
Green onions, sliced	2	2
Baking powder	4 tsp.	20 mL
Salt	1 tsp.	5 mL
Vegetable cocktail juice	1 1/4 cups	300 mL
Cooking oil	1/4 cup	60 mL

Sprinkle chicken thighs and drumsticks with salt and pepper. Put into greased 4 quart (4 L) casserole. Set aside.

Melt butter in large frying pan on medium. Add onion. Cook for 5 to 10 minutes, stirring often, until softened.

Add next 4 ingredients. Heat and stir for 1 to 2 minutes until fragrant.

Add flour and bouillon powder. Heat and stir for 1 minute. Slowly add water, stirring constantly, until boiling and slightly thickened. Pour over chicken. Bake, covered, in 350°F (175°C) oven for about 1 1/2 hours until chicken is fully cooked and internal temperature reaches 170°F (77°C).

Dumplings: Measure first 4 ingredients into medium bowl. Stir. Make a well in centre.

Add vegetable juice and cooking oil to well. Stir until just moistened. Spoon mounds of batter, about 2 tbsp. (30 mL) each, in single layer on top of chicken mixture. Bake, covered, for 20 minutes. Bake, uncovered, for another 5 minutes until wooden pick inserted in centre of dumpling comes out clean. Serves 6.

1 serving: 575 Calories; 22.1 g Total Fat (9.6 g Mono, 5.5 g Poly, 4.8 g Sat); 150 mg Cholesterol; 47 g Carbohydrate; 3 g Fibre; 45 g Protein; 1324 mg Sodium

Mixed Chicken Stew

Two kinds of potatoes and plenty of vegetables in this tasty stew.

Chicken parts, skin removed	3 lbs.	1.36 kg
Chicken bouillon powder	2 tbsp.	30 mL
Ketchup	1 tbsp.	15 mL
Medium onions, cut in chunks	2	2
Medium carrots, sliced	3	3
Sliced celery	1/2 cup	125 mL
Medium potatoes, cubed	3	3
Sweet potatoes, sliced or cubed	1 lb.	454 g
Coarsely grated cabbage, packed	3 cups	750 mL
Salt	1 1/2 tsp.	7 mL
Pepper	1/4 tsp.	1 mL
Garlic powder	1/4 tsp.	1 mL
Ground thyme	1/2 tsp.	2 mL

Put chicken into large pot. Add water to cover. Add bouillon powder. Cover. Bring to a boil. Simmer for about 30 minutes until tender. Remove chicken with slotted spoon. Remove bones. Cut meat into bite-sized pieces and return to pot.

Add remaining ingredients. If it looks like too much liquid, reserve a cupful and add as needed. Cover. Cook slowly for about 1 hour. Makes 12 cups (2.7 L).

1 cup (250 mL): 260 Calories; 7 g Total Fat (2 g Mono, 2 g Poly, 2 g Sat); 70 mg Cholesterol; 20 g Carbohydrate; 3 g Fibre; 26 g Protein; 890 mg Sodium

1. Chicken Paella, page 240
2. Coconut Curry Casserole, page 242

Props courtesy of: Browne & Co.

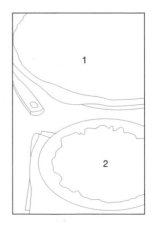

Brunswick Stew

The unexpected vegetable combination is sure to please.

Bacon slices, diced	4	4
Chopped onion	2 1/2 cups	575 mL
Chicken parts, skin removed	4 lbs.	1.8 kg
Chicken bouillon powder	2 tbsp.	30 mL
Canned tomatoes (14 oz., 398 mL), broken up	1	1
Medium potatoes, cubed	3	3
Kernel corn, fresh or frozen	2 cups	500 mL
Canned lima beans (14 oz., 398 mL), drained	1	1
Worcestershire sauce	2 tsp.	10 mL
Salt	1/2 tsp.	2 mL
Pepper	1/4 tsp.	1 mL
Cayenne pepper	1/8 tsp.	0.5 mL

Fry bacon and onion in frying pan. Transfer with slotted spoon to large pot.

Add chicken and enough boiling water to cover. Stir in bouillon powder. Bring to a boil. Cover. Simmer for about 45 minutes until chicken is tender. Remove chicken with slotted spoon. When cool enough to handle, remove bones. Cut meat into bite-sized pieces. Return to pot.

Add next 8 ingredients. Cook, uncovered, until potato is tender and stew has thickened, about 20 minutes. Makes 12 cups (2.7 L).

1 cup (250 mL): 390 Calories; 16 g Total Fat (5 g Mono, 3 g Poly, 4.5 g Sat); 105 mg Cholesterol; 24 g Carbohydrate; 4 g Fibre; 38 g Protein; 970 mg Sodium

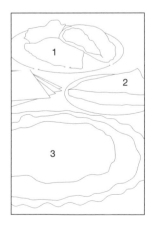

1. Picadillo Pastries, page 231
2. Pizza-style Meatloaf, page 260
3. Honey Garlic Crostata, page 227

Chunky Salsa Corn Stew

No need to serve cornbread on the side. This hearty chili is topped with cornmeal dumplings.
It's a rustic delight the whole family will love.

Cooking oil	1 tbsp.	15 mL
Boneless, skinless chicken thighs, halved	1 lb.	454 g
Salt	1/2 tsp.	2 mL
Pepper	1/4 tsp.	1 mL
Chopped green pepper	2 cups	500 mL
Chopped onion	1 1/2 cups	375 mL
Chili powder	1 tbsp.	15 mL
Ground cumin	1 tsp.	5 mL
Red baby potatoes, halved	1 lb.	454 g
Can of diced tomatoes (14 oz., 398 mL), with juice	1	1
Chunky salsa	1 1/2 cups	375 mL
Prepared chicken broth	1 1/2 cups	375 mL
Frozen kernel corn	1/2 cup	125 mL
Biscuit mix	1 1/3 cups	325 mL
Cornmeal	2/3 cup	150 mL
Milk	2/3 cup	150 mL
Frozen kernel corn, thawed	1/2 cup	125 mL
Chopped fresh cilantro or parsley (or 1 1/2 tsp., 7 mL, dried)	2 tbsp.	30 mL

Heat cooking oil in Dutch oven or large pot on medium. Add chicken. Sprinkle with salt and pepper. Cook, uncovered, for about 5 minutes, stirring occasionally, until starting to brown.

Add next 4 ingredients. Cook for 5 to 10 minutes, stirring occasionally, until vegetables are tender-crisp.

Add next 5 ingredients. Stir. Bring to a boil. Reduce heat to medium-low. Simmer, covered, for about 30 minutes until thickened and potato is tender.

Measure biscuit mix and cornmeal into medium bowl. Stir. Make a well in centre. Add remaining 3 ingredients to well. Stir until just moistened. Drop 2 tbsp. (30 mL) portions onto chicken mixture. Cook, covered, for about 20 minutes until wooden pick inserted into dumpling comes out clean. Serves 4.

1 serving: 710 Calories; 20.5 g Total Fat (9.4 g Mono, 4.4 g Poly, 4.9 g Sat); 77 mg Cholesterol; 96 g Carbohydrate; 10 g Fibre; 35 g Protein; 2134 mg Sodium

Chicken Biscuit Stew

Not only is this recipe lower in calories, fat and sodium than you'd expect, but it's also high in fibre, and it's loaded with vegetables. You definitely can't go wrong with that!

Canola oil	1 tsp.	5 mL
Boneless, skinless chicken thighs, halved	2 lbs.	900 g
All-purpose flour	3 tbsp.	45 mL
Garlic powder	1/2 tsp.	2 mL
Dried dillweed	1/2 tsp.	2 mL
Salt	1/8 tsp.	0.5 mL
Pepper	1/4 tsp.	1 mL
Prepared chicken broth	1 1/2 cups	375 mL
Chopped fresh (or frozen cut) green beans	1 cup	250 mL
Chopped onion	1 cup	250 mL
Chopped unpeeled potato	1 cup	250 mL
Sliced carrot	1 cup	250 mL
Sliced celery	1 cup	250 mL
CHEDDAR RANCH BISCUITS		
Whole wheat flour	1 1/2 cups	375 mL
Grated sharp Cheddar cheese	2/3 cup	150 mL
Baking powder	2 tsp.	10 mL
Cold butter	1 tbsp.	15 mL
Fat-free ranch dressing	3/4 cup	175 mL
Canola oil	1 tbsp.	15 mL

Heat canola oil in large frying pan on medium-high. Add chicken. Cook for about 10 minutes, stirring occasionally, until browned.

Add next 5 ingredients. Heat and stir for 1 minute. Slowly add broth, stirring constantly until smooth. Transfer chicken mixture to greased 3 quart (3 L) casserole.

Add remaining 5 ingredients. Stir. Bake, covered, in 375°F (190°C) oven for about 1 hour until potato and carrot are tender. Stir.

Cheddar Ranch Biscuits: Combine first 3 ingredients in medium bowl. Cut in butter until mixture resembles coarse crumbs.

Add dressing and canola oil. Stir until just moistened. Drop batter onto hot chicken mixture in 8 mounds, using about 1/4 cup (60 mL) for each. Bake, uncovered, for about 20 minutes until wooden pick inserted in centre of biscuit comes out clean. Serves 8.

1 serving: 360 Calories; 11 g Total Fat (4 g Mono, 2 g Poly, 4 g Sat); 106 mg Cholesterol; 36 g Carbohydrate; 5 g Fibre; 29 g Protein; 660 mg Sodium

Sauerkraut Potato Stew

Say hello to Oktoberfest with this rollicking sauerkraut and beer stew.

Cooking oil	2 tsp.	10 mL
Sliced smoked ham sausage	3/4 lb.	340 g
All-purpose flour	1/4 cup	60 mL
Salt	1/2 tsp.	2 mL
Pepper	1/4 tsp.	1 mL
Bone-in chicken thighs, skin removed	6	6
(about 5 oz., 140 g, each)		
Chopped onion	1 1/2 cups	375 mL
Chopped carrot	1/2 cup	125 mL
Cubed peeled potato	3 cups	750 mL
Prepared chicken broth	1 1/2 cups	375 mL
Beer	1 cup	250 mL
Diced peeled cooking apple	1 cup	250 mL
(such as McIntosh)		
Apple juice	1/2 cup	125 mL
Bay leaf	1	1
Caraway seed	1/2 tsp.	2 mL
Jar of wine sauerkraut	1	1
(17 1/2 oz., 500 mL), drained		

Heat cooking oil in Dutch oven or large pot on medium. Add sausage. Cook, uncovered, for about 5 minutes, stirring occasionally, until lightly browned. Transfer with slotted spoon to medium bowl. Set aside.

Combine next 3 ingredients in large resealable freezer bag. Add chicken. Toss until coated. Remove chicken. Discard any remaining flour mixture. Add chicken to same pot. Cook on medium for about 5 minutes per side until browned. Add to sausage.

Add onion and carrot to same pot. Cook for 5 to 10 minutes, stirring often, until onion is softened.

Add next 7 ingredients and chicken mixture. Stir. Bring to a boil. Reduce heat to medium-low. Simmer, covered, for about 15 minutes until potato is tender.

Add sauerkraut. Stir. Cook, uncovered, for about 15 minutes until thickened. Discard bay leaf. Serves 6.

1 serving: 586 Calories; 28.5 g Total Fat (12.5 g Mono, 4.7 g Poly, 9.0 g Sat); 110 mg Cholesterol; 42 g Carbohydrate; 5 g Fibre; 37 g Protein; 1795 mg Sodium

Chicken Hotpot

Tender-crisp carrots, bamboo shoots and bok choy make an outstanding appearance in this mildly hot and tangy hotpot.

Canola oil	2 tsp.	10 mL
Boneless, skinless chicken breast halves, chopped	3/4 lb.	340 g
Sliced carrot	1 cup	250 mL
Sliced fresh shiitake mushrooms	1 cup	250 mL
Can of shoestring-style sliced bamboo shoots (8 oz., 227 mL), drained	1	1
Prepared chicken broth	1/4 cup	60 mL
Rice vinegar	1/4 cup	60 mL
Soy sauce	2 tbsp.	30 mL
Granulated sugar	2 tsp.	10 mL
Finely grated ginger root	1 tsp.	5 mL
Sesame oil (for flavour)	1 tsp.	5 mL
Pepper	1/2 tsp.	2 mL
Sliced bok choy	2 cups	500 mL
Chopped red pepper	1 cup	250 mL
Water	2 tbsp.	30 mL
Cornstarch	1 tbsp.	15 mL

Heat canola oil in large saucepan on medium-high. Add chicken. Cook, uncovered, for 2 to 4 minutes, stirring occasionally, until no longer pink.

Add next 10 ingredients. Stir. Bring to a boil. Reduce heat to medium. Boil gently, partially covered, for 2 to 4 minutes until carrot is almost tender-crisp.

Add bok choy and red pepper. Stir. Cook, covered, for 2 to 4 minutes until vegetables are tender-crisp.

Stir water into cornstarch in small cup. Add to chicken mixture. Heat and stir until boiling and thickened. Makes about 6 cups (1.5 L). Serves 4.

1 serving: 189 Calories; 5.3 g Total Fat (2.1 g Mono, 1.7 g Poly, 0.8 g Sat); 49 mg Cholesterol; 13 g Carbohydrate; 3 g Fibre; 23 g Protein; 543 mg Sodium

Pictured on page 198.

Lemon Chicken Bean Stew

The favourite combination of chicken and lemon has never "bean" so tasty. Bright citrus picks up this simple and satisfying stew. Serve with baby potatoes or a salad.

All-purpose flour	1/4 cup	60 mL
Boneless, skinless chicken thighs, halved	2 lbs.	900 g
Chopped carrot	2 cups	500 mL
Can of white kidney beans	1	1
(19 oz., 540 mL), rinsed and drained		
Prepared chicken broth	1 cup	250 mL
Apple juice	1/2 cup	125 mL
Salt	1/2 tsp.	2 mL
Pepper	1/4 tsp.	1 mL
Chopped fresh parsley (or 2 1/4 tsp.,	3 tbsp.	45 mL
11 mL, flakes)		
Lemon juice	1 tbsp.	15 mL
Grated lemon zest	1 tsp.	5 mL

Measure flour into large resealable freezer bag. Add chicken. Seal bag. Toss until coated. Remove chicken. Discard any remaining flour.

Put carrot into 3 1/2 to 4 quart (3.5 to 4 L) slow cooker. Arrange chicken over top. Scatter beans over chicken.

Combine next 4 ingredients in small bowl. Pour over beans. Cook, covered, on Low for 8 to 9 hours or on High for 4 to 4 1/2 hours.

Add remaining 3 ingredients. Stir. Makes about 5 cups (1.25 L).

1 cup (250 mL): 438 Calories; 15.0 g Total Fat (5.3 g Mono, 3.3 g Poly, 3.9 g Sat); 119 mg Cholesterol; 35 g Carbohydrate; 6 g Fibre; 40 g Protein; 575 mg Sodium

 Chipotle chili peppers are smoked jalapeño peppers. Be sure to wash your hands after handling. Store leftover chipotle chili peppers with sauce in airtight container in refrigerator for up to 1 year.

Curious Chicken Chili

Why is this chili is such a curiosity? Check out the ingredients. You just have to taste this delightful concoction—we know you want to.

Cooking oil	2 tsp.	10 mL
Boneless, skinless chicken thighs, cut into 1/2 inch (12 mm) pieces	1 lb.	454 g
Chopped onions	1 1/2 cups	375 mL
Chopped green pepper	1 cup	250 mL
Diced jalapeño pepper (see Tip, page 166)	1 tbsp.	15 mL
Garlic cloves, minced (or 1/2 tsp., 2 mL, powder)	2	2
Salt	1 tsp.	5 mL
Can of diced tomatoes (14 oz., 398 mL), with juice	1	1
Can of pineapple chunks (14 oz., 398 mL), with juice	1	1
Can of red kidney beans (14 oz., 398 mL), rinsed and drained	1	1
Hot (or cold) strong prepared coffee	1 cup	250 mL
Can of diced green chilies (4 oz., 113 g)	1	1
Tomato paste (see Tip, page 136)	3 tbsp.	45 mL
Chili powder	2 tbsp.	30 mL
Semi-sweet chocolate baking square (1 oz., 28 g), grated	1	1
Ground cumin	1 tsp.	5 mL

Heat cooking oil in large frying pan on medium-high. Add chicken. Cook for about 5 minutes, stirring often, until browned.

Add next 5 ingredients. Cook for about 5 minutes, stirring often, until onion starts to soften. Transfer to 3 1/2 to 4 quart (3.5 to 4 L) slow cooker.

Add remaining 9 ingredients. Stir. Cook, covered, on Low for 4 hours or on High for 2 hours. Makes about 8 cups (2 L).

1 cup (250 mL): 246 Calories; 7.2 g Total Fat (2.4 g Mono, 1.5 g Poly, 2.0 g Sat); 37 mg Cholesterol; 31 g Carbohydrate; 7 g Fibre; 16 g Protein; 505 mg Sodium

Black Bean Chili

A fiesta in every bite! Serve this versatile recipe with warm, crusty rolls or tortilla chips, or on a bed of fresh greens for a quick and easy taco salad.

Cooking oil	2 tsp.	10 mL
Lean ground chicken	1 lb.	454 g
Chopped onion	1 1/2 cups	375 mL
Chopped celery	1/2 cup	125 mL
Chili powder	1 tbsp.	15 mL
Dried oregano	2 tsp.	10 mL
Garlic clove, minced (or 1/4 tsp., 1 mL, powder)	1	1
Can of stewed tomatoes (14 oz., 398 mL)	1	1
Chopped red pepper	1 1/2 cups	375 mL
Frozen kernel corn	1 cup	250 mL
Can of tomato sauce (7 1/2 oz., 213 mL)	1	1
Hot pepper sauce	1/2 tsp.	2 mL
Can of black beans (19 oz.,540 mL), rinsed and drained	1	1
Sliced green onion	1/4 cup	60 mL
Grated sharp Cheddar cheese	1/2 cup	125 mL
Chopped fresh cilantro or parsley (optional)	2 tbsp.	30 mL

Heat cooking oil in large frying pan on medium-high. Add chicken. Scramble-fry for about 5 minutes until no longer pink.

Add onion and celery. Cook for 5 to 10 minutes, stirring often, until onion is softened. Reduce heat to medium.

Add next 3 ingredients. Heat and stir for about 1 minute until fragrant.

Add next 5 ingredients. Stir. Bring to a boil. Reduce heat to medium-low. Simmer, covered, for 15 minutes to blend flavours.

Add beans and green onion. Stir. Cook for about 10 minutes until heated through.

Sprinkle with cheese and cilantro. Makes about 7 cups (1.75 L).

1 cup (250 mL): 345 Calories; 13.7 g Total Fat (1.7 g Mono, 0.9 g Poly, 2.0 g Sat); 8 mg Cholesterol; 35 g Carbohydrate; 8 g Fibre; 23 g Protein; 606 mg Sodium

Pictured on page 143.

Biscuit-topped Chili

Put some heat into what you eat with this salsa-flavoured chili treat—topped off with golden biscuits! Make it a complete meal by adding a side salad. Make it a party by adding a margarita!

Cooking oil	1 tbsp.	15 mL
Lean ground chicken	1 lb.	454 g
Chopped onion	1/4 cup	60 mL
Can of red kidney beans (14 oz., 398 mL), rinsed and drained	1	1
Salsa	1 1/2 cups	375 mL
Can of condensed tomato soup (10 oz., 284 mL)	1	1
All-purpose flour	2 cups	500 mL
Baking powder	1 tbsp.	15 mL
Granulated sugar	2 tsp.	10 mL
Seasoned salt	1 tsp.	5 mL
Pepper	1/4 tsp.	1 mL
Milk	2/3 cup	150 mL
Cooking oil	1/3 cup	75 mL

Heat first amount of cooking oil in large frying pan on medium-high. Add chicken and onion. Scramble-fry for about 8 minutes until chicken is starting to brown and onion is softened.

Add next 3 ingredients. Cook and stir until heated through. Transfer to greased 9 inch (23 cm) deep dish pie plate.

Measure next 5 ingredients into medium bowl. Stir. Make a well in centre.

Add milk and second amount of cooking oil to well. Stir until just moistened. Turn dough out onto lightly floured surface. Knead 8 times. Roll or pat dough to 9 inch (23 cm) diameter circle. Place over chicken mixture. Prick entire surface of dough with fork through to bottom of pan. Bake, uncovered, in 400°F (200°C) oven for 25 to 30 minutes until golden. Serves 4.

1 serving: 859 Calories; 38.5 g Total Fat (12.6 g Mono, 6.9 g Poly, 2.0 g Sat); 2 mg Cholesterol; 90 g Carbohydrate; 11 g Fibre; 36 g Protein; 1403 mg Sodium

Jerk Chicken Sandwiches

Fresh, attractive croissant sandwiches are filled with crisp green lettuce and sweetly spiced jerk chicken—these would make a pretty addition to a luncheon. Use a variety of small rolls if mini-croissants are unavailable.

Brown sugar, packed	1 tbsp.	15 mL
Dried thyme	1 tsp.	5 mL
Ground allspice	1 tsp.	5 mL
Ground ginger	1 tsp.	5 mL
Garlic powder	3/4 tsp.	4 mL
Dried crushed chilies	1/2 tsp.	2 mL
Ground cinnamon	1/2 tsp.	2 mL
Salt	1/2 tsp.	2 mL
Pepper	1/4 tsp.	1 mL
Cooking oil	1 tbsp.	15 mL
Boneless, skinless chicken breast halves (about 4 oz., 113 g, each)	2	2
Mayonnaise	1/2 cup	125 mL
Lime juice	1 tbsp.	15 mL
Mini-croissants, split	12	12
Green leaf lettuce leaves, quartered	3	3
Thinly sliced yellow pepper	1/2 cup	125 mL

Combine first 9 ingredients in small bowl.

Transfer half of brown sugar mixture to large bowl. Add cooking oil to same large bowl. Stir. Add chicken. Toss until coated. Marinate, covered, in refrigerator for 1 hour. Remove chicken. Arrange on greased baking sheet with sides. Discard any remaining marinade. Cook in 425°F (220°C) oven for about 15 minutes until internal temperature reaches 170°F (77°C). Let stand for 5 minutes. Cut crosswise into thin slices.

Add mayonnaise and lime juice to remaining sugar mixture. Stir. Spread over cut sides of croissants. Layer lettuce, yellow pepper and chicken on bottom halves of croissants. Cover with tops. Secure with wooden picks. Makes 12 sandwiches.

1 sandwich: 223 Calories; 14.8 g Total Fat (2.3 g Mono, 0.7 g Poly, 4.5 g Sat); 33 mg Cholesterol; 15 g Carbohydrate; 1 g Fibre; 7 g Protein; 372 mg Sodium

Grilled Chicken Wraps

Tender, moist chicken with a hint of lime and just the right amount of spices to make it memorable.

Chopped fresh cilantro or parsley (or 1 tbsp., 15 mL, dried)	1/4 cup	60 mL
Cooking oil	3 tbsp.	45 mL
Dried crushed chilies (optional)	2 tsp.	10 mL
Ground cumin	1 tsp.	5 mL
Garlic cloves, minced (or 1/2 tsp., 2 mL, powder)	2	2
Boneless, skinless chicken breast halves	1 lb.	454 g
Lime juice	1/4 cup	60 mL
Corn relish	1/4 cup	60 mL
Sour cream	1/4 cup	60 mL
Flour tortillas (10 inch, 25 cm, diameter)	4	4
Large ripe avocado, sliced	1	1
Red medium pepper, seeds and ribs removed, thinly sliced	1	1
Grated medium Cheddar cheese	1 cup	250 mL

Combine first 5 ingredients in medium bowl. Add chicken. Stir. Cover with plastic wrap. Chill for at least 1 hour, stirring occasionally.

Add lime juice to chicken mixture. Stir. Drain and discard liquid. Preheat barbecue to medium. Cook chicken on greased grill for about 5 minutes per side until no longer pink inside. Cut diagonally into thin slices. Cover to keep warm.

Combine corn relish and sour cream in small bowl. Spread about 2 tbsp. (30 mL) on each tortilla.

Divide and layer chicken, avocado, red pepper and cheese across centre of each tortilla, leaving 2 inches (5 cm) at each side. Fold sides over filling. Roll up from bottom to enclose filling. Slice in half diagonally. Serves 8.

1 serving: 337 Calories; 18.3 g Total Fat (8.2 g Mono, 3.3 g Poly, 5.4 g Sat); 59 mg Cholesterol; 21 g Carbohydrate; 2 g Fibre; 23 g Protein; 252 mg Sodium

Variation: Brush wraps with 1 tbsp. (15 mL) cooking oil. Cook wraps on greased grill on medium for 5 to 7 minutes, turning occasionally, until crisp and golden.

BBQ Chicken Buns

Serve these on the patio for good outdoor fun. Good indoor food as well.

Butter (or hard margarine)	1 tbsp.	15 mL
Finely chopped onion	1/2 cup	125 mL
Finely chopped celery	1/4 cup	60 mL
Prepared beef broth	1/2 cup	125 mL
Ketchup	1/2 cup	125 mL
White vinegar	2 tsp.	10 mL
Worcestershire sauce	1 tsp.	5 mL
Chili powder	1 tsp.	5 mL
Salt	1/2 tsp.	2 mL
Pepper	1/8 tsp.	0.5 mL
Chopped pimiento stuffed olives	1/3 cup	75 mL
Chopped cooked chicken (see Tip, page 58)	3 cups	700 mL
Kaiser or hamburger buns, split and buttered	12	12

Melt butter in frying pan. Add onion and celery. Sauté until soft.

Add next 9 ingredients. Stir. Heat through.

Spread a scant 1/4 cup (60 mL) on each bun. Buns prepared with cooled filling may be wrapped in foil and chilled. To heat, place in 350°F (175°C) oven for about 15 minutes until filling is hot. Makes 12.

1 bun: 270 Calories; 7 g Total Fat (2.5 g Mono, 0.5 g Poly, 3 g Sat); 35 mg Cholesterol; 34 g Carbohydrate; 3 g Fibre; 16 g Protein; 840 mg Sodium

 Too cold to barbecue? Use the broiler instead! Your food should cook in about the same length of time, and remember to turn or baste as directed. Set your oven rack so that the food is about 3 to 4 inches (7.5 to 10 cm) away from the element. For most ovens, that is the top rack.

Chicken Salad Bagels

A multi-flavoured filling in a multi-grain bagel—
with a little pepper sauce to put a kick in your step.

Thinly sliced celery	1/4 cup	60 mL
Plain yogurt	2 1/2 tbsp.	37 mL
Raw sunflower seeds	2 tbsp.	30 mL
Green onion, thinly sliced	1	1
Grated lemon zest	1/2 tsp.	5 mL
Dried dillweed	1/2 tsp.	5 mL
Drops or hot pepper sauce	3	3
Finely chopped cooked chicken (see Tip, page 58)	1 cup	250 mL
Romaine lettuce leaves, halved	2	2
Multi-grain bagels, split	2	2

Combine first 7 ingredients in small bowl. Add chicken. Mix well.

Place lettuce on bottom halves of bagels. Spoon chicken mixture over lettuce. Place top halves of bagels over salmon mixture. Cut bagels in half. Serves 2.

1 bagel: 490 Calories; 12 g Total Fat (2.5 g Mono, 4 g Poly, 2.5 g Sat); 55 mg Cholesterol; 64 g Carbohydrate; 5 g Fibre; 31 g Protein; 600 mg Sodium

Chicken Reuben

Just loaded with flavour. The pumpernickel bread is a nice touch.

Salad dressing (or mayonnaise)	1 tbsp.	15 mL
Chili sauce	1 tsp.	5 mL
Sweet pickle relish	3/4 tsp.	4 mL
Onion powder, just a pinch		
Pumpernickel (or rye) bread slices	2	2
Thin slices of cooked chicken (see Tip, page 58)	3	3
Sauerkraut	3 tbsp.	45 mL
Swiss or mozzarella cheese slice	1	1

Mix first 4 ingredients well in small bowl.

Spread 1/2 salad dressing mixture over each bread slice. On 1 slice, layer chicken, sauerkraut and cheese. Top with second slice, salad dressing side down. Fry in greased frying pan over medium-high heat, browning both sides. Makes 1 sandwich.

1 sandwich: 360 Calories; 11 g Total Fat (0.5 g Mono, 1 g Poly, 4 g Sat); 55 mg Cholesterol; 39 g Carbohydrate; 6 g Fibre; 25 g Protein; 1830 mg Sodium

Chicken Sloppy Joes

If they were called Tidy Joes they just wouldn't be as much fun, would they? Unleash your inner child and dive into these saucy open-faced sandwiches.

Cooking oil	1 tbsp.	15 mL
Lean ground chicken	1 lb.	454 g
Chopped green pepper	1/2 cup	125 mL
Chopped onion	1/2 cup	125 mL
Tomato juice	1 cup	250 mL
Can of pizza sauce (7 1/2 oz., 213 mL)	1	1
Ketchup	2 tbsp.	30 mL
Chili powder	1 tsp.	5 mL
Garlic powder	1/4 tsp.	1 mL
Salt	1/4 tsp.	1 mL
Hamburger buns, split and toasted	4	4

Heat cooking oil in large frying pan on medium-high. Add next 3 ingredients. Scramble-fry for 8 to 10 minutes until chicken is no longer pink.

Add next 6 ingredients. Stir. Reduce heat to medium-low. Simmer, covered, for 10 minutes to blend flavours.

Place bun halves on large plate. Spoon chicken mixture over bun halves. Makes 8 sloppy joes. Serves 4.

1 sloppy joe: 219 Calories; 10.8 g Total Fat (1.8 g Mono, 1.0 g Poly, 0.4 g Sat); 0 mg Cholesterol; 17 g Carbohydrate; 2 g Fibre; 13 g Protein; 454 mg Sodium

 tip To julienne, cut into very thin strips that resemble matchsticks.

Clubhouse Sandwich

A delicious twist on an old favourite.

Salad dressing (or mayonnaise)	1 tbsp.	15 mL
Prepared mustard	1/4 tsp.	1 mL
Whole wheat bread slices, toasted and buttered	3	3
Cooked chicken (see Tip, page 58) slices	2	2
Salt, sprinkle		
Pepper, sprinkle		
Bacon slices, crispy-fried	2	2
Lettuce leaf	1	1
Tomato slices	2	2
Salt, sprinkle		
Pepper, sprinkle		
Very thin purple onion slice (or other sweet mild onion)	1	1
Swiss or Monterey Jack cheese slice	1	1
Medium or sharp Cheddar cheese slice	1	1
Thin slices of pickle	4	4

Stir salad dressing and mustard together.

On first slice of toast layer chicken, salt and pepper, bacon and lettuce on buttered side. Spread unbuttered side of second slice of toast with 1/2 mustard mixture. Place mustard side down over lettuce.

On buttered side of second slice of toast layer tomato, salt and pepper, onion, Monterey Jack cheese and Cheddar cheese. Spread remaining mustard mixture on buttered side of third slice and put on top, mustard side down.

Before cutting, press a wooden pick down through each quarter. Cut into quarters. Press pickle slice over each pick. Serve as is or heat in microwave on high for about 10 to 20 seconds to melt cheese a little. Makes 1 sandwich.

1 sandwich: 550 Calories; 26 g Total Fat (4.5 g Mono, 2 g Poly, 11 g Sat); 85 mg Cholesterol; 46 g Carbohydrate; 7 g Fibre; 34 g Protein; 1900 mg Sodium

Chicken Curry Filling

A good sandwich filling with a mild curry flavour.

Finely chopped cooked chicken (see Tip, page 58)	2 cups	500 mL
Salad dressing (or mayonnaise)	1/4 cup	60 mL
Sour cream	2 tbsp.	30 mL
Curry powder	1/4 tsp.	1 mL
Salt	1/2 tsp.	2 mL

Stir all ingredients together well in bowl. If you want a softer spread, add a bit of milk and mix. Makes 1 1/2 cups (375 mL). Serves 5.

1 serving: 140 Calories; 8 g Total Fat (2 g Mono, 1 g Poly, 2 g Sat); 50 mg Cholesterol; 2 g Carbohydrate; 0 g Fibre; 14 g Protein; 380 mg Sodium

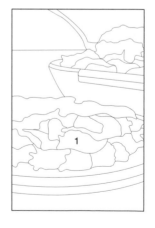

1. Spinach Chicken Lasagna, page 236

Breakfast Burrito

These mild burritos taste great dipped in a zesty sauce or salsa.

Bacon slice, diced	1	1
Finely chopped onion	1 tsp.	5 mL
Large egg, fork beaten	1	1
Diced cooked chicken (see Tip, page 58)	1/4 cup	60 mL
Salt, sprinkle		
Pepper, sprinkle		
Flour tortillas, 7 inch (18 cm)	2	2
Grated medium Cheddar cheese	2 tbsp.	30 mL

Fry bacon and onion until onion is soft.

Add egg, chicken, salt and pepper. Scramble-fry until egg is cooked.

Heat tortillas quickly in another frying pan. Lay on plate. Put half of cheese down centre of each. Divide filling between them. Roll. Serves 1.

1 serving: 550 Calories; 22 g Total Fat (9 g Mono, 3 g Poly, 8 g Sat); 260 mg Cholesterol; 56 g Carbohydrate; 3 g Fibre; 30 g Protein; 730 mg Sodium

Pictured on page 288.

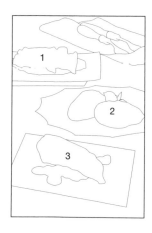

1. Uptown Asparagus Chicken, page 210
2. Lemon Basil Chicken Rolls, page 212
3. Festive Chicken Bake, page 265

Barley Bean Rolls

These crispy, pinwheel burritos are a perfect high-energy snack. Dip in sour cream and salsa.

Can of refried beans (14 oz., 398 mL)	1	1
Whole wheat flour tortillas (7 1/2 inch, 19 cm, diameter)	6	6
Cooked pot barley	2 cups	500 mL
Chopped, cooked, chicken (see Tip, page 58)	1 cup	250 mL
Grated mozzarella and Cheddar cheese blend	3/4 cup	175 mL
Finely chopped pickled jalapeño pepper	1 tbsp.	15 mL

Cooking spray
Paprika, sprinkle

Spread about 1/4 cup (60 mL) refried beans on each tortilla, leaving 1 inch (2.5 cm) edge.

Combine next 4 ingredients in medium bowl. Sprinkle over refried beans. Roll up tightly, jelly-roll style. Secure each roll with 2 wooden picks. Place rolls on greased baking sheet with sides (see Note).

Spray rolls with cooking spray. Sprinkle with paprika. Bake in 350°F (175°C) oven for about 15 minutes until crisp and golden. Makes 6 rolls.

1 roll: 460 Calories; 13 g Total Fat (1.5 g Mono, 0 g Poly, 4.5 g Sat); 30 mg Cholesterol; 65 g Carbohydrate; 13 g Fibre; 23 g Protein; 940 mg Sodium

Note: These rolls freeze well for a quick and convenient snack. Bake from frozen, covered, in 350°F (175°C) oven for 20 minutes. Bake, uncovered, for another 15 minutes until crisp and heated through.

Pictured on page 287.

Chicken Quesadillas

A 'dilla with a difference! Artichokes and cream cheese make a fantastically delicious statement in this great appetizer. Can also be served as a light lunch.

Garlic and herb cream cheese	1/4 cup	60 mL
Flour tortillas (9 inch, 23 cm, diameter)	4	4
Finely chopped cooked chicken (see Tip, page 58)	1 cup	250 mL
Lime juice	2 tbsp.	30 mL
Salt	1/8 tsp.	0.5 mL
Finely diced, seeded tomato	1/2 cup	125 mL
Thinly sliced green onion	1/4 cup	60 mL
Jar of marinated artichoke hearts (6 oz., 170 mL), drained and chopped	1	1
Grated jalapeño Monterey Jack cheese	1 cup	250 mL

Spread cream cheese evenly on each tortilla, almost to edge.

Place chicken in small bowl. Drizzle with lime juice. Sprinkle with salt. Stir. Spread chicken mixture over half of each tortilla.

Layer next 4 ingredients, in order given, over chicken mixture. Fold tortillas in half to cover filling. Press down lightly. Place on greased baking sheet. Bake in 425°F (220°C) oven for 10 to 12 minutes until cheese is melted and edges start to brown. Cut each quesadilla into 4 wedges. Makes 16 wedges.

1 wedge: 114 Calories; 5.0 g Total Fat (1.6 g Mono, 0.5 g Poly, 2.4 g Sat); 17 mg Cholesterol; 11 g Carbohydrate; 1 g Fibre; 6 g Protein; 206 mg Sodium

Grilled Quesadillas

Crispy and golden on the outside with a spicy chicken filling on the inside.

Sour cream	1/3 cup	75 mL
Chili sauce	2 tbsp.	30 mL
Chopped cooked chicken (see Tip, page 58)	3 cups	750 mL
Grated Monterey Jack cheese	1 2/3 cups	400 mL
Flour tortillas (10 inch, 25 cm, diameter)	4	4
Sliced pickled jalapeño peppers	1 tbsp.	15 mL
Medium tomatoes, seeds removed, diced	2	2
Finely chopped green onion	3 tbsp.	45 mL
Chopped fresh parsley (or 1 1/2 tsp., 7 mL, flakes)	2 tbsp.	30 mL
Cooking oil	1 tbsp.	15 mL

Combine sour cream and chili sauce in medium bowl. Add chicken. Toss until coated.

Divide and scatter cheese over 1/2 of each tortilla. Divide and spoon chicken mixture evenly over cheese.

Layer next 4 ingredients over chicken mixture. Fold each tortilla in half to enclose filling.

Preheat barbecue to medium. Brush tops of folded tortillas with 1/2 of cooking oil. Cook quesadillas, top-side down, on greased grill for 5 minutes. Brush with remaining cooking oil. Turn. Cook for about 5 minutes until crisp and golden and cheese is melted. Cut in half to serve. Serves 4.

1 serving: 656 Calories; 33.7 g Total Fat (11.8 g Mono, 5 g Poly, 14.4 g Sat); 152 mg Cholesterol; 36 g Carbohydrate; 3 g Fibre; 51 g Protein; 772 mg Sodium

Chicken Bunwich

These tasty sandwiches are a great way to use up leftover chicken. They can be assembled ahead and stored in the fridge, then heated when you are ready to eat.

Butter (or hard margarine)	1 tbsp.	15 mL
Water	2 tbsp.	30 mL
Sliced or chopped onion	1 cup	250 mL
Diced cooked chicken (see Tip, page 58)	2 cups	500 mL
Finely diced celery	1/2 cup	125 mL
Parsley flakes	1 tsp.	5 mL
Salt	1/4 tsp.	1 mL
Pepper, sprinkle		
Salad dressing (or mayonnaise)	1/2 cup	125 mL
Grated medium Cheddar cheese	1/2 cup	125 mL
Hamburger buns, split and buttered	8	8

Melt butter in frying pan. Add water and onion. Cover. Simmer gently, stirring often, until onion is clear and soft and moisture has evaporated.

Put next 7 ingredients into bowl. Mix. Add onion. Stir gently.

Divide among buns. Wrap each bun in foil. Heat in 350°F (175°C) oven for about 15 minutes until heated through. Makes 8 bunwiches.

1 bunwich: 280 Calories; 13 g Total Fat (3 g Mono, 1.5 g Poly, 4.5 g Sat); 45 mg Cholesterol; 25 g Carbohydrate; 1 g Fibre; 15 g Protein; 500 mg Sodium

 To remove the centre rib from lettuce, kale or Swiss chard, fold the leaf in half along the rib and then cut along the length of the rib.

Quesadillas Olé

A creative combination of ingredients makes these spicy chicken quesadillas just the ticket for dinner.

Cooking oil	1 tsp.	5 mL
Lean ground chicken	1 lb.	454 g
Chopped onion	1/2 cup	125 mL
Garlic clove, minced (or 1/4 tsp., 1 mL powder)	1	1
Frozen kernel corn, thawed	1 cup	250 mL
Medium salsa	1 cup	250 mL
Chili paste (sambal oelek)	1 tsp.	5 mL
Chili powder	1 tsp.	5 mL
Ground cumin	1 tsp.	5 mL
Grated Monterey Jack with jalapeño cheese	1 cup	250 mL
Sun-dried tomato (or plain) flour tortillas (9 inch, 22 cm, diameter)	4	4
Hard margarine (or butter)	2 tsp.	10 mL

Heat cooking oil in large frying pan on medium-high. Add ground chicken. Scramble-fry for 5 to 10 minutes until no longer pink inside. Drain.

Add onion and garlic. Heat and stir for 2 to 3 minutes until liquid is evaporated and onion is softened.

Add next 5 ingredients. Heat and stir for 2 to 3 minutes until liquid is evaporated and onion is softened.

Sprinkle 2 tbsp (30 mL) cheese over half of each tortilla, almost to edge. Scatter chicken mixture over cheese on each. Sprinkle with remaining cheese. Fold unfilled tortilla halves over cheese. Press down lightly.

Melt 1 tbsp. (15 mL) margarine in same frying pan on medium. Carefully place 2 folded tortillas in pan. Cook for about 2 minutes until bottom of each quesadilla is golden and brown spots appear. Carefully turn quesadillas over. Cook for about 2 minutes until golden and cheese is melted. Repeat with remaining margarine and folded tortillas. Makes 4 quesadillas.

1 quesadilla: 552 Calories; 30.9 g Total Fat (5.8 g Mono, 2.1 g Poly, 6.7 g Sat); 27 mg Cholesterol; 37 g Carbohydrate; 4 g Fibre; 33 g Protein; 624 mg Sodium

Spiced Chicken Buns

A special lunch to be sure. If you don't have English muffins,
hamburger buns work just as well.

Canned sliced peaches with juice (14 oz., 398 mL)	1	1
Brown sugar, packed	1/3 cup	75 mL
Lemon juice	1/2 tsp.	2 mL
Brandy flavouring	1/2 tsp.	2 mL
Ground cinnamon	1/8 tsp.	0.5 mL
Butter (or hard margarine)	1/4 cup	60 mL
All-purpose flour	1/4 cup	60 mL
Chicken bouillon powder	1 tsp.	5 mL
Salt	1/2 tsp.	2 mL
Paprika	1/4 tsp.	1 mL
Milk	2 cups	500 mL
Sherry (or alcohol-free sherry)	2 tbsp.	30 mL
Coarsely chopped cooked chicken (see Tip, page 58)	2 cups	500 mL
Ham slices, cut bun size at least 1/8 inch (3 mm) thick from cooked ham	12	12
English muffins, split, toasted and buttered	6	6

Put first 5 ingredients in small saucepan. Stir. Bring to a boil. Simmer 5 minutes. Keep warm.

Melt butter in medium saucepan. Mix in flour, bouillon powder, salt and paprika. Stir in milk until it boils and thickens.

Add sherry and chicken. Return to a simmer.

Lay ham slices over top, overlapping. Cover. Simmer gently to warm ham.

Lay 2 muffin halves on each of 6 plates. Using tongs, remove and place ham slice on each half. Spoon about 1/4 cup (60 mL) chicken sauce over each. Remove peach slices with slotted spoon and put on top of each muffin half. Makes 6 buns.

1 bun: 480 Calories; 16 g Total Fat (4 g Mono, 1.5 g Poly 8 g Sat); 75 mg Cholesterol; 57 g Carbohydrate; 2 g Fibre; 25 g Protein; 1020 mg Sodium

Chicken Taco Wraps

These meal-sized soft tacos are filled with a mix of creamy avocado and salsa. Delicious!

Cooking oil	2 tsp.	10 mL
Lean ground chicken	1 lb.	454 g
Water	1/4 cup	60 mL
Envelope of taco seasoning (1 1/4 oz., 35 g)	1	1
Ripe medium avocado, cut up	1	1
Sour cream	1/3 cup	75 mL
Salsa	1/4 cup	60 mL
Flour tortillas (9 inch, 23 cm, diameter)	4	4
Grated Monterey Jack cheese	1 cup	250 mL
Romaine lettuce leaves, cut crosswise into thin strips	4	4

Heat cooking oil in medium frying pan on medium-high. Add ground chicken. Scramble-fry for 5 to 10 minutes until no longer pink. Drain.

Add water to taco seasoning. Heat and stir for 1 minute to blend flavours. Remove from heat. Cover to keep warm.

Mash avocado with fork in medium bowl. As sour cream and salsa. Mix well. Spread evenly on each tortilla, almost to edge. Spoon chicken mixture across centre of each tortilla.

Sprinkle cheese over chicken mixture. Scatter lettuce over cheese. Fold sides over filling. Roll up from bottom to enclose. Makes 4 wraps.

1 wrap: 730 Calories; 42 g Total Fat (10 g Mono, 2.5 g Poly, 10 g Sat); 120 mg Cholesterol; 54 g Carbohydrate; 6 g Fibre; 34 g Protein; 1380 mg Sodium

Stroganoff Buns

A scrumptious layer of stroganoff chicken layered with lettuce, tomato and cheese. Excellent lunch fare.

Cooking oil	2 tbsp.	30 mL
Finely chopped onion	1 cup	250 mL
Lean ground raw chicken	1 1/4 lbs.	570 g
All-purpose flour	1/3 cup	75 mL
Beef bouillon powder	2 tsp.	10 mL
Salt	3/4 tsp.	4 mL
Pepper	1/4 tsp.	1 mL
Water	1 1/4 cups	300 mL
Canned sliced mushrooms, drained (10 oz., 284 mL)	1	1
Worcestershire sauce	1/4 tsp.	1 mL
Sour cream	1/2 cup	125 mL
Hamburger buns, halved, toasted and buttered	7	7
Shredded lettuce	1 cup	250 mL
Thin tomato slices	14	14
Grated medium or sharp Cheddar cheese	2/3 cup	150 mL

Heat cooking oil in frying pan. Add onion and ground chicken. Sauté until no pink remains in meat and onion is soft.

Mix in flour, bouillon powder, salt and pepper. Stir in water until mixture boils and thickens.

Add mushrooms, Worcestershire sauce and sour cream. Heat through without boiling.

Arrange 2 bun halves on each plate. Top with chicken stroganoff, lettuce, tomato slice and cheese. Makes 3 2/3 cups (825 mL) stroganoff. Makes 7 buns.

1 bun: 410 Calories; 20 g Total Fat (2.5 g Mono, 1 g Poly, 4.5 g Sat); 80 mg Cholesterol; 33 g Carbohydrate; 3 g Fibre; 23 g Protein; 1020 mg Sodium

Greek Lemon Pitas

Lemon lovers, this pita's for you! Lots of lemon flavour in a warm pita pocket filled with all sorts of tasty ingredients.

Lemon juice	1/4 cup	60 mL
Liquid honey	3 tbsp.	45 mL
Garlic clove, minced (or 1/4 tsp., 1 mL, powder)	1	1
Dried oregano	1 tsp.	5 mL
Pepper	1/4 tsp.	1 mL
Boneless, skinless chicken thighs, quartered (about 3 oz, 85 g, each)	8	8
Seasoned salt	1/2 tsp.	2 mL
Bamboo skewers (8 inches, 20 cm, each) soaked in water for 10 minutes	8	8
Thin lemon slices (about 1/2 lemon)	8	8
Salt	1/2 tsp.	2 mL
Plain yogurt	1 cup	250 mL
Chopped Kalamata (or black) olives	1/2 cup	125 mL
Liquid honey	2 tbsp.	30 mL
Chopped fresh parsley (or 3/4 tsp., 4 mL, flakes)	1 tbsp.	15 mL
Chopped fresh mint (or 3/4 tsp., 4 mL, dried)	1 tbsp.	15 mL
Shredded romaine lettuce, lightly packed	2 cups	500 mL
Pita bread (7 inch, 18 cm, diameter), halved and opened	4	4

Combine first 5 ingredients in medium bowl. Add chicken. Stir until coated. Let stand at room temperature for 20 minutes. Drain and discard lemon juice mixture.

Sprinkle chicken with seasoned salt. Thread onto skewers. Fold lemon slices into quarters and thread onto ends of skewers. Preheat gas barbecue to medium (see Tip, page 84). Cook skewers on greased grill for about 15 minutes, turning occasionally, until chicken is no longer pink inside. Remove lemon slices to cutting board. Remove chicken from skewers. Cover to keep warm. Finely chop lemon. Sprinkle with salt.

Combine next 5 ingredients in medium bowl. Add lemon. Stir. Add lettuce and chicken. Toss.

Place pita pockets on warm grill. Heat for 30 seconds. Fill pockets with chicken mixture. Makes 8 pockets.

1 pocket: 265 Calories; 8.7 g Total Fat (3.4 g Mono, 1.7 g Poly, 2.6 g Sat); 60 mg Cholesterol; 27 g Carbohydrate; 1 g Fibre; 19 g Protein; 474 mg Sodium

Chicken Souvlaki Pitas

Chicken souvlaki meets Greek salad. These two favourites are rolled up in one big sloppy pita!

Boneless, skinless chicken breast halves, cut into 24 pieces	1 lb.	454 g
Bamboo skewers (8 inches, 20 cm, each), soaked in water for 10 minutes	4	4
Lemon juice	1/4 cup	60 mL
Olive (or cooking) oil	2 tbsp.	30 mL
Grated lemon zest (see Tip, page 151)	2 tsp.	10 mL
Dried oregano	1 tsp.	5 mL
Garlic cloves, minced (or 1/2 tsp., 2 mL, powder)	2	2
Salt	1/2 tsp.	2 mL
Pepper	1 tsp.	5 mL
Tzatziki	1/4 cup	60 mL
Black olive tapenade	2 tbsp.	30 mL
Pita breads (7 inch, 18 cm, diameter)	4	4
Sliced tomato	2/3 cup	150 mL
Thinly sliced English cucumber (with peel)	1/2 cup	125 mL
Crumbled feta cheese	1/2 cup	125 mL
Julienned yellow pepper	1/4 cup	60 mL
Thinly sliced red onion	1/4 cup	60 mL

Thread chicken onto skewers. Place in large shallow dish.

Combine next 7 ingredients in small bowl. Pour over chicken. Turn until coated. Marinate, covered, in refrigerator for 2 hours, turning occasionally. Preheat barbecue to medium-high. Place skewers on greased grill, discarding any remaining lemon juice mixture. Close lid. Cook for about 12 minutes, turning occasionally, until chicken is no longer pink inside.

Combine tzatziki and tapenade in small bowl. Place pitas on greased grill. Heat for about 30 seconds until softened. Spread with tzatziki mixture. Remove chicken from skewers and arrange across centre of each pita.

Top with remaining 5 ingredients. Fold pitas in half to enclose filling. Secure with wooden picks. Serve immediately. Makes 4 pitas.

1 pita: 410 Calories; 11.8 g Total Fat (3.8 g Mono, 1.3 g Poly, 4.4 g Sat); 82 mg Cholesterol; 39 g Carbohydrate; 2 g Fibre; 35 g Protein; 843 mg Sodium

Modern Caesar Pitas

Don't get your toga in a tangle—this update on an old favourite is sure to please.
What makes these pitas so delightfully different? The added flavours of tahini and walnuts.
All hail Caesar!

Chopped or torn romaine lettuce, lightly packed	3 cups	750 mL
Diced cooked chicken (see Tip, page 58)	1 cup	250 mL
Chopped walnuts	1/4 cup	60 mL
GARLIC SESAME DRESSING		
Olive oil	1 tbsp.	15 mL
Lemon juice	1 tbsp.	15 mL
White wine vinegar	1 tbsp.	15 mL
Tahini (sesame paste)	1 tbsp.	15 mL
Anchovy paste (optional)	1/4 tsp.	1 mL
Garlic clove, minced (or 1/4 tsp., 1 mL, powder)	1	1
Pepper	1/8 tsp.	0.5 mL
Whole wheat pita bread (7 inch, 18 cm, diameter), halved and opened	2	2

Put first 3 ingredients into medium bowl.

Garlic Sesame Dressing: Beat first 7 ingredients with fork in small cup. Makes about 1/4 cup (60 mL) dressing. Pour over lettuce mixture. Toss well.

Spoon lettuce mixture into pita pockets. Makes 4 pitas.

1 pita: 243 Calories; 13.4 g Total Fat (4.9 g Mono, 5.6 g Poly, 2.0 g Sat); 26 mg Cholesterol; 19 g Carbohydrate; 4 g Fibre; 14 g Protein; 182 mg Sodium

Pizza Burgers

When you can't decide between burgers and pizza, you can try this recipe. It looks like a cheeseburger but tastes like a sausage and pepper pizza! Personalize each burger by adding different toppings.

Large egg, fork-beaten	1	1
Crushed seasoned croutons	1/2 cup	125 mL
Finely chopped onion	1/2 cup	125 mL
Fennel seed	2 tsp.	10 mL
Lean ground chicken	1 lb.	454 g
Hot Italian sausage, casing removed	1/2 lb.	225 g
Provolone cheese slices	6	6
Onion buns, split	6	6
Pizza sauce	3/4 cup	175 mL
Small green pepper, cut into 6 rings	1	1
Small red pepper, cut into 6 rings	1	1

Combine first 4 ingredients in medium bowl.

Add chicken and sausage. Mix well. Divide into 6 equal portions. Shape into 4 inch (10 cm) patties. Preheat barbecue to medium. Place patties on greased grill. Close lid. Cook for about 5 minutes per side until internal temperature reaches 170°F (77°C).

Place 1 cheese slice on each patty.

Place bun halves on greased grill. Cook for about 1 minute until golden. Spread pizza sauce on bun halves. Serve patties, topped with pepper rings, in buns. Makes 6 burgers.

1 burger: 596 Calories; 30.9 g Total Fat (7.5 g Mono, 1.7 g Poly, 13.3 g Sat); 127 mg Cholesterol; 39 g Carbohydrate; 3 g Fibre; 38 g Protein; 1234 mg Sodium (need new NI)

Italian Burgers

Spezia, or spice, *is what makes these Italian-inspired patties extra nice!*
Adjust the amount of chilies to suit your preferred heat level. Very flavourful!

Large egg, fork-beaten	1	1
Fresh bread crumbs (see Tip, page 210)	3/4 cup	175 mL
Dijon mustard	2 tsp.	10 mL
Garlic clove, minced (or 1/2 tsp., 1 mL, powder)	1	1
Fennel seed, crushed (see Tip, page 204)	1/2 tsp.	2 mL
Dried crushed chilies	1/2 tsp.	2 mL
Dried oregano	1/2 tsp.	2 mL
Salt	1/2 tsp.	2 mL
Pepper	1/2 tsp.	2 mL
Lean ground chicken	1 lb.	454 g
Sun-dried tomato pesto	2 1/2 tbsp.	37 mL
Sliced roasted red peppers, blotted dry	1 cup	250 mL
Slices of mozzarella cheese	8	8
Lettuce leaves	8	8
Tomato slices	8	8
Hamburger buns, split	8	8

Combine first 9 ingredients in large bowl. Add chicken. Mix well. Divide into 8 equal portions. Shape into 3 inch (7.5 cm) diameter patties.

Arrange patties on greased baking sheet with sides. Broil on top rack in oven for about 5 minutes until top is lightly browned. Turn. Spread pesto on patties. Broil for another 5 minutes until browned.

Arrange red pepper on patties. Place cheese slices over red pepper. Broil for about 2 minutes until cheese is melted.

Serve patties, topped with lettuce and tomato, in buns. Makes 8 burgers.

1 burger: 380 Calories; 19.0 g Total Fat (3.7 g Mono, 1.5 g Poly, 5.3 g Sat); 50 mg Cholesterol; 28 g Carbohydrate; 2 g Fibre; 23 g Protein; 677 mg Sodium

Picture on page 53.

Chicken Bacon Burgers

These colourful chicken burgers loaded with tasty toppings will please the whole family.

Boneless, skinless chicken breasts halves) (about 4 oz., 113 g, each)	4	4
Salt, sprinkle		
Pepper, sprinkle		
Cooking oil	2 tsp.	10 mL
Mango chutney	1/4 cup	60 mL
Salad dressing (or mayonnaise)	3 tbsp.	45 mL
Kaiser rolls, split and toasted (buttered, optional)	4	4
Fresh spinach leaves, lightly packed	1 cup	250 mL
Swiss cheese slices (about 4 oz, (113 g)	4	4
Tomato slices	4	4
Cooked bacon slices	8	8

Place 1 chicken breast half between 2 sheets of waxed paper. Pound with meat mallet to about 1/2 inch (12 mm) thickness. Repeat with remaining chicken breast halves. Sprinkle both sides with salt and pepper.

Heat cooking oil in large frying pan on medium. Add chicken. Cook for 8 to 10 minutes per side until no longer pink inside.

Combine chutney and salad dressing in small cup. Spread on both halves of each roll.

Arrange spinach leaves on top of chutney mixture on bottom half or each roll. Set aside.

Put 1 cheese slice and 1 tomato slice on top of each chicken breast half in pan. Reduce heat to low. Cover. Cook for 2 to 3 minutes until cheese is melted.

Heat bacon slices. Place 1 chicken breast half on top of spinach on each roll. Top with 2 bacon slices. Cover with top halves of rolls. Makes 4 burgers.

1 burger: 597 Calories; 26.7 g Total Fat (10.8 g Mono, 5 g Poly, 8.7 g Sat); 121 mg Cholesterol; 38 g Carbohydrate; 2 g Fibre; 49 g Protein; 1020 mg Sodium

Apple Sage Chicken Burgers

Apple and sage are all the rage in these flavourful chicken burgers. A subtle sweetness lingers—who would have thought that apple and chicken would go so well together?

Mayonnaise	1/2 cup	125 mL
Unsweetened applesauce	2 tbsp.	30 mL
Dijon mustard	1 tsp.	5 mL
Large egg, fork-beaten	1	1
Fine dry bread crumbs	1/2 cup	125 mL
Grated havarti cheese	1/4 cup	60 mL
Unsweetened applesauce	2 tbsp.	30 mL
Dijon mustard	2 tsp.	10 mL
Dried sage	1 tsp.	5 mL
Salt	1/2 tsp.	2 mL
Lean ground chicken	1 lb.	454 g
Hamburger buns, split	4	4
Lettuce leaves	4	4

Combine first 3 ingredients in small bowl. Chill.

Combine next 7 ingredients in large bowl. Add chicken. Mix well. Divide into 4 equal portions. Shape into 4 1/2 inch (11 cm) patties. Preheat barbecue to medium. Place patties on greased grill. Close lid. Cook for about 8 minutes per side until internal temperature reaches 175°F (80°C).

Spread mayonnaise mixture on bun halves. Serve patties, topped with lettuce, in buns. Makes 4 burgers.

1 burger: *581 Calories; 37.3 g Total Fat (0.5 g Mono, 1.0 g Poly, 8.1 g Sat); 145 mg Cholesterol; 33 g Carbohydrate; 2 g Fibre; 27 g Protein; 923 mg Sodium*

1. Tangy Pineapple Chicken, page 285
2. Mushroom Chicken Sauce, page 290
3. Cranberry Chicken, page 292

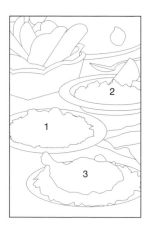

Hurry Chimichurri Patties

Chimichurri is a thick herb sauce that's as common in Argentina as ketchup is in North America. These zesty patties have plenty of fresh herb flavour. Serve on your favourite bun.

Large egg	1	1
Cornflake crumbs	1/3 cup	75 mL
Fine dry bread crumbs	1/3 cup	75 mL
Medium salsa	1/3 cup	75 mL
Basil pesto	2 tbsp.	30 mL
Lean ground chicken	1 lb.	454 g
Cooking oil	1 tsp.	5 mL
CHIMICHURRI SAUCE		
Fresh parsley, lightly packed	1 cup	250 mL
Olive (or cooking) oil	3 tbsp.	45 mL
Fresh oregano leaves	2 tbsp.	30 mL
Balsamic vinegar	1 tbsp.	15 mL
Garlic clove, minced (or 1/4 tsp., 1 mL, powder)	1	1
Dried crushed chilies	1/2 tsp.	2 mL

Beat egg with fork in large bowl. Add next 4 ingredients. Stir well. Add ground chicken. Mix well. Divide and shape into four 5 to 6 inch (12.5 to 15 cm) diameter patties.

Heat cooking oil in large frying pan on medium. Add patties. Cook for about 7 minutes per side until no longer pink inside.

Chimichurri Sauce: Process all 6 ingredients in blender or food processor until paste-like consistency. Makes about 1/2 cup (125 mL) sauce. Serve with patties. Makes 4 patties.

1 pattie: 460 Calories; 32 g Total Fat (9 g Mono, 1.5 g Poly, 2.5 g Sat); 140 mg Cholesterol; 18 g Carbohydrate; 1 g Fibre; 24 g Protein; 420 mg Sodium

Pictured on page 270.

1. Fennel Roast Chicken, page 262

Mediterranean Burgers

These Mediterranean burgers are far from mediocre. Feta, onion, red pepper and a variety of herbs and spices give these burgers an extraordinary amount of flavour!

Butter (or hard margarine)	1 1/2 tsp.	7 mL
Chopped onion	1 cup	250 mL
Roasted red peppers, drained and blotted dry, chopped	3/4 cup	175 mL
Red wine vinegar	2 tbsp.	30 mL
White bread slice, torn into small pieces	1	1
Lemon juice	2 tbsp.	30 mL
Grated lemon zest	2 tsp.	10 mL
Garlic clove, minced (or 1/4 tsp., 1 mL, powder)	1	1
Dried oregano	1 tsp.	5 mL
Dried thyme	1 tsp.	5 mL
Seasoned salt	1 tsp.	5 mL
Pepper	1/2 tsp.	2 mL
Lean ground chicken	1 1/2 lbs.	680 g
Crumbled feta cheese	1/2 cup	125 mL
Cream cheese, softened	1/4 cup	60 mL
Hamburger buns, split	6	6

Melt butter in large frying pan on medium. Add onion. Cook for 5 to 10 minutes, stirring often, until softened.

Add red pepper and vinegar. Stir. Reduce heat to medium-low. Cook for about 15 minutes, stirring occasionally, until onion is very soft. Remove from heat. Cover to keep warm.

Put bread and lemon juice into medium bowl. Stir until bread is moistened. Add next 6 ingredients. Stir. Add chicken. Mix well. Divide into 6 equal portions. Shape into 4 1/2 inch (11 cm) diameter patties.

Put feta and cream cheese into small bowl. Mash until smooth. Preheat gas barbecue to medium (see Tip, page 84). Cook patties on greased grill for 6 to 8 minutes per side until fully cooked and internal temperature reaches 175°F (80°C). Spread cheese mixture on top of patties. Cook for about 1 minute until cheese is softened. Remove to plate. Cover to keep warm.

Toast bun halves on greased grill for about 1 minute until golden. Serve patties, topped with onion mixture, in buns. Makes 6 burgers.

1 burger: 486 Calories; 24.4 g Total Fat (2.3 g Mono, 1.2 g Poly, 5.2 g Sat); 25 mg Cholesterol; 34 g Carbohydrate; 2 g Fibre; 28 g Protein; 1050 mg Sodium

Variation: Use 3/4 cup (175 mL) chèvre in place of feta and cream cheese.

Portobello Chicken Burgers

Can't decide whether to make a chicken or a portobello mushroom burger? Have both at the same time! This makes a great alternative to a traditional beef burger.

Portobello mushrooms (about 6 oz., 170 g, each), stems and gills removed (see Tip, page 117)	4	4
Olive (or cooking) oil	1 tbsp.	15 mL
Salt, sprinkle		
Pepper, sprinkle		
Large egg, fork-beaten	1	1
Grated Parmesan cheese	1/4 cup	60 mL
Fine dry bread crumbs	2 tbsp.	30 mL
Sun-dried tomato pesto	2 tbsp.	30 mL
Finely chopped fresh rosemary	1/4 tsp.	1 mL
Salt	1/4 tsp.	1 mL
Pepper	1/4 tsp.	1 mL
Lean ground chicken	3/4 lb.	340 g
Whole wheat kaiser rolls, split	4	4
Mayonnaise	1/4 cup	60 mL
Romaine leaves	4	4

Brush mushrooms with olive oil. Sprinkle with salt and pepper. Preheat barbecue to medium. Place mushrooms, stem side down, on ungreased grill. Close lid. Cook for about 5 minutes until grill marks appear. Transfer, stem-side up, to large plate.

Combine next 7 ingredients in medium bowl. Add chicken. Mix well. Divide into 4 equal portions. Shape into 4 1/2 inch (11 cm) patties. Press patties firmly into mushrooms. Place on greased grill, patty side down. Close lid. Cook for about 8 minutes until internal temperature of patty reaches 175°F (80°C). Turn. Close lid. Cook for about 3 minutes until mushroom is tender and browned.

Place roll halves on greased grill. Cook for about 1 minute until golden. Spread mayonnaise on roll halves. Serve patties, topped with lettuce, in rolls. Makes 4 burgers.

1 burger: 492 Calories; 27.1 g Total Fat (3.0 g Mono, 1.5 g Poly, 6.1 g Sat); 123 mg Cholesterol; 37 g Carbohydrate; 7 g Fibre; 27 g Protein; 972 mg Sodium

Tuscan Chicken Burgers

Lean chicken is a healthy alternative to beef in these burgers. The spinach, dressing and tomato toppings are so tasty that there's no need to load on any fattening condiments.

Egg whites (large)	2	2
Large flake rolled oats	3/4 cup	175 mL
Finely chopped fresh spinach leaves, lightly packed	1/3 cup	75 mL
Sun-dried tomato (or Italian) dressing	2 tbsp.	30 mL
Grated Parmesan cheese	1 tbsp.	15 mL
Pepper	1/4 tsp.	1 mL
Garlic powder	1/8 tsp.	0.5 mL
Lean ground chicken	1 lb.	454 g
Fresh spinach leaves, lightly packed	1 cup	250 mL
Sun-dried tomato (or Italian) dressing	1 tbsp.	15 mL
Multi-grain (or whole wheat) rolls, split	4	4
Large tomato, sliced	1	1

Combine first 7 ingredients in medium bowl. Add chicken. Mix well. Divide into 4 equal portions. Shape into 4 inch (10 cm) diameter patties. Arrange on greased baking sheet with sides. Spray with cooking spray. Broil on top rack in oven for about 5 minutes per side until internal temperature reaches 175°F (80°C).

Toss second amounts of spinach and dressing in small bowl. Arrange on bottom halves of rolls. Serve patties topped with tomato in rolls. Makes 4 burgers.

1 burger: 445 Calories; 13 g Total Fat (0.5 g Mono, 1.5 g Poly, 2 g Sat); 64 mg Cholesterol; 55 g Carbohydrate; 6 g Fibre; 34 g Protein; 656 mg Sodium (need new NI)

Pictured on page 180.

 Keep your fried foods crisp, rather than greasy, with properly heated oil that has reached 350–375°F (170–190°C). The easiest way to test the temperature is to use a deep-fry thermometer. If you don't have a thermometer, dip the tip of a wooden spoon into the oil. If the oil around the spoon bubbles, the temperature is right. You can also toss a small piece of bread into the oil. If the bread sizzles and turns brown within 1 minute, the oil is ready.

Pineapple Chicken Pizzas

Crispy and tangy pizzas on pita breads.

Teriyaki sauce	1/4 cup	60 mL
Brown sugar, packed	1 tsp.	5 mL
Chili sauce	1/2 tsp.	2 mL
Boneless, skinless chicken breast halves (about 2)	8 oz.	225 g
Satay sauce	2 tbsp.	30 mL
Chili sauce	2 tbsp.	30 mL
Small pita breads (3 inch, 7.5 cm, diameter)	12	12
Finely chopped fresh (or canned, drained) pineapple	1/2 cup	125 mL
Finely chopped green pepper	1/3 cup	75 mL
Grated mozzarella cheese	1 cup	250 mL

Combine first 3 ingredients in medium bowl or resealable freezer bag. Add chicken. Turn to coat. Cover or seal. Marinate in refrigerator for 1 to 3 hours. Drain and discard marinade. Preheat gas barbecues to medium. Cook chicken on greased grill for about 5 minutes per side until no longer pink inside. Finely chop chicken.

Combine satay sauce and second amount of chili sauce in small bowl. Brush 1 side of pitas with satay mixture.

Divide and scatter chicken, pineapple and green pepper over satay mixture. Sprinkle with mozzarella cheese. Place pizzas on greased grill. Close lid. Cook for 3 to 5 minutes until cheese is melted and pitas are crispy. Makes 12 pizzas.

1 pizza: 109 Calories; 3.2 g Total Fat (1 g Mono, 0.4 g Poly, 1.6 g Sat); 19 mg Cholesterol; 12 g Carbohydrate; 1 g Fibre; 8 g Protein; 318 mg Sodium

Mango-stuffed Chicken

*The tropical taste comes alive on
the barbecue!*

Diced ripe mango (or 14 oz., 398 mL, can of sliced mango with syrup, drained and diced)	1 cup	250 mL
Finely chopped salted macadamia nuts (or almonds)	1/2 cup	125 mL
Thinly sliced green onion	2 tbsp.	30 mL
Grated lime (or lemon) zest	1/2 tsp.	2 mL
Curry powder	1/2 tsp.	2 mL
Whole roasting chicken	4 lbs.	1.8 kg
LIME YOGURT MARINADE		
Plain yogurt	1 1/2 cups	375 mL
Lime (or lemon) juice	1/4 cup	60 mL
Ground coriander	1 tbsp.	15 mL
Curry powder	1 tbsp.	15 mL
Finely grated, peeled gingerroot (or 1/2 tsp., 2 mL, ground ginger)	2 tsp.	10 mL
Garlic cloves, minced (or 1 tsp., 5 mL, powder)	4	4
Salt	1 tsp.	5 mL

Put first 5 ingredients into medium bowl. Stir.

Place chicken, backbone-up, on cutting board. Cut down both sides of backbone with kitchen shears or sharp knife to remove (see Tip, page 134). Turn chicken over. Press chicken out flat. Carefully loosen skin but do not remove. Stuff mango mixture between meat and skin, spreading mixture as evenly as possible. Place stuffed chicken in large shallow baking dish.

Lime Yogurt Marinade: Combine all 7 ingredients in small bowl. Makes about 1 3/4 cups (425 mL) marinade. Pour over chicken. Turn until coated. Cover with plastic wrap. Marinate in refrigerator for at least 3 hours, turning occasionally. Drain and discard marinade. Preheat barbecue to medium. Place chicken, skin-side down, on 1 side of greased grill over drip pan. Turn off burner under chicken, leaving opposite burner on medium. Close lid. Cook for 45 minutes. Turn chicken over. Close lid. Cook for 45 to 50 minutes until meat thermometer inserted into breast (not stuffing) reads 185°F (85°C). Remove from heat. Cover with foil. Let stand for 15 minutes. Cut into serving-size portions. Serves 6.

1 serving: 399 Calories; 24.1 g Total Fat (12.2 g Mono, 3.7 g Poly, 5.9 g Sat); 107 mg Cholesterol; 10 g Carbohydrate; 2 g Fibre; 35 g Protein; 320 mg Sodium

Coconut Pesto-stuffed Chicken Breasts

Whisk friends to the tropics with chicken breasts stuffed with a coconut pesto. The coconut-rum wash gives the chicken a deep caramelized colour and just a touch of "spirited" flavour.

Fresh basil, lightly packed	1 1/2 cups	375 mL
Chopped macadamia nuts	1/3 cup	75 mL
Medium sweetened coconut	1/3 cup	75 mL
Pineapple juice	1/4 cup	60 mL
Lime juice	2 tbsp.	30 mL
Salt	1/4 tsp.	1 mL
Boneless, skinless chicken breast halves (about 4 oz., 113 g, each)	4	4
Cooking oil	1 tsp.	5 mL
Paprika	1/2 tsp.	2 mL
Seasoned salt	1/2 tsp.	2 mL
Pepper	1/4 tsp.	1 mL
Coconut rum	1/4 cup	60 mL
Brown sugar, packed	1 1/2 tbsp.	25 mL

In a blender or food processor, process first 6 ingredients until a thick paste forms.

Cut slits horizontally in chicken breasts to form pockets and fill with basil mixture. Secure with wooden picks.

Combine next 4 ingredients and rub over chicken.

Combine rum and brown sugar. Grill chicken on direct medium heat for 5 to 6 minutes per side, brushing occasionally with rum mixture, until chicken is no longer pink inside. Cover with foil and let stand for 5 minutes. Serves 4.

1 serving: 313 Calories; 13.6 g Total Fat (7.8 g Mono, 1.0 g Poly, 3.7 g Sat); 66 mg Cholesterol; 13 g Carbohydrate; 2 g Fibre; 27 g Protein; 404 mg Sodium

Caribbean Chicken

Life is easy when ja-makin' some of this Caribbean-influenced grilled chicken. Similar to Jamaican jerk chicken but much milder. The heat is beautifully tempered by a fresh, fruity topping filled with papaya and avocado.

Onion powder	1 1/2 tsp.	7 mL
Dried thyme	1 tsp.	5 mL
Granulated sugar	1 tsp.	5 mL
Ground allspice	1/2 tsp.	2 mL
Salt	1/2 tsp.	2 mL
Pepper	1/2 tsp.	2 mL
Cayenne pepper	1/4 tsp.	1 mL
Ground cinnamon	1/4 tsp.	1 mL
Ground nutmeg	1/4 tsp.	1 mL
Diced avocado	2 cups	500 mL
Diced papaya	1 1/2 cups	375 mL
Lime juice	3 tbsp.	45 mL
Orange juice	3 tbsp.	45 mL
Grated orange zest	1 tsp.	5 mL
Salt	1/4 tsp.	1 mL
Orange juice	1 1/2 tbsp.	25 mL
Boneless, skinless chicken breast halves (about 4 oz., 113 g, each)	4	4

Combine first 9 ingredients in small bowl. Transfer 1 tsp. (5 mL) spice mixture to medium bowl and set remaining mixture aside.

Add next 6 ingredients to spice mixture in medium bowl. Toss to combine.

Add second amount of orange juice to remaining spice mixture in small bowl. Stir to form a paste. Rub on both sides of chicken. Let stand, covered, in refrigerator for 1 hour. Preheat gas barbecue to medium (see Tip, page 84). Cook chicken on greased grill for about 10 minutes per side until fully cooked and internal temperature reaches 170°F (77°C). Remove to cutting board. Cut chicken crosswise into 1/4 inch (6 mm) strips. Transfer to serving platter. Spoon papaya mixture over chicken. Serves 4.

1 serving: 289 Calories; 13.1 g Total Fat (7.8 g Mono, 1.8 g Poly, 2.2 g Sat); 66 mg Cholesterol; 17 g Carbohydrate; 6 g Fibre; 30 g Protein; 510 mg Sodium

Pineapple Rum Kabobs

There's a reason rum runners risked it all. For fabulously flavoured chicken, of course! OK, maybe we're stretching it a little but when your guests taste these rum-laced kabobs, we're sure they'll brave almost anything for a second helping. Use a ripe pineapple for best results.

Dark (navy) rum	1/4 cup	60 mL
Lime juice	1/4 cup	60 mL
Liquid honey	1/4 cup	60 mL
Brown sugar, packed	1 tbsp.	15 mL
Dijon mustard	1 tbsp.	15 mL
Cooking oil	2 tsp.	10 mL
Boneless, skinless chicken breast halves, cut into 36, 1 inch (2.5 cm) pieces	1 1/2 lbs.	680 g
Medium pineapple, cut into 36, 1 inch (2.5 cm) pieces	1	1
Bamboo skewers (8 inches, 20 cm, each), soaked in water for 10 minutes	12	12

Whisk first 6 ingredients in small bowl. Pour into large resealable freezer bag. Add chicken. Seal bag. Turn until coated. Let stand in refrigerator for 1 hour, turning occasionally. Remove chicken. Transfer rum mixture to small saucepan. Bring to a boil on medium. Reduce heat to medium-low. Simmer, uncovered, for at least 5 minutes.

Thread 3 pieces of chicken and 3 pieces of pineapple alternately onto each skewer. Preheat gas barbecue to medium (see Tip, page 84). Cook kabobs on greased grill for about 12 minutes, turning occasionally and brushing with reserved rum mixture, until chicken is no longer pink inside. Makes 12 kabobs.

1 kabob: 128 Calories; 1.7 g Total Fat (0.7 g Mono, 0.5 g Poly, 0.3 g Sat); 33 mg Cholesterol; 12 g Carbohydrate; 1 g Fibre; 13 g Protein; 49 mg Sodium

Pictured on page 36.

 Because the gills can sometimes be bitter, it is best to remove them from portobellos. First remove the stems, then, using a small spoon, scrape out and discard the gills.

Spice Cupboard Kabobs

Pay attention to your neglected spices and put them to work in these tandoori-style kabobs.
Factor the long marinating time into your planning.

Plain yogurt	3/4 cup	175 mL
Finely chopped onion (or 1 tbsp., 15 mL, flakes)	1/4 cup	60 mL
Lemon juice	3 tbsp.	45 mL
Garlic cloves, minced (or 3/4 tsp., 4 mL, powder)	3	3
All-purpose flour	1 tbsp.	15 mL
Finely grated ginger root (or 1/2 tsp., 2 mL, ground ginger)	2 tsp.	10 mL
Cayenne pepper	1 tsp.	5 mL
Dry mustard	1 tsp.	5 mL
Ground coriander	1 tsp.	5 mL
Ground cumin	1 tsp.	5 mL
Paprika	1 tsp.	5 mL
Ground cinnamon	1/4 tsp.	1 mL
Turmeric	1/4 tsp.	1 mL
Ground cardamom	1/8 tsp.	0.5 mL
Boneless, skinless chicken breasts, cut into 1 inch (2.5 cm) cubes	1 1/2 lbs.	680 g
Bamboo skewers (8 inches, 20 cm, each), soaked in water for 10 minutes	12	12
Salt	1/4 tsp.	1 mL
Chopped fresh cilantro or parsley	1 tbsp.	15 mL

Combine first 14 ingredients in small bowl.

Put chicken into large resealable freezer bag. Add yogurt mixture. Seal bag. Turn until coated. Let stand in refrigerator for at least 6 hours or overnight, turning occasionally. Remove chicken. Discard any remaining yogurt mixture.

Thread chicken onto skewers. Sprinkle with salt. Preheat gas barbecue to medium (see Tip, page 84). Cook kabobs on greased grill for 12 to 14 minutes, turning occasionally, until no longer pink inside. Remove to serving platter.

Sprinkle with cilantro. Makes 12 kabobs.

1 kabob: 72 Calories; 0.7 g Total Fat (0.1 g Mono, 0.1 g Poly, 0.3 g Sat); 36 mg Cholesterol; 1 g Carbohydrate; trace Fibre; 14 g Protein; 81 mg Sodium (need new NI)

Pictured on page 144.

Citrus Spice Chicken

The best zest in town! This'll freshen up any dinner table.

Orange juice	1/2 cup	125 mL
Lime juice	1/4 cup	60 mL
Balsamic vinegar	2 tbsp.	30 mL
Dijon mustard	1 tbsp.	15 mL
Finely chopped chipotle pepper in adobo sauce (see Tip, page 78)	1 tbsp.	15 mL
Garlic cloves, minced (or 1/2 tsp., 2 mL, powder)	2	2
Dried oregano	1 tsp.	5 mL
Chili powder	1/2 tsp.	2 mL
Ground cumin	1/4 tsp.	1 mL
Salt	1/4 tsp.	1 mL
Chicken legs, back attached (about 11 oz., 310 g, each)	4	4
Cooking oil	2 tbsp.	30 mL

Process first 10 ingredients in blender until smooth. Pour into large resealable freezer bag. Add chicken. Seal bag. Turn until coated. Let stand in refrigerator for 2 hours, turning occasionally. Remove chicken. Transfer orange juice mixture to small saucepan. Bring to a boil. Reduce heat to medium-low. Simmer for at least 5 minutes. Set aside.

Pat chicken dry with paper towel. Brush both sides of chicken with cooking oil. Preheat gas barbecue to medium-high. Place chicken on one side of greased grill. Reduce heat on burner under chicken to low, leaving opposite burner on medium. Close lid. Cook for 30 minutes. Turn and brush generously with reserved orange juice mixture. Cook for another 25 minutes until internal temperature reaches 170°F (77°C). Brush with remaining orange juice mixture before serving. Makes 4 legs.

1 leg: 286 Calories; 15.5 g Total Fat (7.0 g Mono, 4.1 g Poly, 2.8 g Sat); 102 mg Cholesterol; 7 g Carbohydrate; 1 g Fibre; 28 g Protein; 302 mg Sodium

Lemon Grass Chicken Skewers

A longer marinating time will intensify the flavour of these splendid skewers— overnight is best. The accompanying salsa is light and refreshing. Superb!

Can of coconut milk (14 oz., 398 mL)	1	1
Finely chopped lemon grass, bulb only (root and stalk removed),	2 1/2 tbsp.	37 mL
Brown sugar, packed	2 tbsp.	30 mL
Soy sauce	1 tbsp.	15 mL
Finely grated ginger root	2 tsp.	10 mL
Garlic clove, minced	1	1
Boneless, skinless chicken thighs, cut in half lengthwise (about 1 lb., 454 g)	6	6
Bamboo skewers (8 inches, 20 cm, each), soaked in water for 10 minutes	12	12
CUCUMBER SALSA		
Lime juice	1/4 cup	60 mL
Cooking oil	2 tbsp.	30 mL
Granulated sugar	2 tbsp.	30 mL
Sweet chili sauce	2 tsp.	10 mL
Salt	1/4 tsp.	1 mL
Finely diced peeled cucumber, seeds removed	2 cups	500 mL
Finely chopped green onion	1/4 cup	60 mL
Chopped fresh cilantro or parsley	2 tbsp.	30 mL
Chopped salted peanuts	2 tbsp.	30 mL

Combine first 6 ingredients in small bowl.

Put chicken into large resealable freezer bag. Add coconut milk mixture. Seal bag. Turn until coated. Let stand in refrigerator for at least 4 hours or overnight, turning occasionally. Remove chicken. Transfer coconut milk mixture to small saucepan. Bring to a boil. Reduce heat to medium. Boil gently for at least 5 minutes, stirring occasionally.

Thread chicken, accordion-style, onto skewers. Preheat gas barbecue to medium (see Tip, page 84). Cook chicken on greased grill for about 10 minutes, turning occasionally and brushing with coconut milk mixture, until no longer pink inside. Discard any remaining coconut milk mixture.

Cucumber Salsa: Combine first 5 ingredients in small bowl.

Add remaining 4 ingredients. Stir. Makes about 2 cups (500 mL) salsa. Serve salsa with skewers using slotted spoon. Makes 12 skewers.

1 skewer with 2 1/2 tbsp. (37 mL) salsa: 135 Calories; 9.5 g Total Fat (3.0 g Mono, 1.6 g Poly, 4.2 g Sat); 25 mg Cholesterol; 6 g Carbohydrate; trace Fibre; 8 g Protein; 156 mg Sodium

Pictured on page 17.

Grilled Greats

Chicken Peanut Satay

This sweet satay does double duty as a main dish or a party-pleasing appie.
The dipping sauce is similar to Thai peanut sauce but is a little milder.

Cooking oil	2 tbsp.	30 mL
Sesame oil (for flavour)	2 tsp.	10 mL
Garlic clove, minced (or 1/4 tsp., 1 mL, powder)	1	1
Finely grated ginger root (or 1/4 tsp., 1 mL, ground ginger)	1 tsp.	5 mL
Dried crushed chilies	1/2 tsp.	2 mL
Grated lime zest	1/2 tsp.	2 mL
Ground coriander	1/2 tsp.	2 mL
Ground turmeric	1/2 tsp.	2 mL
Chicken breast fillets (see Note)	1 1/2 lbs.	680 g
Bamboo skewers (8 inches, 20 cm, each), soaked in water for 10 minutes	12	12
Salt, sprinkle		
Pepper, sprinkle		

SATAY PEANUT SAUCE

Light coconut milk	1 cup	250 mL
Chunky peanut butter	1/2 cup	125 mL
Brown sugar, packed	1 tbsp.	15 mL
Lime juice	1 tbsp.	15 mL
Fish sauce	2 tsp.	10 mL
Rice vinegar	2 tsp.	10 mL
Dried crushed chilies	1/2 tsp.	2 mL

Combine first 8 ingredients in medium bowl. Add chicken. Stir until coated. Let stand, covered, in refrigerator for at least 1 hour, or up to 24 hours.

Thread chicken onto skewers, accordion-style. Discard any remaining seasoning mixture. Sprinkle with salt and pepper. Preheat gas barbecue to medium (see Tip, page 84). Cook on greased grill for 3 to 4 minutes per side until no longer pink inside. Remove to serving plate.

Satay Peanut Sauce: Combine all 7 ingredients in small saucepan on medium. Bring to a boil. Reduce heat to medium-low. Simmer, uncovered, for 3 to 5 minutes, stirring occasionally, until the consistency of thick gravy. Makes about 1 1/3 cups (325 mL) sauce. Serve with satays. Makes 12 satays.

1 satay with 1 1/2 tbsp. (25 mL) sauce: 159 Calories; 9.2 g Total Fat (3.9 g Mono, 2.3 g Poly, 2.2 g Sat); 33 mg Cholesterol; 4 g Carbohydrate; 1 g Fibre; 16 g Protein; 160 mg Sodium

Note: Chicken breast halves may be used instead of chicken fillets. Cut breasts lengthwise into 1/4 inch (6 mm) thick strips.

Minted Cider Chicken

A hint of mint adds a touch of spring to this mildly sweet, glazed chicken.

Finely chopped fresh mint	1/4 cup	60 mL
Red jalapeño jelly, melted	1/4 cup	60 mL
Apple cider vinegar	2 tbsp.	30 mL
Frozen concentrated apple juice, thawed	1 tbsp.	15 mL
Garlic clove, minced (or 1/4 tsp., 1 mL, powder)	1	1
Salt	1/4 tsp.	1 mL
Pepper	1/8 tsp.	0.5 mL
Chicken drumsticks (or bone-in thighs) (about 3 oz., 85 g, each)	12	12

Combine first 7 ingredients in small bowl.

Preheat gas barbecue to medium-high (see Tip, page 84). Cook chicken on greased grill for about 30 minutes, turning occasionally, until starting to brown. Brush with mint mixture. Cook for another 15 minutes, turning occasionally and brushing with mint mixture, until fully cooked and internal temperature reaches 170°F (77°C). Makes 12 drumsticks.

1 drumstick: 75 Calories; 2.0 g Total Fat (0.7 g Mono, 0.5 g Poly, 0.5 g Sat); 32 mg Cholesterol; 4 g Carbohydrate; trace Fibre; 10 g Protein; 82 mg Sodium

Grilled Chicken in Pandanus Leaves

Pandanus leaves add a woodsy vanilla-like note to this dish, as well as a remarkable visual. Fascinating presentation, superb flavour.

Oyster sauce	2 tbsp.	30 mL
Soy sauce	2 tbsp.	30 mL
Tom yum paste	2 tbsp.	30 mL
Brown sugar, packed	1 tbsp.	15 mL
Garlic cloves, minced	2	2
Sesame oil	1 tsp.	5 mL
Pepper	1/4 tsp.	1 mL
Boneless, skinless chicken thigs (about 3 oz., 85 g, each), halved	8	8
Pandanus leaves, cut into 5 x 1 inch (12.5 x 12.5 cm) pieces	32	32

(continued on next page)

Combine first 7 ingredients in large resealable freezer bag. Add chicken and marinate in refrigerator for 6 hours or overnight. Drain and discard marinade.

Place 2 pandanus leaves, overlapping lengthwise, on work surface. Place 1 chicken piece in centre of leaves. Bring both ends up and secure with a wooden pick. Repeat steps. Cook on greased grill on medium for 7 minutes per side until meat thermometer reads 170°F (77°C). Makes 16 pieces.

1 piece: 77 Calories; 4.6 g Total Fat (1.2 g Mono, 0.7 g Poly, 1.2 g Sat); 28 mg Cholesterol; 1 g Carbohydrate; trace Fibre; 8 g Protein; 174 mg Sodium

Sesame Ginger Chicken

Ginger and sesame mingle magnificently in the marvellous marinade.

Soy sauce	1/3 cup	75 mL
Rice vinegar	3 tbsp.	45 mL
Sesame oil	3 tbsp.	45 mL
Brown sugar, packed	2 tbsp.	30 mL
Finely grated ginger root (or 3/4 tsp., 4 mL, ground ginger)	1 tbsp.	15 mL
Garlic cloves, minced (or 1/2 tsp., 2 mL, powder)	2	2
Boneless, skinless chicken breast halves (about 4 oz., 113 g, each)	4	4
Sesame seeds, toasted (see Tip, page 22)	1 tbsp.	15 mL

Combine first 6 ingredients in large resealable freezer bag. Add chicken. Seal bag. Turn until coated. Let stand in refrigerator for at least 6 hours or overnight, turning occasionally. Remove chicken. Transfer soy sauce mixture to small saucepan. Bring to a boil. Reduce heat to medium. Boil gently, uncovered, for at least 5 minutes, until thickened and reduced by half.

Preheat gas barbecue to medium (see Tip, page 84). Cook chicken on greased grill for 15 to 17 minutes, turning occasionally and brushing with reserved soy sauce mixture, until fully cooked and internal temperature reaches 170°F (77°C). Sprinkle with sesame seeds. Serves 4.

1 serving: 271 Calories; 13.0 g Total Fat (4.9 g Mono, 5.1 g Poly, 2.1 g Sat); 66 mg Cholesterol; 10 g Carbohydrate; trace Fibre; 28 g Protein; 1735 mg Sodium

Smoky Bacon Drumsticks

Everything's better wrapped in bacon! Especially these juicy drumsticks, enhanced by seductive, smoky paprika.

Smoked sweet paprika	1 tbsp.	15 mL
Garlic powder	1 tsp.	5 mL
Salt	1 tsp.	5 mL
Pepper	1/2 tsp.	2 mL
Chicken drumsticks (about 3 oz., 85 g, each), skin removed	12	12
Bacon slices	12	12

Combine first 4 ingredients in small cup.

Rub paprika mixture over drumsticks. Wrap 1 bacon slice around each drumstick. Secure with wooden picks. Preheat barbecue to medium. Place chicken on greased grill. Close lid. Cook for about 35 minutes, turning occasionally, until internal temperature reaches 170°F (77°C). Remove and discard wooden picks. Makes 12 drumsticks

1 drumstick: 108 Calories; 5.6 g Total Fat (2.3 g Mono, 1.0 g Poly, 1.7 g Sat); 42 mg Cholesterol; trace Carbohydrate; trace Fibre; 13 g Protein; 376 mg Sodium

1. Chicken Ratatouille, page 159
2. Chicken and Apricot Pilaf, page 192
3. Chicken and Olives, page 158

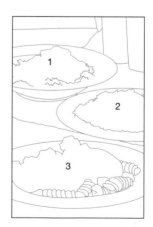

Yakitori

Plan ahead to grill these for old friends in the late afternoon of a hot summer's day.
So quick, you won't miss a moment's conversation.

Mirin	1/4 cup	60 mL
Thick teriyaki basting sauce	1/4 cup	60 mL
Chili paste (sambal oelek)	1 1/2 tsp.	7 mL
Garlic powder	1/8 tsp.	0.5 mL
Boneless, skinless chicken thighs	1 lb.	454 g
Bamboo skewers (8 inches, 20 cm, each), soaked in water for 10 minutes	8	8
Sesame seeds, toasted (see Tip, page 22)	1 tsp.	5 mL

Combine first 4 ingredients in small bowl.

Place chicken between 2 sheets of plastic wrap. Pound with mallet or rolling pin until flattened. Cut in half lengthwise. Place in medium bowl. Add 1/4 cup (60 mL) mirin mixture. Turn until coated. Marinate, covered, in refrigerator for 30 minutes.

Thread chicken, accordion-style, onto skewers. Preheat barbecue to high. Place skewers on greased grill. Cook for about 2 minutes per side, brushing with remaining mirin mixture, until no longer pink inside.

Sprinkle with sesame seeds. Makes 8 skewers.

1 skewer: 114 Calories; 4.4 g Total Fat (1.6 g Mono, 1.0 g Poly, 1.2 g Sat); 37 mg Cholesterol; 5 g Carbohydrate; 0 g Fibre; 11 g Protein; 257 mg Sodium

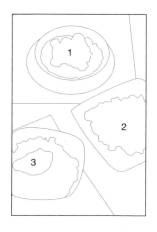

1. Ginger Pineapple Meatballs, page 184
2. Cashew Chicken, page 186
3. Hoisin Chicken Pot, page 164

Hickory Chicken and Apricots

Forgo the smokehouse—we tell you exactly how to get that genuine hickory taste using your barbecue. You won't believe how well apricots and pecans combine with a smoky hickory flavour. Canned sliced peaches also work well.

APRICOT STUFFING

Can of apricot halves in light syrup, (14 oz., 398 mL) drained and syrup reserved, finely chopped	1	1
Fresh bread crumbs	2/3 cup	150 mL
Chopped pecans, toasted (see Tip, page 22)	1/2 cup	125 mL
Finely chopped onion	1/2 cup	125 mL
Chopped fresh parsley (or 2 1/4 tsp., 11 mL, flakes)	3 tbsp.	45 mL
Brown sugar, packed	2 tsp.	10 mL
Salt	1/4 tsp.	1 mL
Pepper, sprinkle		
Whole chicken	4 lbs.	1.8 kg
Hickory wood chips (see Note 1)	1 1/2 cup	375 mL
Water		
Reserved syrup from apricots	2/3 cup	150 mL
Soy sauce	1 1/2 tbsp.	25 mL
Dijon mustard	1 tbsp.	15 mL
Liquid honey	1 tbsp.	15 mL

Apricot Stuffing: Combine first 8 ingredients in medium bowl. Makes about 2 1/3 cups (575 mL) stuffing.

Loosely fill body cavity of chicken with stuffing. Secure with wooden picks or small metal skewers. Tie wings with butcher's string close to body. Tie legs to tail.

Soak wood chips in water for 20 minutes. Drain. Put chips in smoker box (see Note 2). Close smoker box. Place smoker box over 1 side of grill in gas barbecue. Heat barbecue to medium for about 20 minutes until chips are smoking. Adjust burner under smoker box as necessary to keep it smoking and to maintain temperature of about 350°F (175°C). Place a small piece of greased foil on grill opposite smoker box. Place chicken on foil. Turn off burner under chicken. Close lid. Cook for 1 3/4 hours. Have a water spray bottle on hand to lightly douse any flames that may occur from wood chips in smoker box.

(continued on next page)

Combine remaining 4 ingredients in small bowl. Brush over chicken. Cook for about 15 minutes, brushing with soy sauce mixture, until chicken is fully cooked and meat thermometer inserted into thickest part of breast reads 185°F (85°C). Temperature of stuffing should reach at least 165°F (74°C). Transfer chicken to cutting board. Remove stuffing to serving bowl. Cover to keep warm. Cover chicken with foil. Let stand for 10 minutes before carving. Serves 6.

1 serving: 798 Calories; 52.8 g Total Fat (22.9 g Mono, 12.0 g Poly, 13.7 g Sat); 227 mg Cholesterol; 21 g Carbohydrate; 2 g Fibre; 58 g Protein; 708 mg Sodium

Note 1: Wood chips for your barbecue can be found in the barbecue section of department stores or in barbecue specialty stores.

Note 2: If you do not own a smoker box, you can make your own using a foil pan. Fill the pan with the soaked wood chips and cover with a sheet of foil. Poke holes in the top to allow smoke to escape.

Grilled Hoisin Drumsticks

No hoisin around—these slowly marinated drumsticks are just too good! The caramelized hoisin glaze is so sweet and, dare we say, scandalously sticky, that you'll want to have a few napkins at the ready.

Cooking oil	1/3 cup	75 mL
Rice wine (or dry sherry)	3 tbsp.	45 mL
Garlic cloves, minced	3	3
Finely grated ginger root	1 tsp.	5 mL
Chicken drumsticks (about 3 oz., 85 g, each)	12	12
Brown sugar, packed	2/3 cup	150 mL
Soy sauce	1/2 cup	125 mL
Hoisin sauce	1/3 cup	75 mL
Ketchup	1/3 cup	75 mL

Combine first 4 ingredients in large resealable freezer bag. Add chicken. Seal bag. Turn until coated. Let stand in refrigerator for 6 hours or overnight, turning occasionally. Remove chicken. Discard any remaining cooking oil mixture.

Combine remaining 4 ingredients in small bowl. Preheat gas barbecue to medium (see Tip, page 84). Cook chicken on greased grill for 25 minutes, turning occasionally. Brush with soy sauce mixture. Cook for another 15 minutes, turning often and brushing with soy sauce mixture, until fully cooked and internal temperature reaches 170°F (77°C). Makes 12 drumsticks.

1 drumstick: 195 Calories; 6.0 g Total Fat (2.3 g Mono, 1.6 g Poly, 1.3 g Sat); 66 mg Cholesterol; 17.3 g Carbohydrate; trace Fibre; 18 g Protein; 1189 mg Sodium

Pictured on page 53.

Beer Can Chicken

Check the barbecue section of your local department store for a roasting stand that is specially made to hold the beer can and chicken safely.

Can of beer (12 1/2 oz., 355 mL)	1	1
Apple juice	1/4 cup	60 mL
Apple cider vinegar	2 tbsp.	30 mL
Cooking oil	2 tbsp.	30 mL
Worcestershire sauce	2 tsp.	10 mL
Montreal chicken spice	2 tbsp.	30 mL
Brown sugar, packed	2 tsp.	10 mL
Dried oregano	1 tsp.	5 mL
Dry mustard	1 tsp.	5 mL
Onion powder	1 tsp.	5 mL
Whole chicken	4 lbs.	1.8 kg

Pour 2/3 cup (150 mL) beer into a spray bottle, leaving remaining beer in can. Set can aside. Add next 4 ingredients to spray bottle. Swirl gently to combine. Set aside.

Combine next 5 ingredients in small bowl. Sprinkle 1 tbsp. (15 mL) seasoning mixture inside chicken cavity. Rub remaining seasoning mixture over surface of chicken. Let stand, covered, in refrigerator for 30 minutes. Stand the chicken, tail end down, over beer can and press down to insert can into body cavity of chicken. Preheat gas barbecue to medium. Place drip pan under grill on one side of barbecue. Balance chicken upright over drip pan, so that bottom of beer can rests on grill. Turn burner under chicken to low, leaving opposite burner on medium. Close lid. Cook for 1 1/2 to 1 3/4 hours, spraying chicken with beer mixture every 20 minutes, until browned and meat thermometer inserted in thickest part of breast reads 185°F (85°C). Carefully remove chicken from beer can by inserting a carving fork through chicken above level of top of beer can and lifting chicken off of can (see Note). Transfer chicken to cutting board. Cover with foil. Let stand for 10 minutes before carving. Serves 6.

1 serving: 754 Calories; 50.4 g Total Fat (21.6 g Mono, 11.1 g Poly, 13.4 g Sat); 227 mg Cholesterol; 10 g Carbohydrate; trace Fibre; 57 g Protein; 607 mg Sodium

Note: Be careful when removing the beer can from the chicken. The can will be full of very hot liquid.

Mango Salsa Chicken

Refreshing, delicious and pretty to look at! Spicy citrus and mango salsa is the perfect match for tender chicken. The salsa also goes well with salads, wraps, quesadillas and grilled fish.

Boneless, skinless chicken breast halves (about 4 oz., 113 g, each)	4	4
Olive oil	2 tbsp.	30 mL
Lime juice	1 1/2 tbsp.	25 mL
Grated lime zest	1 1/2 tsp.	7 mL
Cajun seasoning	1 tsp.	5 mL
LIME MANGO SALSA		
Chopped frozen mango, thawed (see Note)	1 cup	250 mL
Finely diced red onion	1/4 cup	60 mL
Garlic clove, minced (or 1/4 tsp., 1 mL, powder)	1	1
Finely diced jalapeño pepper (see Tip, page 166)	2 tbsp.	30 mL
Olive oil	2 tbsp.	30 mL
Lime juice	1 1/2 tbsp.	25 mL
Chopped fresh cilantro or parsley	1 tbsp.	15 mL
Grated lime zest	1 1/2 tsp.	7 mL

Preheat gas barbecue to medium (see Tip, page 84). Score both sides of each chicken breast several times with sharp knife. Combine next 4 ingredients in small bowl. Brush over chicken breasts. Cook chicken on greased grill for about 6 minutes per side, brushing with lime mixture, until no longer pink inside.

Lime Mango Salsa: Combine all 8 ingredients in small bowl. Makes 1 1/2 cups (375 mL) salsa. Serve with chicken. Serves 4.

1 serving: 281 Calories; 15.5 g Total Fat (10.5 g Mono, 1.6 g Poly, 2.3 g Sat), 65 mg Cholesterol; 10 g Carbohydrate; 1 g Fibre; 26 g Protein; 197 mg Sodium

Note: If frozen mango is unavailable, use fresh or canned mango instead. Chopped oranges or pineapple also work well.

Pictured on page 252.

Chicken Aztec

We know that Aztec life was anything but tranquil, but you've got to pay homage to a culture that used chocolate for currency! Savour the secrets of the Ancients and taste the mysterious, dark accents chocolate and cocoa provide when paired with chicken.

Cooking oil	1 tbsp.	15 mL
Brown sugar, packed	2 tsp.	10 mL
Lime juice	2 tsp.	10 mL
Chili powder	1 tsp.	5 mL
Cocoa	1 tsp.	5 mL
Ground cinnamon	1 tsp.	5 mL
Boneless, skinless chicken breast halves (about 4 oz., 113 g, each)	4	4
Melted butter (or hard margarine)	3 tbsp.	45 mL
Chopped fresh cilantro or parsley	2 tbsp.	30 mL
Finely chopped green onion	1 tbsp.	15 mL
Lime juice	1 tbsp.	15 mL
Finely diced jalapeño pepper (see Tip, page 166)	1 tsp.	5 mL
Grated semi-sweet chocolate	1 tsp.	5 mL

Combine first 6 ingredients in small bowl.

Brush on both sides of chicken. Preheat gas barbecue to medium (see Tip, page 84). Cook chicken on greased grill for about 10 minutes per side until fully cooked and internal temperature reaches 170°F (77°C). Remove to serving plate. Cover to keep warm.

Combine remaining 6 ingredients in small bowl. Spoon over chicken. Serves 4.

1 serving: 254 Calories; 14.3 g Total Fat (4.8 g Mono, 1.8 g Poly, 6.4 g Sat); 88 mg Cholesterol; 5 g Carbohydrate; 1 g Fibre; 26 g Protein; 133 mg Sodium

Pictured on page 36.

 tip   Never substitute non-fat sour cream in a cooked recipe that calls for light or regular sour cream—it can negatively effect taste and texture.

Cedar Plank Chicken

Amaze your friends with the delicious novelty of serving dinner on an aromatic plank. They won't believe how moist and delicious chicken can be with a little help from a cedar! (Keep in mind that long soaking and marinating times are required.)

Cedar plank (see Note)	1	1
Red jalapeño jelly	1/2 cup	125 mL
Italian dressing	1/2 cup	125 mL
Grated orange zest	2 tbsp.	30 mL
Bone-in chicken breast halves (about 10 oz., 285 g, each)	4	4
Brown sugar, packed	1 tbsp.	15 mL
Dried sage	1/2 tsp.	2 mL
Paprika	1/2 tsp.	2 mL
Salt	1/2 tsp.	2 mL
Pepper	1/2 tsp.	2 mL
Cooking oil	1 tbsp.	15 mL

Place cedar plank in sink or large container. Add enough water to cover. Weight planks with heavy cans to keep submerged. Let stand for at least 6 hours or overnight.

Put jalapeño jelly in small microwave-safe bowl. Microwave on high (100%) for about 1 minute until melted. Add dressing and orange zest. Stir. Pour into large resealable freezer bag. Add chicken. Seal bag. Turn until coated. Let stand in refrigerator for 4 to 6 hours, turning occasionally. Remove chicken. Discard any remaining dressing mixture.

Combine next 5 ingredients in small cup. Rub on both sides of chicken.

Brush cooking oil on one side of plank. Arrange chicken, skin side up, on greased side of plank. Preheat gas barbecue to medium. Place plank on ungreased grill. Close lid. Cook for about 50 minutes until chicken is fully cooked and internal temperature reaches 170°F (77°C). Serves 4.

1 serving: 331 Calories; 13.6 g Total Fat (6.6 g Mono, 3.9 g Poly, 2.0 g Sat); 119 mg Cholesterol; 9 g Carbohydrate; trace Fibre; 41 g Protein; 515 mg Sodium

Note: Cedar planks specifically designed for barbecuing can be purchased in the meat department of large grocery stores. Or use an untreated western red cedar plank found in building supply stores. Never use a treated cedar plank. Planks should be about 16 x 6 x 1/2 inches (40 x 15 x 1.2 cm) and are good for 1 use each.

Pictured on page 36.

Orange Basil Chicken

This juicy dish is spatchcocked—meaning cut open and pressed flat before it's grilled.
Use kitchen shears to make the job easy.

Butter (or hard margarine), softened	3 tbsp.	45 mL
Chopped fresh basil	2 tbsp.	30 mL
Grated orange zest	1 tsp.	5 mL
Ground cumin	1/2 tsp.	2 mL
Salt	1/4 tsp.	1 mL
Pepper	1/4 tsp.	1 mL
Whole chicken	4 lbs.	1.8 kg
Frozen concentrated orange juice, thawed	2 tbsp.	30 mL
Maple (or maple-flavoured) syrup	2 tbsp.	30 mL

Combine first 6 ingredients in small bowl.

Place chicken, backbone up, on cutting board. Cut down both sides of backbone, using kitchen shears or knife, to remove. Turn chicken over. Press chicken flat. Carefully loosen skin but do not remove (see Tip, below). Stuff butter mixture between meat and skin, spreading mixture as evenly as possible. Preheat gas barbecue to medium. Place chicken, skin side down, on 1 side of greased grill. Turn off burner under chicken, leaving opposite burner on medium. Close lid. Cook for 45 minutes. Carefully turn chicken over.

Combine concentrated orange juice and maple syrup in small cup. Brush over chicken. Cook for another 30 minutes, brushing occasionally with orange juice mixture, until meat thermometer inserted into thickest part of breast reads 185°F (85°C). Transfer chicken to cutting board. Cover with foil. Let stand for 15 minutes before carving. Serves 6.

1 serving: 728 Calories; 51.3 g Total Fat (20.4 g Mono, 10.0 g Poly, 16.6 g Sat); 242 mg Cholesterol; 7 g Carbohydrate; trace Fibre; 57 g Protein; 351 mg Sodium

 To loosen chicken skin, lift the edge of the skin and gently slide your fingers as far as possible underneath it. Be careful not to tear it.

Fiesta Chicken and Salsa

Fresh and fun! Sour cream and lime make the chicken moist and tender, and the crisp, colourful salsa is a perfect contrast. The whole family will love this one.

COOL CORN SALSA

Diced avocado	1 cup	250 mL
Can of kernel corn (7 oz., 199), drained	1	1
Diced English cucumber (with peel)	1/2 cup	125 mL
Diced tomato	1/2 cup	125 mL
Thinly sliced green onion	3 tbsp.	45 mL
Lime juice	1 tbsp.	15 mL
Granulated sugar	1 tsp.	5 mL
Salt	1/4 tsp.	1 mL

FIESTA CHICKEN

Sour cream	1/2 cup	125 mL
Envelope of taco seasoning mix (1 1/4 oz., 35 g)	1	1
Lime juice	1 tbsp.	15 mL
Boneless, skinless chicken breast halves (about 4 oz., 113 g, each)	6	6

Cool Corn Salsa: Combine all 8 ingredients in medium bowl. Stir. Makes about 3 cups (750 mL). Chill.

Fiesta Chicken: Combine first 3 ingredients in small bowl. Place chicken in large resealable freezer bag. Pour sour cream mixture over top. Seal bag. Turn until coated. Marinate in refrigerator for 2 hours, turning occasionally. Remove chicken. Discard any remaining sour cream mixture. Preheat barbecue to medium. Place chicken on greased grill. Close lid. Cook for about 8 minutes per side until internal temperature reaches 170°F (77°C). Serve with Cool Corn Salsa. Serves 6.

1 serving: 255 Calories; 8.7 g Total Fat (2.8 g Mono, 0.8 g Poly, 3.3 g Sat); 79 mg Cholesterol; 12 g Carbohydrate; 2 g Fibre; 28 g Protein; 624 mg Sodium

Rotisserie Chicken

A dinner solution that requires minimal time and effort, and produces deliciously moist and tender results! Take a chicken, add a simple rub, then skewer and truss the bird on the rotisserie and you're good to go.

Paprika	1 tbsp.	15 mL
Garlic powder	2 tsp.	10 mL
Onion powder	2 tsp.	10 mL
Pepper	2 tsp.	10 mL
Celery salt	1 tsp.	5 mL
Whole chicken	4 lbs.	1.8 kg
Cooking oil	1 tbsp.	15 mL

Combine first 5 ingredients in small cup.

Rub chicken with cooking oil. Sprinkle 1 tbsp. (15 mL) paprika mixture into cavity of chicken. Rub remaining paprika mixture over chicken. Place drip pan filled 2/3 with water on 1 burner. Preheat barbecue to medium-high. Set up chicken on rotisserie (see Note) over drip pan. Close lid. Cook for about 30 minutes until starting to brown. Reduce heat to medium. Cook for about 1 hour until meat thermometer inserted in thickest part of thigh reaches 185°F (85°C). Transfer chicken to cutting board. Cover with foil. Internal temperature should rise to at least 185°F (85°C). Let stand for 10 minutes. Serves 6.

1 serving: 251 Calories; 11.1 g Total Fat (4.4 g Mono, 2.7 g Poly, 2.6 g Sat); 103 mg Cholesterol; 2 g Carbohydrate; 1 g Fibre; 34 g Protein; 268 mg Sodium

Note: Refer to your barbecue manual for instructions on rotisserie use.

 If a recipe calls for less than an entire can of tomato paste, freeze the unopened can for 30 minutes. Open both ends and push the contents through one end. Slice off only what you need. Freeze the rest in a resealable freezer bag or plastic wrap for future use.

Southwestern Spuds

How does something so simple taste so good?

Large potatoes (with skin)	4	4
Cooking oil	2 tsp.	10 mL
Sliced fresh white mushrooms	1 cup	250 mL
Chopped green pepper	1.2 cup	125 mL
Chopped cooked chicken (see Tip, page 58)	2 cups	500 mL
Medium salsa	1 cup	250 mL
Sour cream	1 cup	250 mL
Grated medium Cheddar cheese	1/2 cup	125 mL

With fork, poke several holes randomly in each potato. Wrap each with paper towel. Microwave on high (100%) for about 15 minutes, turning potatoes over at halftime, until tender.

Meanwhile, heat cooking oil in large frying pan on medium-high. Add mushrooms and green pepper. Cook for about 2 minutes, stirring occasionally, until vegetables start to soften.

Add chicken and salsa. Heat and stir for about 3 minutes until heated through. Reduce heat to medium-low.

Add sour cream. Stir well. Remove from heat. Cover to keep warm. Cut potatoes in half lengthwise. Without damaging skin, carefully mash inside of each potato with fork. Place 2 potato halves on each of 4 plates. Spoon chicken mixture onto each potato half.

Sprinkle cheese over top. Serves 4.

1 serving: 473 Calories; 21.8 g Total Fat (7.2 g Mono, 2.6 g Poly, 10.2 g Sat); 106 mg Cholesterol; 38 g Carbohydrate; 5 g Fibre; 33 g Protein; 374 mg Sodium

"Osso Bucco" Chicken

No bones about it, this chicken version of osso bucco is delightful.

All-purpose flour	1/4 cup	60 mL
Seasoned salt	1/2 tsp.	2 mL
Bone-in chicken thighs, skin removed (about 5 oz., 140 g, each)	8	8
Cooking oil	2 tbsp.	30 mL
Chopped onion	2 cups	500 mL
Chopped carrot	1 cup	250 mL
Garlic clove, minced (or 1/4 tsp., 1 mL, powder)	1	1
Dried sage	1 tsp.	5 mL
Can of Italian-style stewed tomatoes (19 oz., 540 mL)	1	1
Can of condensed chicken broth (10 oz., 284 mL)	1	1
Dry (or alcohol-free) white wine	1 cup	250 mL
Bay leaf	1	1
Chopped fresh parsley	1/4 cup	60 mL
Grated lemon zest	1 tbsp.	15 mL

Combine flour and seasoned salt in large resealable freezer bag. Add chicken. Toss until coated. Remove chicken. Discard any remaining flour mixture.

Heat cooking oil in large frying pan on medium-high. Arrange chicken in pan, spaced apart. Cook for about 5 minutes, turning at halftime, until browned on both sides. Remove to plate. Set aside. Reduce heat to medium.

Add next 4 ingredients to same frying pan. Cook for about 5 minutes, stirring occasionally, until carrot starts to soften.

Add next 4 ingredients. Stir. Bring to a boil, scraping any brown bits from bottom of pan. Add chicken. Reduce heat to medium-low. Simmer, covered, for about 1 hour, stirring occasionally, until chicken is tender. Remove chicken to serving bowl using slotted spoon. Cover to keep warm. Cook sauce, uncovered, on medium for about 10 minutes until thickened. Discard bay leaf. Pour sauce mixture over chicken.

Combine parsley and lemon zest in small cup. Sprinkle over chicken and sauce before serving. Serves 4.

1 serving: 539 Calories; 23.9 g Total Fat (10.5 g Mono, 5.9 g Poly, 5.2 g Sat); 143 mg Cholesterol; 26 g Carbohydrate; 2 g Fibre; 43 g Protein; 799 mg Sodium

Pictured on page 143.

Chicken Kiev

You'll need to allow extra time to prepare this dish, but it's worth the wait. A classic.

Large chicken breasts, halved, skin and bones removed	4	4
Parsley flakes	1 tbsp.	15 mL
Chives	1 tbsp.	15 mL
Worcestershire sauce	1/2 tsp.	2 mL
Salt	1/2 tsp.	2 mL
Pepper	1/4 tsp.	1 mL
Garlic powder (or 1/2 clove, minced)	1/8 tsp.	0.5 mL
Butter (or hard margarine), softened	1/2 cup	125 mL
All-purpose flour	1/3 cup	75 mL
Large eggs, beaten	2	2
Fine dry bread crumbs	1 cup	250 mL
Cooking oil for deep-frying		
MUSHROOM SAUCE		
Butter (or hard margarine)	2 tbsp.	30 mL
Sliced fresh mushrooms	2 cups	500 mL
All-purpose flour	2 tsp.	10 mL
Chicken bouillon powder	1 tsp.	5 mL
Paprika	1/8 tsp.	0.5 mL
Light cream	3/4 cup	175 mL
Soy sauce	1 tsp.	5 mL

Pound each chicken breast between 2 sheets of waxed paper to flatten 1/4 inch (6 mm) thick. Do not puncture or tear.

In small bowl mix next 7 ingredients. Shape into 8 balls or rectangular shapes. Chill in freezer for a few minutes until firm. Place ball at long (wide) end of each breast. Fold sides over first then bring up front and back fastening with wooden picks.

Roll in flour, dip in egg and coat with crumbs. Chill for about 1 hour.

Deep-fry, 2 at a time, in 375°F (190°C) hot oil for about 3 minutes until golden. Drain on paper towels.

Mushroom Sauce: Melt butter in frying pan. Add mushrooms. Sauté until soft.

Mix in flour, bouillon powder and paprika. Stir in cream and soy sauce until it boils. Spoon over chicken. Makes 8 servings.

Variation: For a simple filling, mix butter with 2 tbsp. (30 mL) chopped chives.

1 serving: 720 Calories; 48 g Total Fat (14 g Mono, 4 g Poly, 24 g Sat); 280 mg Cholesterol; 34 g Carbohydrate; 2 g Fibre; 40 g Protein; 1850 mg Sodium

Butter Chicken Curry

Absolutely delicious! Lean chicken is coated in a spice mix for maximum flavour.

Canola oil	1 tbsp.	15 mL
Curry powder	1 tbsp.	15 mL
Finely grated ginger root (or 3/4 tsp., 4 mL, ground ginger)	1 tbsp.	15 mL
Brown sugar, packed	1 tsp.	5 mL
Ground cumin	1/2 tsp.	2 mL
Salt	1/2 tsp.	2 mL
Boneless, skinless chicken breast halves, quartered	1 lb.	454 g
Butter	1 tsp.	5 mL
Canola oil	1 tsp.	5 mL
Finely chopped onion	1 1/2 cups	375 mL
Garlic cloves, minced (or 1/2 tsp., 2 mL, powder)	2	2
Tomato paste (see Tip, page 136)	3 tbsp.	45 mL
Curry powder	1 tsp.	5 mL
Brown sugar, packed	1/2 tsp.	2 mL
Ground cinnamon	1/4 tsp.	1 mL
Prepared chicken broth	1 cup	250 mL
Plain Balkan-style yogurt	1/2 cup	125 mL
Chopped fresh cilantro (optional)	1 tbsp.	15 mL

Combine first 6 ingredients in medium bowl. Add chicken. Toss until coated. Place on greased baking sheet with sides. Cook in 450°F (230°C) oven for about 10 minutes until no longer pink inside.

Heat butter and second amount of canola oil in large frying pan on medium. Add onion and garlic. Cook for about 10 minutes, stirring often, until onion is softened and browned.

Add next 4 ingredients. Heat and stir for 1 minute. Add broth. Stir. Bring to a boil. Reduce heat to medium-low. Add chicken. Cook for about 5 minutes, stirring occasionally, until heated through. Remove from heat.

Stir in yogurt and cilantro. Serves 4.

1 serving: 243 Calories; 7 g Total Fat (3.5 g Mono, 1.5 g Poly, 1.5 g Sat); 69 mg Cholesterol; 14 g Carbohydrate; 3 g Fibre; 30 g Protein; 577 mg Sodium

Curried Chicken and Peaches

Not sure what to make for dinner? Try this sweet curried chicken over rice
for a quick and colourful meal.

Cooking oil	1 tsp.	5 mL
Chicken breasts, cut into 1/2 inch (12 mm) slices	1 lb.	454 g
Cooking oil	1 tsp.	5 mL
Chopped onion	1 cup	250 mL
All-purpose flour	1 tbsp.	15 mL
Curry powder	2 tsp.	10 mL
Salt	1/4 tsp.	1 mL
Can of diced tomatoes (14 oz., 398 mL), drained	1	1
Can of sliced peaches in juice (14 oz., 398 mL), drained and juice reserved, chopped	1	1
Reserved peach juice	1/2 cup	125 mL
Peach yogurt	1/2 cup	125 mL
Chopped green onion	1/4 cup	60 mL

Heat cooking oil in large frying pan on medium-high. Add chicken. Cook for about 3 minutes per side until browned. Transfer to plate. Cover to keep warm.

Add second amount of cooking oil to same frying pan. Add onion. Cook for 2 minutes, stirring often.

Add next 3 ingredients. Heat and stir for about 1 minute until fragrant.

Add next 3 ingredients. Stir. Bring to a boil. Reduce heat to medium. Boil gently, uncovered, for about 5 minutes until thickened. Add chicken. Heat and stir for about 1 minute until chicken is no longer pink inside.

Add yogurt and green onion. Stir. Makes about 4 1/2 cups (1.1 L).

1 cup (250 mL): 236 Calories; 4 g Total Fat (1.5 g Mono, 0.5 g Poly, 1 g Sat); 40 mg Cholesterol; 31 g Carbohydrate; 2 g Fibre; 18 g Protein; 890 mg Sodium

Pictured on page 269.

Elegant Chicken

Incredibly good—the sauce is the secret.

All-purpose flour	2 tbsp.	30 mL
Paprika	1/8 tsp.	0.5 mL
Salt	1/8 tsp.	0.5 mL
Pepper, sprinkle		
Boneless, skinless chicken breast halves (about 4 oz., 113 g, each)	4	4
Hard margarine (butter browns too fast)	1 tbsp.	15 mL
HAZELNUT SAUCE		
Sliced fresh mushrooms	1 cup	250 mL
Dry white (or alcohol-free) wine	1/2 cup	125 mL
Condensed cream of mushroom soup (1/2 of 10 oz., 284 mL, can)	2/3 cup	150 mL
Garlic powder	1/4 tsp.	1 mL
Sliced hazelnuts (filberts), toasted (see Tip, page 22)	2 tbsp.	30 mL

Combine first 4 ingredients in plastic bag. Add chicken. Toss to coat chicken in flour mixture.

Melt margarine in frying pan on medium. Add chicken. Cook for 8 to 10 minutes per side until no longer pink inside. Remove to serving bowl. Cover to keep warm.

Hazelnut Sauce: Put mushrooms and wine into same frying pan. Stir to loosen brown bits. Boil gently for 3 to 4 minutes until mushrooms are softened and liquid is reduced.

Add soup, garlic powder and hazelnuts. Stir. Return to a boil. Pour over chicken. Serves 4.

1 serving: 284 Calories; 10.5 g Total Fat (4.8 g Mono, 2.4 g Poly, 2.2 g Sat); 82 mg Cholesterol; 8 g Carbohydrate; trace Fibre; 33 g Protein; 419 mg Sodium

Pictured on page 251.

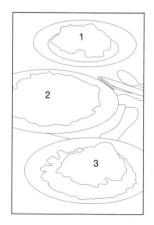

1. "Osso Bucco" Chicken, page 138
2. Black Bean Chili, page 80
3. Pineapple Chicken Bliss, page 207

Chicken Mole

The chocolate adds a new dimension to this savoury sauce, a staple of Mexican cuisine.

Hard margarine (butter browns too fast)	2 tbsp.	30 mL
Boneless, skinless chicken breast halves	1 1/2 lbs.	680 g
Cans of tomato sauce (7 1/2 oz., 213 mL, each)	2	2
Medium onion, chopped	1	1
Medium green pepper, chopped	1	1
Ground almonds	1/4 cup	60 mL
Whole cloves	2	2
Chili powder	2 tsp.	10 mL
Salt	1 tsp.	5 mL
Pepper	1/4 tsp.	1 mL
Hot pepper sauce	1/4 tsp.	1 mL
Garlic powder	1/4 tsp.	1 mL
Unsweetened chocolate baking square (1 oz., 28 g), cut up	1/2	1/2

Melt margarine in frying pan on medium. Add chicken. Cook for 4 to 5 minutes per side until browned. Cut into bite-sized pieces. Return to frying pan.

Add remaining 11 ingredients. Heat and stir until simmering and chocolate is melted. Reduce heat. Cover. Simmer for 30 minutes. Serves 6.

1 serving: 182 Calories; 8.2 g Total Fat (4.2 g Mono, 1.1 g Poly, 2.1 g Sat); 41 mg Cholesterol; 11 g Carbohydrate; 2 g Fibre; 18 g Protein; 902 mg Sodium

Pictured on page 251.

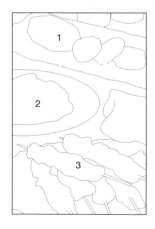

1. Sun-dried Tomato Chicken Roll, page 258
2. Spinach Orzo Salad, page 47
3. Spice Cupboard Kabobs, page 118

Kochujang Chicken

An exotic and earthy Korean dish.

Korean hot pepper paste	2 tbsp.	30 mL
Granulated sugar	1 tbsp.	15 mL
Sake	1 tbsp.	15 mL
Soy sauce	1 tbsp.	15 mL
Garlic cloves, minced	2	2
Finely grated ginger root	1 tsp.	5 mL
Boneless, skinless chicken thighs, thinly sliced (see Tip, page 47)	1 lb.	454 g
Sesame oil	1 tbsp.	15 mL
Sliced fresh shitake mushrooms	3 cups	750 mL
Thinly sliced green pepper	1 cup	250 mL
Thinly sliced onion	1 cup	250 mL
Julienned carrot	1/2 cup	125 mL
Thinly sliced cabbage kimchee	1 tbsp.	15 mL
Finely chopped small red chili peppers (see Tip, page 166)	1 tbsp.	15 mL

Combine first 6 ingredients in medium bowl. Add chicken, stir and marinate in the refrigerator, covered, for 30 minutes. Drain and discard marinade.

Heat a wok or large frying pan on medium-high. Add sesame oil. Add chicken and stir-fry for 1 minute.

Add remaining 6 ingredients and stir-fry for 5 minutes until onion and mushrooms are softened. Makes about 6 cups (1.5 L).

1 cup (250 mL): 245 Calories; 8.5 g Total Fat (2.2 g Mono, 1.3 g Poly, 1.9 g Sat); 50 mg Cholesterol; 24 g Carbohydrate; 6 g Fibre; 17 g Protein; 813 mg Sodium

Wine and Rosemary Chicken

Tender chicken in a subtle white wine and rosemary sauce. Garnish with a sprig of rosemary for a pretty presentation.

Cooking oil	2 tsp.	10 mL
Boneless, skinless chicken thighs, halved	1 lb.	454 g
Baby carrots	1 1/2 cups	375 mL
Chopped onion	1 cup	250 mL
Dry (or alcohol-free) white wine	1 cup	250 mL
Low-sodium prepared chicken broth	1/2 cup	125 mL

(continued on next page)

Fresh rosemary sprigs	2	2
Garlic cloves, minced (or 1/2 tsp., 2 mL, powder)	2	2
Lemon pepper	1/2 tsp.	2 mL
Water	1 tbsp.	15 mL
Cornstarch	2 tsp.	10 mL
Light sour cream	2 tbsp.	30 mL

Heat cooking oil in large pot or Dutch oven on medium-high. Add chicken. Cook for about 10 minutes, stirring occasionally, until browned.

Add next 7 ingredients. Stir. Bring to a boil. Reduce heat to medium-low. Cover. Simmer for about 40 minutes, stirring occasionally, until chicken and carrots are tender.

Stir water into cornstarch in small cup until smooth. Add to chicken mixture. Heat and stir on medium for about 1 minute until sauce is boiling and thickened. Discard rosemary sprigs.

Add sour cream. Stir well. Serves 4.

1 serving: 285 Calories; 9.7 g Total Fat (3.7 g Mono, 2.5 g Poly, 2.6 g Sat); 104 mg Cholesterol; 13 g Carbohydrate; 2 g Fibre; 26 g Protein; 206 mg Sodium

Chicken Sausage Patties

These tasty patties are a great hit with kids.

Finely chopped onion	1/2 cup	125 mL
Brown sugar	2 tbsp.	30 mL
Soy sauce	1 tbsp.	15 mL
Seasoned salt	3/4 tsp.	4 mL
Garlic powder	1/4 tsp.	1 mL
Ground sage	1/2 tsp.	2 mL
Dry bread crumbs	1/3 cup	75 mL
Ground raw chicken	1 lb.	454 g

Measure first 7 ingredients in medium bowl. Mix well.

Add chicken. Mix thoroughly. Divide into 8 patties. Fry in greased frying pan until no pink remains in meat. Makes 8 patties.

1 pattie: 150 Calories; 8 g Total Fat (0 g Mono, 0 g Poly, 0 g Sat); 45 mg Cholesterol; 7 g Carbohydrate; 0 g Fibre; 11 g Protein; 330 mg Sodium

Shrimp-sauced Chicken

A touch of gourmet.

Chicken breasts, halved, skin and bones removed	2	2
All-purpose flour	1/4 cup	60 mL
Hard margarine (butter browns too fast)	2 tbsp.	30 mL
Salt, sprinkle		
Pepper, sprinkle		
SHRIMP SAUCE		
Butter (or hard margarine)	3 tbsp.	45 mL
All-purpose flour	3 tbsp.	45 mL
Salt	1/2 tsp.	2 mL
Pepper	1/8 tsp.	0.5 mL
Onion powder	1/8 tsp.	0.5 mL
Dill weed	1/8 tsp.	0.5 mL
Milk	1 cup	250 mL
Salad dressing (or mayonnaise)	1/4 cup	60 mL
Canned small shrimp (4 oz., 113 g), rinsed and drained	1	1

Pound chicken between 2 pieces of waxed paper or plastic to make fairly thin.

Coat with flour and cook in margarine in frying pan, browning both sides. Sprinkle with salt and pepper.

Shrimp Sauce: Melt butter in saucepan. Mix in flour, salt, pepper, onion powder and dill weed.

Stir in milk and salad dressing until it boils and thickens.

Carefully stir in shrimp. Heat through. Serve over chicken. Serves 4.

1 serving: 400 Calories; 20 g Total Fat (5 g Mono, 5 g Poly, 8 g Sat); 155 mg Cholesterol; 16 g Carbohydrate; 0 g Fibre; 37 g Protein; 880 mg Sodium

West Indian Chicken Curry

The warm flavour of cinnamon and the sweetness of sugar work in harmony with curry spices to make a delightful and satisfying chicken, potato and tomato curry.

Baby potatoes, halved	1/2 lb.	225 g
Cooking oil	2 tbsp.	30 mL
Chopped onion	2 cups	500 mL
Curry powder	2 tbsp.	30 mL
Brown sugar, packed	1 tbsp.	15 mL
Garlic cloves, minced	2	2
(or 1/2 tsp., 2 mL, powder)		
Salt	1/2 tsp.	2 mL
Pepper	1/2 tsp.	2 mL
Ground cinnamon	1/4 tsp.	1 mL
Cayenne pepper	1/8 tsp.	0.5 mL
Boneless, skinless chicken breast halves, cut into 1 inch (2.5 cm) pieces	1 lb.	454 g
Can of diced tomatoes (14 oz., 398 mL), with juice	1	1
Plain yogurt	1/2 cup	125 mL

Pour water into small saucepan until about 1 inch (2.5 cm) deep. Add potatoes. Cover. Bring to a boil. Reduce heat to medium. Boil gently for 12 to 15 minutes until tender. Drain.

Meanwhile, heat cooking oil in large saucepan on medium-high. Add onion. Cook, uncovered, for 3 minutes, stirring often.

Add next 7 ingredients. Stir.

Add chicken. Stir. Reduce heat to medium. Cook, uncovered, for about 5 minutes, stirring occasionally, until chicken is browned.

Add tomatoes and potato. Heat and stir, scraping any brown bits from bottom of pan, until boiling. Reduce heat to medium-low. Cook, covered, for about 8 minutes, stirring occasionally, until heated through.

Add yogurt. Stir. Makes about 5 cups (1.25 L).

1 cup (250 mL): 261 Calories; 7.4 g Total Fat (3.6 g Mono, 2.0 g Poly, 1.0 g Sat); 55 mg Cholesterol; 24 g Carbohydrate; 2 g Fibre; 25 g Protein; 532 mg Sodium

Pictured on page 269.

Thai Coconut Chicken

By using lower-fat ingredients, you can enjoy this delicious Thai dish without any guilt!

Prepared chicken broth	1 1/4 cups	300 mL
Lime juice (see Tip, page 151)	3 tbsp.	45 mL
Soy sauce	2 tbsp.	30 mL
Finely grated ginger root	1 tbsp.	15 mL
Grated lime zest	1 tbsp.	15 mL
Garlic cloves, minced (or 1/2 tsp., 2 mL, powder)	2	2
Pepper	1/4 tsp.	1 mL
Boneless, skinless chicken breast halves	4	4
Brown sugar, packed	1/4 cup	60 mL
Reduced-fat peanut butter	2 tbsp.	30 mL
Sweet chili sauce	1 tbsp.	15 mL
Light coconut milk	1/2 cup	125 mL
Cornstarch	2 tsp.	10 mL

Grated lime zest, for garnish

Combine first 7 ingredients in medium frying pan. Bring to a boil. Reduce heat to medium.

Add chicken. Cook, covered, for 12 to 15 minutes, turning at halftime, until chicken is no longer pink inside. Transfer chicken to serving plate. Cover to keep warm.

Whisk next 3 ingredients into broth mixture until smooth. Bring to a boil.

Stir coconut milk into cornstarch in small cup. Slowly add to broth mixture, stirring constantly with whisk, until boiling and slightly thickened. Serve with chicken.

Garnish with lime zest. Serves 4.

1 serving: 304 Calories; 7.6 g Total Fat (0.7 g Mono, 0.7 g Poly, 2.7 g Sat); 82 mg Cholesterol; 22 g Carbohydrate; 1 g Fibre; 35 g Protein; 1012 mg Sodium

Poached Lemon Chicken

Lemon and white wine sauce gently infused with rosemary
adds sophisticated flavour to tender chicken.

Water	1 tbsp.	15 mL
Cornstarch	1 tbsp.	15 mL
Parsley flakes	1 1/2 tsp.	7 mL
Prepared chicken broth	1 1/2 cups	375 mL
Dry white (or alcohol-free) wine	1/2 cup	125 mL
Sprigs of fresh rosemary	2	2
Boneless, skinless chicken breasts halves (about 4 oz., 113 g, each)	4	4
Lemon pepper	1 tsp.	5 mL
Thin lemon slices	12	12

Stir water into cornstarch and parsley in small cup. Set aside.

Measure broth and wine into medium frying pan. Stir. Add rosemary sprigs.

Place chicken breast halves in wine mixture. Sprinkle with lemon pepper. Place 3 lemon slices on each chicken breast half. Bring to a boil on medium-high. Reduce heat to medium-low. Cover. Simmer for 10 to 15 minutes until chicken is no longer pink inside. Discard lemon slices and rosemary sprigs. Remove chicken with slotted spoon to large serving dish. Cover to keep warm. Increase heat to medium-high. Stir cornstarch mixture. Add to broth mixture. Heat and stir for about 1 minute until boiling and thickened. Remove to small serving bowl. Serve with chicken. Serves 4.

1 serving: 194 Calories; 2.7 g Total Fat (0.8 g Mono, 0.6 g Poly, 0.7 g Sat); 77 mg Cholesterol; 3 g Carbohydrate; trace Fibre; 32 g Protein; 532 mg Sodium

 tip When a recipe calls for grated zest and juice, it's easier to grate the fruit first, then juice it. Be careful not to grate down to the pith (white part of the peel), which is bitter and best avoided.

Polynesian Apricot Chicken

Multi-tasking makes quick work of this suppertime favourite—chop the veggies while the chicken is cooking. Sweet and savoury flavours combine with just a touch of heat. Serve over rice for a complete meal.

Dried apricots, quartered	3/4 cup	175 mL
Olive oil	1 tbsp.	15 mL
Boneless, skinless chicken thighs, quartered	1 lb.	454 g
Chopped onion	1 1/2 cups	375 mL
Chopped green pepper	1 cup	250 mL
Garlic clove, minced (or 1/4 tsp., 1 mL, powder)	1	1
Finely grated ginger root (or 1/4 tsp., 1 mL, ground ginger)	1 tsp.	5 mL
Chili powder	1/2 tsp.	2 mL
Ground cumin	1/2 tsp.	2 mL
Can of diced tomatoes (14 oz., 398 mL), with juice	1	1

Put apricot into small heatproof bowl. Cover with boiling water. Stir. Cover. Set aside.

Heat olive oil in large frying pan on medium. Add chicken. Cook for 8 to 10 minutes, stirring occasionally, until lightly browned. Transfer to plate. Cover to keep warm.

Add next 6 ingredients to same frying pan. Stir. Cook, covered, for about 5 minutes, stirring occasionally, until green pepper is tender-crisp.

Drain apricot. Add to green pepper mixture. Add chicken and tomatoes with juice. Stir. Increase heat to medium-high. Boil gently, uncovered, for about 10 minutes until sauce is slightly thickened. Serves 4.

1 serving: 308 Calories; 12.1 g Total Fat (5.8 g Mono, 2.3 g Poly, 2.9 g Sat); 74 mg Cholesterol; 29 g Carbohydrate; 3 g Fibre; 23 g Protein; 363 mg Sodium

Pictured on page 252.

Chicken Stroganoff

Everybody will be "Russian" to the kitchen to get a whiff of this delicious, creamy chicken dish literally made for royalty. It is purported that the dish was named after Count Stroganov, a member of a very wealthy, well-known Russian family. Great served over egg noodles.

All-purpose flour	1/4 cup	60 mL
Paprika	1/2 tsp.	2 mL
Salt	1/2 tsp.	2 mL
Pepper	1/2 tsp.	2 mL
Boneless, skinless chicken thighs, cut into short strips	1 lb.	454 g
Cooking oil	2 tbsp.	30 mL
Sliced fresh white mushrooms	2 cups	500 mL
Chopped onion	1 1/2 cups	375 mL
Prepared chicken broth	1 cup	250 mL
Dry sherry	3 tbsp.	45 mL
Dijon mustard	1 tsp.	5 mL
Soy sauce	1 tsp.	5 mL
Sour cream	1/2 cup	125 mL
Dried dillweed	1/2 tsp.	2 mL

Combine first 4 ingredients in large resealable freezer bag. Add chicken. Toss until coated. Remove chicken. Discard any remaining flour mixture.

Heat cooking oil in Dutch oven or large pot on medium-high. Add chicken. Cook, uncovered, for about 5 minutes, stirring occasionally, until chicken is browned. Add mushrooms and onion. Cook for 5 to 10 minutes, stirring often, until onion is softened.

Add next 4 ingredients. Heat and stir for 5 minutes, scraping any brown bits from bottom of pan. Reduce heat to medium-low. Simmer, partially covered, for about 10 minutes, stirring occasionally, until thickened.

Add sour cream and dill. Stir. Makes about 4 cups (1 L).

1 cup (250 mL): 358 Calories; 20.9 g Total Fat (7.4 g Mono, 4.2 g Poly, 6.5 g Sat); 94 mg Cholesterol; 14 g Carbohydrate; 1 g Fibre; 25 g Protein; 582 mg Sodium

Sesame Chicken Cutlets

Cutlets are no longer blah when you add some Asian flair! Sesame, ginger and soy sauce add character to this pan-fried favourite.

Large egg	1	1
Soy sauce	1 tbsp.	15 mL
Fine dry bread crumbs	1/2 cup	125 mL
Sesame seeds	1/4 cup	60 mL
Salt	1 tsp.	5 mL
Pepper	1/2 tsp.	2 mL
Ground ginger	1/4 tsp.	1 mL
Chicken breast cutlets (about 4 oz., 113 g, each)	4	4
Cooking oil	3 tbsp.	45 mL

Beat egg and soy sauce with fork in small shallow dish.

Combine next 5 ingredients in separate small shallow dish.

Dip cutlets into egg mixture. Press both sides of cutlets into crumb mixture until coated. Discard any remaining egg and crumb mixture.

Heat cooking oil in large frying pan on medium. Add cutlets. Cook for 3 to 4 minutes per side until golden and no longer pink inside. Makes 4 cutlets.

1 cutlet: 350 Calories; 19 g Total Fat (9 g Mono, 6 g Poly, 2.5 g Sat); 120 mg Cholesterol; 12 g Carbohydrate; 2 g Fibre; 32 g Protein; 1010 mg Sodium

Chicken Cakes

Don't get all crabby about it! Believe us, you don't have to turn to crustaceans to make a delightful, little breaded cake. These chicken cakes are tender and just a little bit spicy.

SPICY DILL SAUCE		
Mayonnaise	1/2 cup	125 mL
Dry sherry	1 tbsp.	15 mL
Chopped fresh dill (or 1/4 tsp., 1 mL, dried)	1 tsp.	5 mL
Cayenne pepper	1/4 tsp.	1 mL
Salt	1/4 tsp.	1 mL
CAKES		
Boneless, skinless chicken breast halves	1 lb.	454 g
Prepared chicken broth	1 1/2 cups	375 mL

(continued on next page)

Large egg, fork-beaten	1	1
Fine dry bread crumbs	1/3 cup	75 mL
Finely chopped onion	1/4 cup	60 mL
Finely chopped celery	2 tbsp.	30 mL
Finely chopped red pepper	2 tbsp.	30 mL
Chopped fresh dill (or 3/4 tsp., 4 mL, dried)	1 tbsp.	15 mL
Garlic clove, minced (or 1/4 tsp., 1 mL, powder)	1	1
Worcestershire sauce	1 tsp.	5 mL
Salt	1/2 tsp.	2 mL
Pepper	1/4 tsp.	1 mL
All-purpose flour	3 tbsp.	45 mL
Large eggs	2	2
Fine dry bread crumbs	1/3 cup	75 mL
Cooking oil	1 tbsp.	15 mL

Spicy Dill Sauce: Combine all 5 ingredients in small bowl. Makes about 1/2 cup (125 mL) sauce.

Cakes: Put chicken into small saucepan. Add broth. Bring to a boil. Reduce heat to medium-low. Simmer, covered, for about 10 minutes until no longer pink inside. Drain (see Note). Cool. Finely chop chicken. Set aside.

Combine next 10 ingredients in medium bowl. Add chicken and 3 tbsp. (45 mL) Spicy Dill Sauce. Stir gently until well combined. Divide into 8 equal portions. Shape into 1/2 inch (12 mm) thick cakes. Place cakes on baking sheet lined with waxed paper.

Measure flour onto plate. Beat eggs in small shallow dish. Measure bread crumbs onto separate plate. Press both sides of cakes into flour. Dip into egg. Press both sides of cakes into bread crumbs until coated. Discard any remaining flour, egg and bread crumbs.

Heat cooking oil in large frying pan on medium. Arrange cakes in single layer in frying pan. Cook for about 4 minutes per side until golden. Remove cakes to plate lined with paper towel to drain. Serve with remaining Spicy Dill Sauce. Makes 8 cakes.

1 cake with 2 tsp. (10 mL) sauce: 248 Calories; 15.8 g Total Fat (8.3 g Mono, 4.8 g Poly, 2.0 g Sat); 99 mg Cholesterol; 9 g Carbohydrate; trace Fibre; 17 g Protein; 454 mg Sodium

Note: You can save the leftover chicken broth for another use. It makes an excellent broth for a bowl of chicken noodle soup!

Chicken Parmesan Schnitzel

A simple supper, indeed! Chicken schnitzel is easy to make and sure to please the entire family. Perfect with a squeeze of fresh lemon and a sprinkle of parsley.

All-purpose flour	1/2 cup	125 mL
Paprika	1 tsp.	5 mL
Seasoned salt	1 tsp.	5 mL
Pepper	1/4 tsp.	1 mL
Large eggs	2	2
Water	1 tbsp.	15 mL
Fine dry bread crumbs	1/2 cup	125 mL
Grated Parmesan cheese	1/2 cup	125 mL
Chicken breasts	4	4
Cooking oil	4 tsp.	20 mL
Butter (or hard margarine)	4 tsp.	20 mL
Lemon wedges (optional)	4	4

Combine first 4 ingredients on plate.

Beat eggs and water with fork in small shallow bowl.

Combine bread crumbs and cheese on separate plate.

Place chicken breasts between two sheets of waxed paper or plastic wrap and pound with a rolling pin or mallet to flatten. Press both sides of chicken into flour mixture. Dip into egg mixture. Press both sides of chicken into crumb mixture until coated. Discard any remaining flour, egg and crumb mixture.

Heat 1 tsp. (5 mL) each of cooking oil and butter in large frying pan on medium. Add chicken. Cook, in batches, for about 2 minutes per side, adding cooking oil and butter 1 tsp. (5 mL) each at a time, as required for each batch, until no longer pink inside.

Serve with lemon wedges. Makes 4 schnitzel.

1 schnitzel: 540 Calories; 18 g Total Fat (7 g Mono, 3 g Poly, 7 g Sat); 265 mg Cholesterol; 23 g Carbohydrate; 1 g Fibre; 66 g Protein; 890 mg Sodium

Alfredo-sauced Chicken

A great meal. Full of noodles, chicken and peas in a honey-garlic sauce.

Cooking oil	2 tbsp.	30 mL
Small boneless chicken breast halves, skin removed, cut in short narrow strips	6	6
Fettuccine	1 lb.	500 g
Boiling water	4 qts.	4 L
Cooking oil	1 tbsp.	15 mL
Salt	1 tbsp.	15 mL
Butter (or hard margarine)	1/2 cup	125 mL
Whipping cream	1 cup	250 mL
Honey	1/4 cup	60 mL
White wine (or alcohol-free wine)	1/4 cup	60 mL
Garlic powder	1/4 tsp.	1 mL
Frozen peas	1 cup	250 mL
Grated Parmesan cheese	1/2 cup	125 mL
Parsley flakes	1 tsp.	5 mL
Salt	1 tsp.	5 mL
Pepper	1/4 tsp.	1 mL

Heat cooking oil in frying pan. Add chicken. Sauté for about 5 minutes until no pink remains.

Cook fettuccine in boiling water, cooking oil and salt in large uncovered pot for 5 to 7 minutes until tender but firm. Drain. Return noodles to pot.

Add next 6 ingredients to chicken. Heat and stir until it simmers. Stir into pasta in pot.

Add remaining ingredients to pasta. Toss to mix well. Makes generous 12 cups (2.7 L) to serve 6.

1 serving: 700 Calories; 42 g Total Fat (13 g Mono, 3.5 g Poly, 20 g Sat); 230 mg Cholesterol; 45 g Carbohydrate; 4 g Fibre; 70 g Protein; 1990 mg Sodium

Chicken and Olives

Do you know someone who's absolutely mad for olives? Well, make this creamy tomato dish decked with olives and you'll have a friend for life! Goes great over couscous or pasta.

Cooking oil	1 tbsp.	15 mL
Chicken drumsticks, skin removed (see Tip, page 188) about 3 oz. (85 g) each	12	12
Chopped onion	2 cups	500 mL
Sliced fresh white mushrooms	1 1/2 cups	375 mL
Diced pepperoni	1 cup	250 mL
Can of Italian-style stewed tomatoes (19 oz., 540 mL)	1	1
Can of condensed cream of mushroom soup (10 oz., 284 mL)	1	1
Dry (or alcohol-free) white wine	1 cup	250 mL
Large pitted green olives, halved	1/3 cup	75 mL
Pitted whole black olives, halved	1/3 cup	75 mL
Bay leaf	1	1
Dried oregano	1/2 tsp.	2 mL
Chopped fresh parsley	1/4 cup	60 mL

Heat cooking oil in large frying pan on medium. Add chicken. Cook for about 15 minutes, turning occasionally, until browned. Remove to plate. Cover to keep warm.

Add next 3 ingredients to same frying pan. Cook for 5 to 10 minutes, stirring often, until onion is softened.

Add next 7 ingredients and chicken. Stir. Bring to a boil. Reduce heat to medium-low. Simmer, covered, for 15 to 20 minutes until internal temperature of chicken reaches 170°F (77°C). Discard bay leaf.

Sprinkle with parsley. Serves 6.

1 serving: 485 Calories; 23.2 g Total Fat (10.1 g Mono, 4.2 g Poly, 6.3 g Sat); 150 mg Cholesterol; 18 g Carbohydrate; 2 g Fibre; 43 g Protein; 1315 mg Sodium

Pictured on page 125.

Chicken Ratatouille

In need of a vacation? Send your taste buds on a trip with this robust dish that's full of bold Mediterranean flavours. This versatile dish goes great with crusty bread or pasta. Serve with lemon wedges.

All-purpose flour	1/4 cup	60 mL
Salt	1/2 tsp.	2 mL
Pepper	1/4 tsp.	1 mL
Boneless, skinless chicken thighs (about 3 oz., 85 g, each)	8	8
Cooking oil	1 tbsp.	15 mL
Diced eggplant (with peel)	2 cups	500 mL
Chopped onion	1 cup	250 mL
Can of diced tomatoes (with juice) (14 oz., 398 mL)	1	1
Chopped green pepper	1 cup	250 mL
Sliced fresh white mushrooms	1 cup	250 mL
Granulated sugar	1 1/2 tsp.	7 mL
Dried basil	1 tsp.	5 mL
Dried thyme	1/2 tsp.	2 mL
Garlic powder	1/2 tsp.	2 mL
Salt	1/2 tsp.	2 mL

Combine first 3 ingredients in large resealable freezer bag. Add chicken. Toss until coated. Remove chicken. Discard any remaining flour mixture.

Heat cooking oil in large frying pan on medium-high. Add chicken. Cook for about 2 minutes per side until browned. Remove to plate.

Add eggplant and onion to same frying pan. Cook for about 5 minutes, stirring often and scraping any brown bits from bottom of pan, until browned and starting to soften.

Add remaining 8 ingredients and chicken. Stir. Bring to a boil. Reduce heat to medium-low. Simmer, covered, for about 30 minutes until chicken is no longer pink inside and vegetables are tender. Serves 4.

1 serving: 361 Calories; 16.5 g Total Fat (6.9 g Mono, 4.1 g Poly, 3.9 g Sat); 112 mg Cholesterol; 20 g Carbohydrate; 3 g Fibre; 34 g Protein; 879 mg Sodium

Pictured on page 125.

Artichoke Chicken

Artichoke is a popular ingredient in Italian cuisine. This simple yet satisfying recipe combines artichoke with chicken and onions for an easy supper that'll quickly become a favourite.

Boneless, skinless chicken breast halves	1 lb.	454 g
Salt	1/8 tsp.	0.5 mL
Pepper	1/8 tsp.	0.5 mL
Olive oil	2 tsp.	10 mL
Can of artichoke hearts (14 oz., 398 mL), drained and chopped	1	1
Finely chopped onion	1/2 cup	125 mL
Garlic cloves, minced (or 1/2 tsp., 2 mL, powder)	2	2
Prepared chicken broth	1/2 cup	125 mL
Prepared chicken broth	2 tbsp.	30 mL
Cornstarch	1 tbsp.	15 mL
Lemon juice	1 tbsp.	15 mL

Cut each chicken breast crosswise into 3 equal pieces. Sprinkle with salt and pepper.

Heat olive oil in large frying pan on medium-high. Add chicken. Cook for about 2 minutes per side until browned. Add next 3 ingredients. Cook for about 5 minutes, stirring often, until onion is softened. Reduce heat to medium-low.

Add first amount of broth. Stir. Cook, covered, for about 5 minutes until chicken is no longer pink inside.

Combine remaining 3 ingredients in small cup. Add to chicken mixture. Heat and stir until boiling and thickened. Serves 4.

1 serving: 180 Calories; 3.5 g Total Fat (2.0 g Mono, 0.5 g Poly, 0.5 g Sat); 65 mg Cholesterol; 8 g Carbohydrate; 2 g Fibre; 28 g Protein; 450 mg Sodium

1. Creole Chicken Jambalaya, page 194
2. Chicken Spinach Rolls, page 213
3. Nutty Chicken Stew, page 68

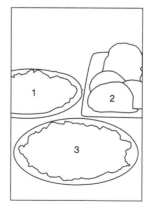

Chicken Couscous Cakes

Full of hearty chicken, rice and veggies, these colourful chicken patties certainly take the cake!

Whole wheat couscous	1/4 cup	60 mL
Boiling water	1/2 cup	125 mL
Canola oil	1 tsp.	5 mL
Finely chopped onion	1 cup	250 mL
Finely chopped red pepper	1 cup	250 mL
Chopped cooked chicken (see Tip, page 58)	2 cups	500 mL
Cooked wild rice	1 cup	250 mL
Fine dry whole wheat bread crumbs (see Tip, page 210)	1/2 cup	125 mL
Garlic and herb no-salt seasoning	1 tbsp.	15 mL
Large egg, fork-beaten	1	1
Grated jalapeño Monterey Jack cheese	1/2 cup	125 mL

Measure couscous into small heatproof bowl. Add boiling water. Stir. Let stand, covered, for about 5 minutes until liquid is absorbed. Fluff with fork. Set aside.

Heat canola oil in large frying pan on medium. Add onion and red pepper. Cook for about 5 minutes, stirring often, until onion starts to soften. Transfer to large bowl.

Add next 4 ingredients and couscous. Stir.

Add egg and cheese. Mix well. Divide into 12 equal portions. Shape into 3 inch (7.5 cm) diameter cakes. Arrange on greased baking sheet with sides. Spray cakes with cooking spray. Bake in 375°F (190°C) oven for about 20 minutes until firm. Makes 12 cakes.

1 cake: 109 Calories; 4.2 g Total Fat (1.5 g Mono, 0.7 g Poly, 1.5 g Sat); 37 mg Cholesterol; 9 g Carbohydrate; 1 g Fibre; 9 g Protein; 74 mg Sodium

Pictured on page 287.

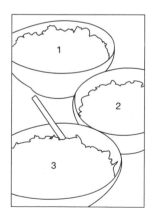

1. Spaghetti Chicken Stir-fry, page 172
2. Bourbon Chicken Pilaf, page 191
3. Asian Chicken Supreme, page 174

Hoisin Chicken Pot

The sparkling flavours of hoisin and ginger make this dish a star attraction.

Chinese dried mushrooms	4	4
Boiling water	1 cup	250 mL
Cooking oil	1 tbsp.	15 mL
Bone-in chicken thighs, skin removed (about 5 oz., 140 g, each)	8	8
Chopped fresh white mushrooms	1 cup	250 mL
Medium onions, cut into 8 wedges each	2	2
Garlic cloves, minced	2	2
Finely grated ginger root	2 tsp.	10 mL
Prepared chicken broth	2 cups	500 mL
Can of sliced water chestnuts (8 oz., 227 mL), drained	1	1
Hoisin sauce	1/2 cup	125 mL
Star anise	3	3
Chopped bok choy	8 cups	2 L
Chili paste (sambal oelek)	2 tsp.	10 mL
Finely chopped green onion	2 tbsp.	30 mL
Sesame seeds, toasted (see Tip, page 22)	1 tbsp.	15 mL

Put dried mushrooms into small heatproof bowl. Add boiling water. Stir. Let stand for about 20 minutes until softened. Drain. Remove and discard stems. Chop caps. Set aside.

Heat cooking oil in large saucepan or Dutch oven on medium-high. Add chicken. Cook, uncovered, for 3 to 4 minutes per side until browned. Remove to plate. Reduce heat to medium.

Add fresh mushrooms. Cook for about 3 minutes, stirring occasionally, until browned. Add next 3 ingredients. Cook for about 5 minutes, stirring occasionally, until onion starts to soften.

Add next 4 ingredients, dried mushrooms and chicken. Stir. Bring to a boil. Reduce heat to medium-low. Simmer, partially covered, for about 30 minutes until chicken is tender.

Add bok choy and chili paste. Stir. Cook for about 10 minutes, stirring occasionally, until bok choy is tender. Discard anise. Sprinkle with green onion and sesame seeds. Serves 4.

1 serving: 536 Calories; 23.2 g Total Fat (9.3 g Mono, 6.1 g Poly, 5.4 g Sat); 144 mg Cholesterol; 35 g Carbohydrate; 5 g Fibre; 47 g Protein; 1131 mg Sodium

Pictured on page 126.

Creamy Spinach Meat Sauce

This velvety sauce is strong to the finish because it's made with spinach! Great for serving on toast or in puff pastry shells. Use a bit more milk to thin this sauce if you want to serve it over pasta.

Olive (or cooking) oil	2 tsp.	10 mL
Lean ground chicken	1 lb.	454 g
Chopped onion	1/2 cup	125 mL
Garlic cloves, minced (or 1/2 tsp., 2 mL, powder)	2	2
Ground coriander	1/2 tsp.	2 mL
Ground cumin	1/2 tsp.	2 mL
Ground nutmeg	1/4 tsp.	1 mL
Salt	3/4 tsp.	4 mL
Pepper	1/8 tsp.	0.5 mL
All-purpose flour	2 tbsp.	30 mL
Can of evaporated milk (13 1/2 oz., 385 mL)	1	1
Milk	1 cup	250 mL
Box of frozen chopped spinach (10 oz., 300 g), thawed and squeezed dry	1	1

Heat olive oil in large frying pan on medium-high. Add next 8 ingredients. Scramble-fry for about 8 minutes until chicken is no longer pink and onion is softened.

Sprinkle with flour. Heat and stir for 1 minute. Reduce heat to medium.

Slowly add evaporated milk, stirring constantly, until smooth. Add milk. Heat and stir for about 5 minutes until boiling and thickened.

Add spinach. Stir. Simmer, uncovered, for about 2 minutes, stirring occasionally, until heated through. Makes about 4 cups (1 L).

1 cup (250 mL): 443 Calories; 26.0 g Total Fat (4.1 g Mono, 0.5 g Poly, 5.3 g Sat); 31 mg Cholesterol; 22 g Carbohydrate; 2.8 g Fibre; 31 g Protein; 739 mg Sodium

Creamy Spinach Noodles

Though this recipe may contain a few of the family's highly contested ingredients, this creamy pasta dish will have your family eating—and enjoying—spinach and blue cheese.

Broad egg noodles	3 cups	750 mL
Olive oil	1 tsp.	5 mL
Chopped onion	1 cup	250 mL
Garlic clove, minced (or 1/4 tsp., 1 mL, powder)	1	1
Alfredo pasta sauce	1 1/2 cups	375 mL
Box of frozen chopped spinach (10 oz., 300 g), thawed and squeezed dry	1	1
Chopped cooked chicken (see Tip, page 58)	1 cup	250 mL
Crumbled blue cheese	2 tbsp.	30 mL
Lemon juice	1 tbsp.	15 mL
Pepper	1/4 tsp.	1 mL

Cook noodles according to package directions. Drain, reserving 1/2 cup (125 mL) cooking water. Return noodles to same pot. Cover to keep warm.

Heat olive oil in large frying pan on medium. Add onion and garlic. Cook for about 5 minutes, stirring often, until onion is softened.

Add remaining 6 ingredients and reserved cooking water. Bring to a boil. Reduce heat to medium-low. Simmer, uncovered, for about 5 minutes, stirring occasionally, until heated through. Add noodles. Stir. Makes about 6 cups (1.5 L).

1 cup (250 mL): 250 Calories; 11.0 g Total Fat (1.5 g Mono, 1.0 g Poly, 6.0 g Sat); 65 mg Cholesterol; 23 g Carbohydrate; 2 g Fibre; 15 g Protein; 470 mg Sodium

 Hot peppers contain capsaicin in the seeds and ribs. Removing the seeds and ribs will reduce the heat. Wear rubber gloves when handling hot peppers and avoid touching your eyes. Wash your hands well afterwards.

Lemon Asparagus Tortellini

Lemon can make even the creamiest dishes taste light and fresh. Delicious!

Water	12 cups	3 L
Salt	1 1/2 tsp.	7 mL
Fresh cheese-filled tortellini	12 1/2 oz.	350 g
Butter (or hard margarine)	2 tbsp.	30 mL
Finely chopped onion	1 cup	250 mL
Boneless, skinless chicken breast, cut into 3/4 inch (2 cm) cubes	1/2 lb.	225 g
Garlic cloves, minced	2	2
Salt	1/2 tsp.	2 mL
Pepper	1/4 tsp.	1 mL
Dry (or alcohol-free) white wine	2/3 cup	150 mL
Grated lemon zest	2 tsp.	10 mL
Fresh asparagus, trimmed of tough ends and cut into 2 inch (5 cm) pieces	1 lb.	454 g
Whipping cream	1 1/2 cups	375 mL
Finely chopped green onion	1 tbsp.	15 mL
Chopped fresh dill (or 1/2 tsp., 2 mL, dried)	1 1/2 tsp.	7 mL
Grated Parmesan cheese	2 tbsp.	30 mL
Finely chopped green onion	1 tbsp.	15 mL
Chopped fresh dill (or 1/2 tsp., 2 mL, dried)	1 1/2 tsp.	7 mL
Pepper, sprinkle		

Combine water and salt in Dutch oven or large pot. Bring to a boil. Add tortellini. Boil, uncovered, for about 8 minutes, stirring occasionally, until tender but firm. Drain. Set aside.

Melt butter in large frying pan on medium. Add next 5 ingredients. Cook for 5 to 10 minutes, stirring often, until onion starts to turn golden and chicken is no longer pink.

Add wine and lemon zest. Stir. Cook for about 5 minutes, stirring occasionally, until wine is reduced by half.

Add asparagus and whipping cream. Stir. Bring to a boil. Reduce heat to medium-low. Simmer, uncovered, for about 3 minutes until asparagus is tender-crisp.

Add first amounts of green onion and dill. Stir. Add tortellini. Cook and stir for about 2 minutes until heated through.

Sprinkle remaining 4 ingredients over top. Serve immediately. Makes about 7 cups (1.75 L).

1 cup (250 mL): 439 Calories; 25.9 g Total Fat (7.4 g Mono, 1.2 g Poly, 15.5 g Sat); 115 mg Cholesterol; 31 g Carbohydrate; 2 g Fibre; 18 g Protein;435 mg Sodium

Apricot Chicken Pasta

This light yet creamy dinner has the added delights of sweet apricot and tender chicken. Pasta lovers will leave the table well satisfied.

Water	12 cups	3 L
Salt	1 1/2 tsp.	7 mL
Whole wheat spaghetti	8 oz.	225 g
Canola oil	2 tsp.	10 mL
Chicken breast cutlets, cut into thin strips	1 lb.	454 g
Canola oil	2 tsp.	10 mL
Sliced fresh white mushrooms	1 cup	250 mL
Chopped onion	1/2 cup	125 mL
All-purpose flour	2 tbsp.	30 mL
Skim milk	2 cups	500 mL
Box of frozen chopped spinach (10 oz., 300 g), thawed and squeezed dry	1	1
Chopped dried apricot	1/2 cup	125 mL
Ground nutmeg	1/4 tsp.	1 mL
Salt	1/2 tsp.	2 mL
Pepper	1/4 tsp.	1 mL
Grated lemon zest	2 tsp.	10 mL

Combine water and salt in Dutch oven. Bring to a boil. Add spaghetti. Boil, uncovered, for 10 to 12 minutes, stirring occasionally, until tender but firm. Drain. Return to same pot. Cover to keep warm.

Meanwhile, heat first amount of canola oil in large frying pan on medium-high. Add chicken. Cook for 3 to 5 minutes, stirring occasionally, until browned. Transfer to plate. Cover to keep warm. Reduce heat to medium.

Add second amount of canola oil to same frying pan. Add mushrooms and onion. Cook for about 5 minutes, stirring often, until onion is softened.

Add flour. Heat and stir for 1 minute. Slowly add milk, stirring constantly, until smooth. Heat and stir until boiling and thickened.

Add next 5 ingredients and chicken. Cook for about 2 minutes, stirring occasionally, until heated through. Add to spaghetti. Stir until coated.

Add lemon zest. Stir well. Makes about 7 cups (1.75 L). Serves 4.

1 serving: 494 Calories; 6.4 g Total Fat (2.9 g Mono, 1.7 g Poly, 0.7 g Sat); 47 mg Cholesterol; 69 g Carbohydrate; 8 g Fibre; 45 g Protein; 528 mg Sodium (need new NI)

Pictured on page 198.

Chili Chicken Pasta

*Like chili? Like pasta? After you try this clever one-pot dish, you'll wonder
why you've never combined them before.*

Cooking oil	2 tsp.	10 mL
Lean ground chicken	1 lb.	454 g
Chopped onion	1 cup	250 mL
Garlic cloves, minced (or 1/2 tsp., 2 mL, powder)	2	2
Can of diced tomatoes (28 oz., 796 mL), with juice	1	1
Can of kidney beans (19 oz., 540 mL), rinsed and drained	1	1
Prepared chicken broth	1 cup	250 mL
Water	1 cup	250 mL
Tomato paste (see Tip, page 136)	1 tbsp.	15 mL
Chili powder	2 tsp.	10 mL
Chopped pickled jalapeño pepper slices	2 tsp.	10 mL
Granulated sugar	1/2 tsp.	2 mL
Salt	1/4 tsp.	1 mL
Pepper	1/4 tsp.	1 mL
Cavatappi pasta	2 cups	500 mL
Grated jalapeño Monterey Jack cheese	1 cup	250 mL

Heat cooking oil in Dutch oven on medium. Add next 3 ingredients. Cook, uncovered, for about 10 minutes, stirring occasionally, until chicken is no longer pink.

Add next 10 ingredients. Stir. Bring to a boil.

Add pasta. Stir. Cook, covered, on medium-low for about 20 minutes, stirring occasionally, until pasta is tender but firm. Remove from heat. Let stand, covered, for 10 minutes.

Sprinkle with cheese. Makes about 9 2/3 cups (2.4 L).

1 cup (250 mL): 249 Calories; 9.0 g Total Fat (0.7 g Mono, 0.5 g Poly, 3.3 g Sat); 41 mg Cholesterol; 27 g Carbohydrate; 3 g Fibre; 16 g Protein; 614 mg Sodium

Pictured on page 179.

Red Curry Chicken Rotini

You can almost taste the tropical sunshine in this bright and fruity curry dish with hearty chicken, creamy coconut, sweet apple and mango.

Water	12 cups	3 L
Salt	1 1/2 tsp.	7 mL
Rotini pasta	4 cups	1 L
Cooking oil	1 tbsp.	15 mL
Boneless, skinless chicken thighs, cut into 1 inch (2.5 cm) pieces	1 lb.	454 g
Diced peeled tart apple (such as Granny Smith)	1 1/2 cups	375 mL
Chopped frozen mango, thawed	1 cup	250 mL
Thinly sliced onion	1 cup	250 mL
Thinly sliced red pepper	1 cup	250 mL
Garlic clove, minced (or 1/4 tsp., 1 mL, powder)	1	1
Can of coconut milk (14 oz., 398 mL)	1	1
Prepared chicken broth	1 cup	250 mL
Fish sauce	2 tbsp.	30 mL
Sweet chili sauce	2 tbsp.	30 mL
Red curry paste	1 tsp.	5 mL
Lime juice	1 tbsp.	15 mL
Chopped fresh basil	1 tbsp.	15 mL

Combine water and salt in Dutch oven. Bring to a boil. Add pasta. Boil, uncovered, for 12 to 14 minutes, stirring occasionally, until tender but firm. Drain. Return to same pot. Cover to keep warm.

Heat cooking oil in large frying pan on medium-high. Add chicken. Cook for 5 to 8 minutes, stirring occasionally, until starting to brown. Drain all but 1 tbsp. (15 mL) drippings.

Add next 5 ingredients. Reduce heat to medium. Cook for 5 to 10 minutes, stirring occasionally, until onion and apple are softened.

Add next 5 ingredients. Stir. Bring to a boil. Simmer, uncovered, for about 10 minutes until sauce is slightly thickened.

Add lime juice. Stir. Add to pasta. Toss. Transfer to serving bowl. Sprinkle with basil. Makes about 8 cups (2 L).

1 cup (250 mL): 367 Calories; 17.6 g Total Fat (3.1 g Mono, 1.7 g Poly, 10.8 g Sat); 37 mg Cholesterol; 37 g Carbohydrate; 3 g Fibre; 16 g Protein; 564 mg Sodium

Pictured on page 179.

Sage Chicken Ravioli

Wonton wrappers provide a much-appreciated shortcut in making homemade ravioli. A light butter and pine nut topping adds the perfect finishing touch.

Finely chopped green onion	2 tbsp.	30 mL
Finely chopped red pepper	2 tbsp.	30 mL
Chopped fresh sage (or 1/4 tsp., 1 mL, dried)	1 tsp.	5 mL
Garlic powder	1/8 tsp.	0.5 mL
Salt	1/4 tsp.	1 mL
Pepper	1/8 tsp.	0.5 mL
Lean ground chicken thigh	3/4 lb.	340 g
Wonton wrappers	48	48
Large egg	1	1
Water	1 tbsp.	15 mL
Water	12 cups	3 L
Salt	1 1/2 tsp.	7 mL
Butter (or hard margarine)	1/4 cup	60 mL
Pine nuts	1/4 cup	60 mL
Grated Parmesan cheese	2 tbsp.	30 mL
Chopped fresh sage (or 3/4 tsp., 4 mL, dried)	1 tbsp.	15 mL
Grated lemon zest	1/2 tsp.	2 mL

Combine first 6 ingredients in medium bowl. Add chicken. Mix well.

Arrange 24 wrappers on work surface. Place about 1 tbsp. (15 mL) chicken mixture in centre of each wrapper.

Whisk egg and first amount of water in small bowl. Brush over edges of wrappers. Cover with remaining wrappers. Press edges to seal. Makes 24 ravioli.

Combine remaining water and salt in Dutch oven. Bring to a boil. Add half of ravioli. Boil, uncovered, for about 5 minutes, stirring occasionally, until chicken mixture is no longer pink and wrappers are tender but firm. Transfer with slotted spoon to sieve. Drain. Transfer to serving bowl. Cover to keep warm. Repeat with remaining ravioli.

Melt butter in small frying pan on medium. Add pine nuts. Heat and stir for about 1 minute until nuts are browned (see Tip, page 50). Add remaining 3 ingredients. Stir. Pour over ravioli. Stir gently until coated. Serves 4.

1 serving: 480 Calories; 31.0 g Total Fat (5.0 g Mono, 4.0 g Poly, 9.0 g Sat); 135 mg Cholesterol; 27 g Carbohydrate; 1 g Fibre; 23 g Protein; 560 mg Sodium

Spaghetti Chicken Stir-fry

Who needs chow mein noodles when spaghetti makes the perfect partner for these crisp, saucy stir-fried veggies. Simple and healthy.

Water	8 cups	2 L
Salt	1 tsp.	5 mL
Spaghetti, broken into thirds	6 oz.	170 g
Cooking oil	2 tsp.	10 mL
Boneless, skinless chicken breast halves, thinly sliced	3/4 lb.	340 g
Sliced carrot	1 cup	250 mL
Sliced onion	1 cup	250 mL
Finely grated ginger root	2 tsp.	10 mL
Garlic clove, minced (or 1/4 tsp., 1 mL, powder)	1	1
Can of cut baby corn (14 oz., 398 mL), drained	1	1
Chopped fresh asparagus (1 inch, 2.5 cm, pieces)	1 cup	250 mL
Small broccoli florets	1 cup	250 mL
Fresh bean sprouts	1 cup	250 mL
Sliced green onion	1/2 cup	125 mL
Prepared chicken broth	1/4 cup	60 mL
Soy sauce	2 tbsp.	30 mL
Sesame oil (for flavour)	2 tsp.	10 mL

Combine water and salt in large saucepan. Bring to a boil. Add pasta. Boil, uncovered, for 10 to 12 minutes, stirring occasionally, until tender but firm. Drain. Return to same pot.

Heat large frying pan or wok on medium-high until very hot. Add cooking oil. Add chicken. Stir-fry for about 3 minutes until no longer pink. Transfer to medium bowl. Cover to keep warm.

Reduce heat to medium. Add next 4 ingredients to same frying pan. Stir-fry for 2 minutes.

Add next 3 ingredients. Stir-fry for about 3 minutes until vegetables are tender-crisp.

Add remaining 5 ingredients, chicken and pasta. Stir-fry for 1 to 2 minutes until combined and heated through. Makes about 9 cups (2.25 L).

1 cup (250 mL): 209 Calories; 3.6 g Total Fat (0.9 g Mono, 0.8 g Poly, 0.5 g Sat); 22 mg Cholesterol; 32 g Carbohydrate; 3 g Fibre; 15 g Protein; 379 mg Sodium

Pictured on page 162.

Chicken Tetrazzini

A lighter cream sauce reduces the total fat,
while whole wheat spaghetti and colourful vegetables add fibre.

Water	12 cups	3 L
Salt	1 1/2 tsp.	7 mL
Whole wheat spaghetti, broken in half	8 oz.	225 g
Canola oil	2 tsp.	10 mL
Sliced fresh brown (or white) mushrooms	2 cups	500 mL
Chopped onion	1 cup	250 mL
Diced red pepper	1 cup	250 mL
Prepared chicken broth	1 1/2 cups	375 mL
Dry (or alcohol-free) white wine	1/4 cup	60 mL
Pepper	1/4 tsp.	1 mL
Diced cooked chicken breast	2 cups	500 mL
Frozen peas, thawed	1 cup	250 mL
Block light cream cheese, softened	4 oz.	125 g
Light sour cream	1/2 cup	125 mL
Grated Parmesan cheese	1/4 cup	60 mL

Combine water and salt in Dutch oven. Bring to a boil. Add pasta. Boil, uncovered, for 10 to 12 minutes, stirring occasionally, until tender but firm. Drain. Return to same pot. Cover to keep warm.

Heat canola oil in large frying pan on medium. Add mushrooms and onion. Cook for about 10 minutes, stirring often, until onion is softened. Add red pepper. Stir. Cook for 2 minutes.

Add next 3 ingredients. Bring to a boil.

Add next 4 ingredients. Stir. Cook for about 5 minutes, stirring occasionally, until heated through. Add pasta. Toss.

Sprinkle Parmesan cheese over top. Stir. Makes about 7 1/2 cups (1.9 L).

1 cup (250 mL): 290 Calories; 12 g Total Fat (2.5 g Mono, 1.5 g Poly, 5 g Sat); 50 mg Cholesterol; 29 g Carbohydrate; 4 g Fibre; 17 g Protein; 240 mg Sodium)

Pictured on page 180.

Asian Chicken Supreme

Tomato-sauced pasta spiked with Asian flavours. Fusion cuisine at its finest!

Sesame (or cooking) oil	1 tbsp.	15 mL
Lean ground chicken	1 lb.	454 g
Garlic cloves, minced	3	3
(or 3/4 tsp., 4 mL, powder)		
Finely grated ginger root	2 tsp.	10 mL
(or 1/2 tsp., 2 mL, ground ginger)		
Pepper	1/4 tsp.	1 mL
Julienned carrot (see Tip, page 86)	1 cup	250 mL
Thinly sliced red pepper	1 cup	250 mL
Thinly sliced onion	1/2 cup	125 mL
Vegetable broth	2 cups	500 mL
Spaghettini	8 oz.	225 g
Can of diced tomato	1	1
(14 oz., 398 mL), with juice		
Water	1 cup	250 mL
Soy sauce	2 tbsp.	30 mL
Dry-roasted peanuts, chopped	1/4 cup	60 mL
Chopped green onion	2 tbsp.	30 mL

Heat sesame oil in large frying pan on medium. Add next 4 ingredients. Scramble-fry for 5 to 10 minutes until chicken is no longer pink.

Add next 3 ingredients. Cook for about 3 minutes, stirring occasionally, until onion is starting to soften.

Add next 5 ingredients. Stir. Bring to a boil. Reduce heat to medium-low. Simmer, covered, for about 15 minutes, stirring often, until pasta is tender but firm.

Sprinkle with peanuts and green onion. Makes about 7 1/2 cups (1.9 L).

1 cup (250 mL): 267 Calories; 9.9 g Total Fat (1.2 g Mono, 0.8 g Poly, 2.0 g Sat); 40 mg Cholesterol; 31 g Carbohydrate; 2 g Fibre; 16 g Protein; 721 mg Sodium

Pictured on page 162.

Lemon Tahini Chicken

The nutty flavours of sesame paste and fresh lemon pair with tender chicken
and pasta for a truly divine combination.

Water	12 cups	3 L
Salt	1 1/2 tsp.	7 mL
Radiatore pasta	4 cups	1 L
Cooking oil	2 tsp.	10 mL
Boneless, skinless chicken thighs, cut into 1 inch (2.5 cm) pieces	3/4 lb.	340 g
Garlic cloves, minced (or 3/4 tsp., 4 mL, powder)	3	3
Chopped roasted red pepper	1/2 cup	125 mL
Tahini (sesame paste)	1/2 cup	125 mL
Lemon juice	3 tbsp.	45 mL
Grated lemon zest	1 tsp.	5 mL
Salt	1 tsp.	5 mL
Pepper	1/2 tsp.	2 mL
Chopped fresh parsley	1/4 cup	60 mL

Combine water and salt in Dutch oven. Bring to a boil. Add pasta. Boil, uncovered, for 7 to 9 minutes, stirring occasionally, until tender but firm. Drain, reserving 1 1/4 cups (300 mL) cooking water. Return pasta to same pot. Cover to keep warm.

Heat cooking oil in medium frying pan on medium. Add chicken. Cook for 5 to 10 minutes, stirring occasionally, until chicken is starting to brown.

Add garlic. Heat and stir for 1 minute until fragrant.

Add next 6 ingredients and reserved cooking water. Stir. Cook for about 5 minutes, stirring occasionally, until chicken is no longer pink inside and sauce is slightly thickened. Add to pasta.

Add parsley. Stir. Makes about 7 cups (1.75 L). Serve immediately.

1 cup (250 mL): 346 Calories; 14.7 g Total Fat (5.6 g Mono, 5.2 g Poly, 2.4 g Sat); 32 mg Cholesterol; 35 g Carbohydrate; 2 g Fibre; 17 g Protein; 578 mg Sodium

Chicken Meatball Sauce

This isn't your kids' spaghetti sauce and meatballs! Rekindle your old childhood romance with the sophisticated flavours of this stylish cinnamon, nutmeg and balsamic vinegar sauce that's all grown up.

Large egg, fork-beaten	1	1
Fine dry bread crumbs	1/2 cup	125 mL
Parsley flakes	1 tsp.	5 mL
Dried oregano	1/2 tsp.	2 mL
Lean ground chicken	1 lb.	454 g
Olive (or cooking) oil	1 tbsp.	15 mL
Chopped onion	1/2 cup	125 mL
Grated carrot	1/2 cup	125 mL
Garlic cloves, minced (or 1/2 tsp., 2 mL, powder)	2	2
Can of diced tomatoes (28 oz., 796 mL), with juice	1	1
Can of tomato sauce (7 1/2 oz., 213 mL)	1	1
Balsamic vinegar	1/4 cup	60 mL
Granulated sugar	2 tsp.	10 mL
Ground cinnamon	1/2 tsp.	2 mL
Ground nutmeg	1/2 tsp.	2 mL
Pepper	1/4 tsp.	1 mL
Bay leaves	2	2

Combine first 4 ingredients in large bowl. Add chicken. Mix well. Roll into 1 inch (2.5 cm) balls.

Heat olive oil in large frying pan on medium-high. Add meatballs. Cook for about 5 minutes, turning often, until well browned. Transfer with slotted spoon to plate lined with paper towel to drain. Makes about 35 meatballs.

Add next 3 ingredients to same frying pan. Cook on medium for 3 to 5 minutes, stirring often, until onion starts to soften. Add meatballs.

Process next 7 ingredients in blender until smooth. Add to meatball mixture. Add bay leaves. Stir. Bring to a boil. Reduce heat to medium-low. Simmer, uncovered, for 20 to 25 minutes, stirring occasionally, until sauce is thickened and internal temperature of chicken reaches 175°F (80°C). Discard bay leaves. Makes about 6 cups (1.5 L).

1 cup (250 mL): 262 Calories; 13.9 g Total Fat (2.2 g Mono, 0.4 g Poly, 0.7 g Sat); 31 mg Cholesterol; 18 g Carbohydrate; 1 g Fibre; 17 g Protein; 506 mg Sodium

Sweet Chicken Curry

*Take your friends and family to India with an Asian-themed dinner. Add basmati rice,
naan bread and cucumber salad for a lively Indian meal.*

Cooking oil	1 tbsp.	15 mL
Boneless, skinless chicken thighs, cut into 3/4 inch (2 cm) pieces	1 lb.	454 g
Chopped onion	1 cup	250 mL
Chopped celery	1/3 cup	75 mL
Curry powder	1 1/2 tsp.	7 mL
Ground ginger	1 tsp.	5 mL
Garlic clove, minced (or 1/4 tsp., 1 mL, powder)	1	1
Dried crushed chilies	1/2 tsp.	2 mL
Chopped peeled cooking apple (such as McIntosh)	1 cup	250 mL
Prepared chicken broth	1 cup	250 mL
Can of tomato sauce (7 1/2 oz., 213 mL)	1	1
Golden raisins	1/4 cup	60 mL
Plain yogurt	1/2 cup	125 mL
Chopped fresh cilantro or parsley (or 1 1/2 tsp., 7 mL, dried)	2 tbsp.	30 mL
Chopped unsalted peanuts	1/4 cup	60 mL
Chopped fresh cilantro or parsley	2 tbsp.	30 mL

Heat cooking oil in large frying pan on medium-high. Add chicken. Cook for about
5 minutes, stirring occasionally, until browned.

Add next 6 ingredients. Cook for about 5 minutes, stirring often, until onion and celery
start to soften.

Add next 4 ingredients. Stir. Bring to a boil. Reduce heat to medium-low. Simmer,
uncovered, for about 15 minutes until thickened and apple is tender.

Add yogurt and first amount of cilantro. Cook and stir until heated through.

Sprinkle individual servings with peanuts and second amount of cilantro. Makes about
4 1/2 cups (1.1 L).

*1 cup (250 mL): 321 Calories; 16.2 g Total Fat (7.1 g Mono, 4.1 g Poly, 3.6 g Sat); 70 mg Cholesterol; 22 g Carbohydrate;
3 g Fibre; 24 g Protein; 544 mg Sodium*

Chicken and Greens

Forget about the chicken and the egg, this is all about the chicken and the peanut! Smooth, spicy peanut sauce, chicken, tender-crisp veggies and chopped peanuts make this stir-fry extraordinary.

Low-sodium soy sauce	1 1/2 tbsp.	25 mL
Cornstarch	1 tbsp.	15 mL
Peanut sauce	2 tbsp.	30 mL
Oyster sauce	2 tbsp.	30 mL
Cooking oil	2 tbsp.	30 mL
Boneless, skinless chicken breast halves, cut into thin strips	1 lb.	454 g
Shredded suey choy (Chinese cabbage)	4 cups	1 L
Chopped bok choy	4 cups	1 L
Chopped unsalted peanuts	2 tbsp.	30 mL

Stir soy sauce into cornstarch in small bowl. Add peanut sauce and oyster sauce. Stir. Set aside.

Heat wok or large frying pan on medium-high until very hot. Add cooking oil. Add chicken. Stir-fry for 3 to 5 minutes until no longer pink.

Add suey choy and bok choy. Stir-fry for about 2 minutes until tender-crisp. Stir cornstarch mixture. Add to chicken mixture. Heat and stir for about 1 minute until boiling and thickened. Transfer to large serving dish.

Sprinkle with peanuts. Serves 4.

1 serving: 280 Calories; 12 g Total Fat (6 g Mono, 3 g Poly, 1.5 g Sat); 63 mg Cholesterol; 12 g Carbohydrate; 2 g Fibre; 30 g Protein; 560 mg Sodium

Pictured on page 216.

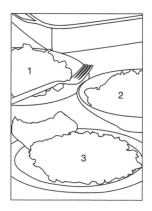

1. Chili Chicken Pasta, page 169
2. Red Curry Chicken Rotini, page 170
3. Bruschetta Chicken, page 235

Speedy Chicken Carbonara

Rather than turning to commercially produced high-salt sauces, this recipe teaches the true method for making a carbonara sauce from scratch—and a touch of chili heat adds a dash of adventure.

Spaghetti	12 oz.	340 g
Egg yolks (large)	4	4
Grated Parmesan cheese	1/2 cup	125 mL
Finely chopped fresh parsley	1/4 cup	60 mL
Chili paste (sambal oelek)	1/2 tsp.	2 m
Bacon slices, chopped	6	6
Chopped cooked chicken (see Tip, page 58)	1 1/2 cups	375 mL
Prepared chicken broth, heated	1 cup	250 mL

Cook pasta according to package directions. Drain. Return to same pot. Cover to keep warm.

Combine next 4 ingredients in small bowl. Set aside.

Cook bacon in large frying pan on medium until crisp. Remove with slotted spoon to plate lined with paper towel to drain. Drain and discard all but 1 tbsp. (15 mL) drippings.

Add chicken and pasta to same frying pan. Reduce heat to medium-low. Cook and stir for about 2 minutes until heated through.

Whisk hot broth into egg mixture. Add to pasta mixture. Add bacon. Toss until coated. Serve immediately. Makes about 6 cups (1.5 L).

1 cup (250 mL): 420 Calories; 14.0 g Total Fat (6.0 g Mono, 2.0 g Poly, 5.0 g Sat); 190 mg Cholesterol; 44 g Carbohydrate; 2 g Fibre; 26 g Protein; 350 mg Sodium

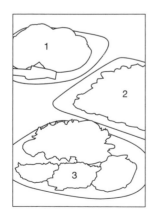

1. Tuscan Chicken Burgers, page 112
2. Chicken Tetrazzini, page 173
3. Cordon Bleu Chicken, page 263

Chicken Cacciatore

Catch the scent of this savoury cacciatore and you'll be the one caught in its tantalizing spell. The herbed tomato sauce will have you ensnared. You won't be able to break free—but that's OK, you won't mind at all! Goes great over pasta or rice.

Cooking oil	2 tsp.	10 mL
Boneless, skinless chicken thighs, quartered	1 1/2 lbs.	680 g
Sliced fresh white mushrooms	1 1/2 cups	375 mL
Chopped onion	1 cup	250 mL
Garlic cloves, minced (or 1/2 tsp., 2 mL, powder)	2	2
Dry (or alcohol-free) white wine	1/4 cup	60 mL
Can of diced tomatoes (28 oz., 796 mL), with juice	1	1
Chopped green pepper	1 1/2 cups	375 mL
Tomato paste (see Tip, page 136)	1/4 cup	60 mL
Bay leaf	1	1
Dried basil	1 tsp.	5 mL
Dried oregano	1 tsp.	5 mL
Granulated sugar	1 tsp.	5 mL
Dried rosemary, crushed	1/2 tsp.	2 mL
Salt	1/2 tsp.	2 mL
Pepper	1/4 tsp.	1 mL

Heat cooking oil in large saucepan or Dutch oven on medium-high. Add chicken. Cook, uncovered, for about 5 minutes, stirring occasionally, until chicken starts to brown.

Add next 3 ingredients. Cook for 5 to 10 minutes, stirring occasionally, until onion is softened and liquid from mushrooms has evaporated.

Add wine. Heat and stir for 1 minute.

Add remaining 10 ingredients. Stir. Bring to a boil. Reduce heat to medium-low. Cook, partially covered, for about 30 minutes, stirring occasionally, until chicken is no longer pink inside and green pepper is tender. Discard bay leaf. Makes about 8 cups (2 L).

1 cup (250 mL): 186 Calories; 7.7 g Total Fat (3.1 g Mono, 1.9 g Poly, 1.9 g Sat); 56 mg Cholesterol; 11 g Carbohydrate; 2 g Fibre; 17 g Protein; 481 mg Sodium

Lemon Ginger Chicken

Different yet familiar, soothing yet refreshing—you'll wish you'd discovered this fine flavour combination sooner. Serve with rice or noodles.

Boneless, skinless chicken breast halves (about 4 oz., 113 g, each)	4	4
All-purpose flour	1/4 cup	60 mL
Salt	1/4 tsp.	1 mL
Pepper	1/4 tsp.	1 mL
Olive (or canola) oil	2 tsp.	10 mL
Prepared chicken broth	1/2 cup	125 mL
Lemon juice	1/4 cup	60 mL
Brown sugar, packed	2 tbsp.	30 mL
Soy sauce	1 tbsp.	15 mL
Finely grated ginger root	1 tsp.	5 mL
Grated lemon zest	1 tsp.	5 mL
Dry mustard	1/4 tsp.	1 mL
Prepared chicken broth	1/4 cup	60 mL
Cornstarch	1 1/2 tsp.	7 mL

Place chicken between 2 sheets of plastic wrap. Pound with mallet or rolling pin to 1/4 inch (6 mm) thickness.

Combine next 3 ingredients on large plate. Press both sides of chicken into flour mixture until coated. Discard any remaining flour mixture.

Heat olive oil in large frying pan on medium-high. Add chicken. Cook for 2 to 4 minutes per side until no longer pink inside. Transfer to plate. Cover to keep warm. Reduce heat to medium.

Add next 7 ingredients to same frying pan. Heat and stir, scraping any brown bits from bottom of pan, until boiling.

Stir second amount of broth into cornstarch in small cup. Add to lemon juice mixture. Heat and stir until boiling and thickened. Reduce heat to medium-low. Add chicken. Turn to coat both sides. Cook for 1 to 2 minutes until heated through. Serves 4.

1 serving: 232 Calories; 4.8 g Total Fat (2.3 g Mono, 0.8 g Poly, 1.0 g Sat); 82 mg Cholesterol; 12 g Carbohydrate; trace Fibre; 33 g Protein; 632 mg Sodium

Pictured on page 198.

Ginger Pineapple Meatballs

Talk about a well-balanced meal! These tangy meatballs are not too sweet, not too sour, and not too spicy. Serve this saucy delight over jasmine rice.

Large egg, fork-beaten	1	1
Fine dry bread crumbs	1/2 cup	125 mL
Finely chopped red pepper	1/4 cup	60 mL
Grated onion	1/4 cup	60 mL
Ground ginger	1/2 tsp.	2 mL
Salt	1/2 tsp.	2 mL
Pepper	1/4 tsp.	1 mL
Lean ground chicken	1 lb.	454 g
Cooking oil	2 tsp.	10 mL
Can of crushed pineapple (14 oz., 398 mL), with juice	1	1
Sweet chili sauce	1/2 cup	125 mL
Lime juice	1 tbsp.	15 mL
Finely grated ginger root (or 1/2 tsp., 2 mL, ground ginger)	2 tsp.	10 mL
Salt	1/4 tsp.	1 mL
Soy sauce	1 tbsp.	15 mL
Cornstarch	2 tsp.	10 mL
Sliced green onion	1/4 cup	60 mL

Combine first 7 ingredients in medium bowl. Add chicken. Mix well. Roll into 1 inch (2.5 cm) balls.

Heat cooking oil in large frying pan on medium-high. Add meatballs. Cook for 5 to 10 minutes, turning often, until fully cooked and internal temperature reaches 175°F (80°C). Transfer with slotted spoon to plate lined with paper towel to drain. Makes about 40 meatballs.

Add next 5 ingredients to same frying pan.

Stir soy sauce into cornstarch in small cup. Add to pineapple mixture. Heat and stir until boiling and thickened. Add meatballs. Stir until coated. Reduce heat to medium-low. Cook for about 5 minutes until heated through.

Sprinkle with green onion. Serves 4.

1 serving: 423 Calories; 19.7 g Total Fat (2.2 g Mono, 1.1 g Poly, 0.7 g Sat); 47 mg Cholesterol; 35 g Carbohydrate; 4 g Fibre; 24 g Protein; 1439 mg Sodium

Pictured on page 126.

Fragrant Chicken and Rice

Now, this is what we call aromatherapy! As this wholesome, zesty rice dish simmers, revel in the soothing and delicious fragrance that will silently draw everyone to the kitchen!

Cooking oil	1 tbsp.	15 mL
Boneless, skinless chicken thighs, cut into 1 inch (2.5 cm) pieces	1 lb.	454 g
Chopped onion	2 cups	500 mL
Ground cinnamon	1/2 tsp.	2 mL
Ground coriander	1/2 tsp.	2 mL
Ground cumin	1/2 tsp.	2 mL
Garlic powder	1/4 tsp.	1 mL
Pepper	1/4 tsp.	1 mL
Prepared chicken broth	2 1/2 cups	625 mL
Can of chickpeas (garbanzo beans), 19 oz., 540 mL, rinsed and drained	1	1
Long grain white rice	1 cup	250 mL
Chopped dried apricot	1/2 cup	125 mL
Salt	1/4 tsp.	1 mL
Sliced natural almonds, toasted (see Tip, page 22)	1/2 cup	125 mL
Chopped fresh chives	2 tbsp.	30 mL
Grated lemon zest	1/2 tsp.	2 mL

Heat cooking oil in large frying pan on medium. Add chicken. Cook for about 5 minutes, stirring occasionally, until starting to brown. Remove to plate.

Add onion to same frying pan. Cook for 5 to 10 minutes, stirring occasionally, until softened.

Add next 5 ingredients. Heat and stir for about 1 minute until fragrant.

Add next 5 ingredients and chicken. Stir. Bring to a boil. Reduce heat to medium-low. Simmer, covered, for 30 minutes, without stirring. Remove from heat. Let stand, covered, for about 5 minutes until liquid is absorbed and rice is tender. Fluff with fork.

Add remaining 3 ingredients. Toss gently. Makes about 8 cups (2 L).

1 cup (250 mL): 387 Calories; 11.4 g Total Fat (5.2 g Mono, 3.1 g Poly, 1.9 g Sat); 37 mg Cholesterol; 50 g Carbohydrate; 5.2 g Fibre; 21 g Protein; 508 mg Sodium

Chicken Supreme

Supremely satisfying, with a touch of heat, this dish certainly lives up to its name! And we've made sure there's plenty of sauce to serve over rice or noodles.

Water	1 cup	250 mL
Low-sodium soy sauce	3 tbsp.	45 mL
Cornstarch	2 tbsp.	30 mL
Hoisin sauce	2 tbsp.	30 mL
Dried crushed chilies	1/2 tsp.	2 mL
Onion powder	1/2 tsp.	2 mL
Cooking oil	2 tsp.	10 mL
Boneless, skinless chicken breast halves, cut into bite-sized pieces	3/4 lb.	340 g
Cooking oil	1 tsp.	5 mL
Fresh mixed stir-fry vegetables	6 cups	1.5 L
Medium onion, cut into thin wedges	1	1
Garlic cloves, minced (or 1/2 tsp., 2 mL, powder)	2	2

Combine first 6 ingredients in small bowl. Set aside.

Heat large frying pan or wok on medium-high until very hot. Add first amount of cooking oil. Add chicken. Stir-fry for about 4 minutes until no longer pink. Remove to separate small bowl. Cover to keep warm.

Add second amount of cooking oil to hot frying pan. Add remaining 3 ingredients. Stir-fry for about 8 minutes until vegetables are tender-crisp. Add chicken. Stir cornstarch mixture. Add to chicken mixture. Heat and stir until boiling and thickened. Serves 4.

1 serving (250 mL): 221 Calories; 5.4 g Total Fat (2.4 g Mono, 1.7 g Poly, 0.8 g Sat); 50 mg Cholesterol; 21 g Carbohydrate; 5 g Fibre; 23 g Protein; 609 mg Sodium

Pictured on page 216.

Cashew Chicken

If Asian flavour is what you're craving, don't bother with take-out. Keep your cash in your pocket and your cashews in your wok. Best served over rice.

Dry sherry	2 tbsp.	30 mL
Soy sauce	1 tbsp.	15 mL
Cornstarch	2 tsp.	10 mL
Chili paste (sambal oelek)	1 tsp.	5 mL
Finely grated ginger root (or 1/4 tsp., 1 mL, ground ginger)	1 tsp.	5 mL

(continued on next page)

Garlic clove, minced (or 1/4 tsp., 1 mL, powder)	1	1
Sesame oil (optional)	2 tsp.	10 mL
Boneless, skinless chicken breast halves, cut into 1/2 inch (12 mm) pieces	1 1/2 lbs.	680 g
Prepared chicken broth	1/2 cup	125 mL
Cornstarch	1 tbsp.	15 mL
Hoisin sauce	1 tbsp.	15 mL
Soy sauce	1 tbsp.	15 mL
Chili paste (sambal oelek)	1 tsp.	5 mL
Dry sherry	1 tsp.	5 mL
Cooking oil	1 tbsp.	15 mL
Cooking oil	1 tbsp.	15 mL
Coarsely chopped onion	1 1/2 cups	375 mL
Small green pepper, cut into 3/4 inch (2 cm) pieces	1	1
Small red pepper, cut into 3/4 inch (2 cm) pieces	1	1
Can of bamboo shoots (8 oz., 227 mL), drained	1	1
Finely grated ginger root (or 1/4 tsp., 1 mL, ground ginger)	1 1/2 tsp.	7 mL
Salted cashews	1 1/4 cups	300 mL
Chopped green onion	1/4 cup	60 mL

Whisk first 7 ingredients in a medium bowl. Add chicken. Stir until coated. Let stand at room temperature for 15 minutes.

Stir next 6 ingredients in small bowl until smooth. Set aside.

Heat wok or large frying pan on medium-high until very hot. Add first amount of cooking oil. Add chicken mixture. Stir-fry for 2 to 3 minutes until chicken is no longer pink.

Add second amount of cooking oil to hot wok. Add next 5 ingredients. Stir-fry for 1 minute. Cook, covered, for 2 to 3 minutes, stirring occasionally, until peppers are tender-crisp. Stir broth mixture. Add to chicken mixture. Heat and stir for about 1 minute until boiling and thickened.

Add cashews and green onion. Stir. Serves 6.

1 serving: 554 Calories; 21.1 g Total Fat (6.0 g Mono, 6.6 g Poly, 4.9 g Sat); 245 mg Cholesterol; 29 g Carbohydrate; 8 g Fibre; 66 g Protein; 1387 mg Sodium

Pictured on page 126.

Ginger Pear Chicken

This tender, moist chicken has just a little heat from ginger.

Salt	1/2 tsp.	2 mL
Pepper	1/4 tsp.	1 mL
Ground ginger	1/4 tsp.	1 mL
Boneless, skinless chicken breast halves (about 4 oz., 113 g, each)	4	4
Olive (or cooking) oil	1 tbsp.	15 mL
Chopped onion	1/2 cup	125 mL
Finely grated ginger root	1 tbsp.	15 mL
Diced peeled pear	2 cups	500 mL
Apple (or pear) cider	1 cup	250 mL
Balsamic vinegar	2 tbsp.	30 mL
Brown sugar, packed	1 tbsp.	15 mL
Chopped fresh thyme (or 1/4 tsp., 1 mL, dried)	1 tsp.	5 mL

Stir first 3 ingredients together in small cup. Sprinkle over chicken.

Heat olive oil in large frying pan on medium-high. Add chicken. Cook for about 4 minutes, turning at halftime, until browned on both sides. Reduce heat to medium. Cook for another 6 to 8 minutes until chicken is fully cooked and internal temperature reaches 170°F (77°C). Remove to plate. Cover to keep warm.

Add onion and grated ginger to same frying pan. Cook for 2 to 3 minutes, stirring often, until onion starts to brown.

Add pear. Cook for 1 to 2 minutes, stirring occasionally, until pear starts to soften.

Add remaining 4 ingredients. Stir. Bring to a boil. Reduce heat to medium. Boil gently, uncovered, for about 10 minutes until pear is softened and liquid is reduced by half. Add chicken. Cook, covered, for about 5 minutes until heated through. Serves 4.

1 serving: 263 Calories; 5.4 g Total Fat (3.0 g Mono, 0.7 g Poly, 1.0 g Sat); 66 mg Cholesterol; 27 g Carbohydrate; 3 g Fibre; 26 g Protein; 367 mg Sodium

 tip To remove the skin from a drumsticks, grasp the skin with a paper towel. This will allow you to grip the otherwise slippery surface.

Mushroom Rice Skillet

Make your entire dinner using just your stovetop and a large frying pan. Rice, chicken, vegetables and minimal cleanup. How much easier can it get?

Cooking oil	1 tsp.	5 mL
Sliced fresh white mushrooms	2 cups	500 mL
Cooking oil	2 tsp.	10 mL
Boneless, skinless chicken thighs, cut into 1/2 inch (12 mm) strips	1 lb.	454 g
Chopped onion	2 cups	500 mL
Chopped tomato	2 cups	500 mL
Prepared chicken broth	2 cups	500 mL
Can of condensed cream of mushroom soup (10 oz., 284 mL)	1	1
Long grain brown rice	1/2 cup	125 mL
Wild rice	1/2 cup	125 mL
Parsley flakes	1 tsp.	5 mL
Dried thyme	1/4 tsp.	1 mL
Pepper	1/4 tsp.	1 mL

Heat first amount of cooking oil in large frying pan on medium. Add mushrooms. Cook for about 10 minutes, stirring occasionally, until starting to brown. Remove to small bowl.

Add second amount of cooking oil to same frying pan. Add chicken. Cook for 5 to 10 minutes, stirring occasionally, until browned. Transfer with slotted spoon to plate.

Add onion to same frying pan. Cook for 5 to 10 minutes, stirring often, until softened.

Add remaining 8 ingredients, mushrooms and chicken. Stir. Bring to a boil. Reduce heat to medium-low. Simmer, covered, for about 1 hour, stirring occasionally, until rice is tender. Makes about 6 1/2 cups (1.6 L).

1 cup (250 mL): 306 Calories; 11.2 g Total Fat (4.1 g Mono, 2.9 g Poly, 2.5 g Sat); 46 mg Cholesterol; 33 g Carbohydrate; 3 g Fibre; 19 g Protein; 570 mg Sodium

Chicken Adobo

Adobo a-go-go! Get your groove on with this Filipino favourite.

Coarsely chopped onion	1 1/2 cups	375 mL
Water	1 cup	250 mL
Rice vinegar	1/2 cup	125 mL
Ketchup	3 tbsp.	45 mL
Soy sauce	3 tbsp.	45 mL
Garlic cloves, minced	3	3
Bay leaves	2	2
Sesame oil (for flavour)	1 tsp.	5 mL
Whole cloves	3	3
Dried crushed chilies	1/4 tsp.	1 mL
Chicken legs, back attached (about 11 oz., 310 g, each), skin removed	4	4
Water	1/4 cup	60 mL
Cornstarch	2 tbsp.	30 mL
Sesame seeds, toasted (see Tip, page 22)	2 tsp.	10 mL

Combine first 10 ingredients in Dutch oven or large pot. Bring to a boil on medium. Reduce heat to medium-low.

Add chicken. Simmer, covered, for about 45 minutes, turning chicken at halftime, until chicken is tender. Transfer chicken with slotted spoon to serving platter. Cover to keep warm. Discard bay leaves and cloves. Carefully process sauce with hand blender or in blender until smooth (see Safety Tip).

Stir water into cornstarch in small cup. Add to sauce. Heat and stir on medium for about 2 minutes until boiling and thickened. Pour over chicken.

Sprinkle with sesame seeds. Serves 4.

1 serving: 554 Calories; 21.1 g Total Fat (6.0 g Mono, 6.6 g Poly, 4.9 g Sat); 245 mg Cholesterol; 29 g Carbohydrate; 8 g Fibre; 66 g Protein; 1387 mg Sodium

Safety Tip: Follow manufacturer's instructions for processing hot liquids.

Bourbon Chicken Pilaf

Infuse your pasta with flavour as it boils. Using a pilaf method transforms ordinary pasta into a tangy taste sensation.

Boneless, skinless chicken thighs, cut into bite-sized pieces	1 lb.	454 g
Sesame oil (for flavour)	1 tsp.	5 mL
Seasoned salt	1/4 tsp.	1 mL
Cooking oil	2 tsp.	10 mL
Chopped onion	1 cup	250 mL
Garlic cloves, minced (or 1/2 tsp., 2 mL, powder)	2	2
Bourbon whiskey	1/4 cup	60 mL
Chicken broth	1 cup	250 mL
Orange juice	1 cup	250 mL
Maple (or maple-flavoured) syrup	2 tbsp.	30 mL
Soy sauce	2 tbsp.	30 mL
Dried crushed chilies	1/4 tsp.	1 mL
Salt	1/4 tsp.	1 mL
Pepper	1/4 tsp.	1 mL
Tiny shell pasta	1 1/2 cups	375 mL
Chopped red pepper	2 cups	500 mL

Combine first 3 ingredients in small bowl.

Heat first amount of cooking oil in large frying pan on medium. Add chicken mixture. Cook for 5 to 8 minutes, stirring occasionally, until browned. Transfer with slotted spoon to separate small bowl. Cover to keep warm.

Add onion and garlic to same frying pan. Cook for 5 to 10 minutes, stirring occasionally, until onion is softened.

Add bourbon. Heat and stir for 30 seconds until liquid is evaporated.

Add next 7 ingredients. Stir. Bring to a boil.

Add pasta and chicken. Stir. Reduce heat to medium-low. Cook, covered, for 15 minutes, stirring often.

Add red pepper. Stir. Cook, covered, for about 5 minutes until pasta is tender but firm. Makes about 6 cups (1.5 L).

1 cup (250 mL): 274 Calories; 8.9 g Total Fat (3.1 g Mono, 1.9 g Poly, 1.9 g Sat); 50 mg Cholesterol; 26 g Carbohydrate; 2 g Fibre; 17 g Protein; 798 mg Sodium

Pictured on page 162.

Chicken and Apricot Pilaf

Spend an Arabian night supping on this appetizing dish with real flair. The fragrant spices and sweet dried fruit are guaranteed to woo you in at least 1001 ways!

Cooking oil	1 tbsp.	15 mL
Lean ground chicken	1 lb.	454 g
Chopped onion	1 cup	250 mL
Cinnamon stick (4 inches, 10 cm), see Note	1	1
Whole green cardamom, bruised (see Tip, page 225)	2	2
Curry powder	1 tbsp.	15 mL
Prepared chicken broth	1 3/4 cups	425 mL
Converted white rice	1 cup	250 mL
Chopped dried apricot	1/3 cup	75 mL
Dark raisins	1/3 cup	75 mL
Salt	1/4 tsp.	1 mL
Frozen peas, thawed	2/3 cup	150 mL
Slivered almonds, toasted (see Tip, page 22)	1/3 cup	75 mL
Chopped fresh mint (or 2 tsp., 10 mL, dried)	2 1/2 tbsp.	37 mL

Heat cooking oil in large saucepan on medium-high. Add chicken and onion. Scramble-fry for about 10 minutes until chicken is no longer pink and onion is softened. Drain.

Add next 3 ingredients. Heat and stir for about 1 minute until fragrant.

Add next 5 ingredients. Stir. Bring to a boil. Reduce heat to medium-low. Simmer, covered, for about 15 minutes, without stirring, until rice is tender. Discard cinnamon stick and cardamom.

Add remaining 3 ingredients. Stir. Let stand, covered, for about 5 minutes until heated through. Makes about 6 cups (1.5 L).

1 cup (250 mL): 360 Calories; 11 g Total Fat (4 g Mono, 1.5 g Poly, 2 g Sat); 65 mg Cholesterol; 47 g Carbohydrate; 3 g Fibre; 19 g Protein; 340 mg Sodium

Note: If you don't have any cinnamon sticks or cardamom pods on hand, you can use 1/4 tsp. (1 mL) each of ground cinnamon and ground cardamom instead.

Pictured on page 125.

Spinach Chicken Skillet

The well-blended flavours of chicken, nutmeg and dill just seem to pop when sprinkled with lemon—it's a whole new taste sensation! If you don't have a large frying pan with a lid, use the lid from your Dutch oven or wok.

Olive (or cooking) oil	1 tbsp.	15 mL
Boneless, skinless chicken breast halves, cut into 1 inch (2.5 cm) cubes	1 lb.	454 g
Salt	1/2 tsp.	2 mL
Pepper	1/4 tsp.	1 mL
Chopped onion	2 cups	500 mL
Grated lemon zest	2 tsp.	10 mL
Prepared chicken broth	3 cups	750 mL
Converted white rice	1 1/2 cups	375 mL
Ground nutmeg	1/4 tsp.	1 mL
Coarsely chopped fresh spinach leaves, lightly packed	2 cups	500 mL
Chopped fresh dill (or 1 1/2 tsp., 7 mL, dried)	2 tbsp.	30 mL
Lemon juice	1 tbsp.	15 mL

Heat olive oil in large frying pan on medium-high. Add chicken. Sprinkle with salt and pepper. Cook for about 5 minutes, stirring occasionally, until starting to brown.

Add onion and lemon zest. Cook for about 5 minutes, stirring often, until onion starts to soften.

Add next 3 ingredients. Stir. Bring to a boil. Reduce heat to medium-low. Simmer, covered, for 20 minutes, without stirring. Remove from heat.

Add spinach and dill. Stir. Let stand, covered, for about 10 minutes until liquid is absorbed and rice is tender.

Add lemon juice. Stir. Makes about 8 cups (2 L).

1 cup (250 mL): 267 Calories; 3.7 g Total Fat (1.8 g Mono, 0.6 g Poly, 0.7 g Sat); 33 mg Cholesterol; 38 g Carbohydrate; 2 g Fibre; 19 g Protein; 456 mg Sodium

Creole Chicken Jambalaya

Everyone loves the spicy flavours of jambalaya, and you'll appreciate this full-meal recipe, which features healthy doses of okra, tomatoes, celery, green pepper and onion.

Cooking oil	1 tbsp.	15 mL
Bone-in chicken thighs (about 5 oz., 140 g, each), skin removed	6	6
Chopped celery	1 cup	250 mL
Chopped green pepper	1 cup	250 mL
Chopped onion	1 cup	250 mL
Hot Italian sausage, casing removed	1/2 lb.	225 g
Can of diced tomatoes (28 oz., 796 mL), with juice	1	1
Sliced fresh (or frozen) okra	2 cups	500 mL
Prepared chicken broth	1 1/4 cups	300 mL
Chopped kale leaves, lightly packed (see Tip, page 95)	1 cup	250 mL
Tomato paste (see Tip, page 136)	3 tbsp.	45 mL
Dried thyme	1 tsp.	5 mL
Hot pepper sauce	1 tsp.	5 mL
Worcestershire sauce	1 tsp.	5 mL
Garlic cloves, minced (or 1/2 tsp., 2 mL, powder)	2	2
Granulated sugar	1/2 tsp.	2 mL
Long-grain white rice	3/4 cup	175 mL
Bay leaf	1	1

Heat cooking oil in Dutch oven on medium-high. Add chicken. Cook for about 8 minutes, turning occasionally, until browned. Transfer to large plate. Reduce heat to medium.

Add next 4 ingredients to same pot. Scramble-fry for about 8 minutes until sausage is no longer pink.

Add next 10 ingredients. Heat and stir, scraping any brown bits from bottom of pan, until boiling.

Add rice, bay leaf and chicken. Stir. Bring to a boil. Reduce heat to medium-low. Simmer, covered, without stirring, for about 30 minutes until rice is tender and internal temperature of chicken reaches 170°F (77°C). Remove and discard bay leaf. Makes about 10 cups (2.5 L). Serves 6.

1 serving: 470 Calories; 19 g Total Fat (3.5 g Mono, 2 g Poly, 6 g Sat); 145 mg Cholesterol; 35 g Carbohydrate; 4 g Fibre; 39 g Protein; 1260 mg Sodium

Pictured on page 161.

Chicken and Apple Curry

We know that apples have often been seen as a symbol of temptation, but serve them with sweet mango and crunchy pistachios in a creamy curry and they're pretty near irresistible!

Cooking oil	1 tbsp.	15 mL
Boneless, skinless chicken thighs, cut into 1 inch (2.5 cm) cubes	1 lb.	454 g
Sliced fresh white mushrooms	2 cups	500 mL
Chopped onion	1 cup	250 mL
All-purpose flour	2 tbsp.	30 mL
Curry powder	2 tsp.	10 mL
Prepared chicken broth	1 1/2 cups	375 mL
Chopped peeled cooking apple (such as McIntosh)	1 1/2 cups	375 mL
Mango chutney, larger pieces chopped	1/4 cup	60 mL
Chopped pistachios, toasted (see Tip, page 22)	1/2 cup	125 mL
Plain yogurt	1/4 cup	60 mL
Chopped fresh cilantro or parsley	2 tbsp.	30 mL

Heat cooking oil in large saucepan on medium-high. Add chicken. Cook, uncovered, for about 5 minutes, stirring often, until browned.

Add mushrooms and onion. Cook for about 5 minutes, stirring often, until onion is softened.

Sprinkle with flour and curry powder. Heat and stir for 1 minute.

Slowly stir in broth. Bring to a boil, stirring constantly and scraping any brown bits from bottom of pan until thickened.

Add apple and chutney. Stir. Reduce heat to medium-low. Simmer, uncovered, for about 10 minutes, stirring occasionally, until apple is tender.

Add remaining 3 ingredients. Stir. Makes about 4 1/2 cups (1.1 L).

1 cup (250 mL): 353 Calories; 18.4 g Total Fat (8.5 g Mono, 4.8 g Poly, 3.6 g Sat); 68 mg Cholesterol; 23 g Carbohydrate; 3 g Fibre; 25 g Protein; 335 mg Sodium

Ginger Chicken Stir-fry

Ginger chicken with pea pods—so hot, it's cool!

Boneless, skinless chicken breast halves	1 lb.	454 g
Sesame (or cooking) oil	1 tbsp.	15 mL
Sugar snap peas, trimmed	2 cups	500 mL
Apple juice	1/2 cup	125 mL
Chopped green onion	1/3 cup	75 mL
Honey	2 tbsp.	30 mL
Soy sauce	2 tbsp.	30 mL
Finely grated ginger root	2 tsp.	10 mL
Dried crushed chilies	1/2 tsp.	2 mL
Seasoned salt	1/2 tsp.	2 mL
Water	1/4 cup	60 mL
Cornstarch	1 1/2 tsp.	7 mL

Place 1 chicken breast between 2 sheets of plastic wrap. Pound with mallet or rolling pin to 1/4 inch (6 mm) thickness. Repeat with remaining chicken. Cut chicken crosswise into thin strips.

Heat wok or large frying pan on medium-high until very hot. Add sesame oil. Add chicken. Stir-fry for 4 to 5 minutes until no longer pink.

Add next 8 ingredients. Stir. Cook for about 3 minutes, stirring often, until peas are tender-crisp.

Stir water into cornstarch in small cup. Add to chicken mixture. Heat and stir until boiling and thickened. Serves 4.

1 serving: 287 Calories; 5.4 g Total Fat (1.8 g Mono, 1.9 g Poly, 1.0 g Sat); 66 mg Cholesterol; 30 g Carbohydrate; 2 g Fibre; 28 g Protein; 912 mg Sodium

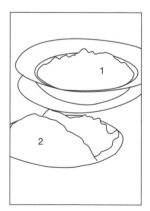

1. Souper Chicken Stew, page 67
2. Chicken Sweet Potato Pie, page 226

Sweet Orange Chicken

You won't have to get up with the chickens to make this quick and easy stir-fry—it takes but minutes to prep and cook! The sweet, spicy glaze will have everyone asking for seconds!

Water	1 tbsp.	15 mL
Cornstarch	2 tsp.	10 mL
Cooking oil	1 tsp.	5 mL
Boneless, skinless chicken thighs, quartered	1 lb.	454 g
Thinly sliced carrot	3/4 cup	175 mL
Orange juice	3/4 cup	175 mL
Brown sugar, packed	1 tbsp.	15 mL
Balsamic vinegar	2 tsp.	10 mL
Hoisin sauce	2 tsp.	10 mL
Salt	1/8 tsp.	0.5 mL
Pepper	1/4 tsp.	1 mL

Stir water into cornstarch in small cup. Set aside.

Heat large frying pan or wok on medium-high until very hot. Add cooking oil. Add chicken. Stir-fry for about 5 minutes until browned. Add carrot.

Combine remaining 6 ingredients in small bowl. Add to chicken mixture. Stir. Bring to a boil. Reduce heat to medium-low. Simmer, covered, for about 6 minutes until chicken is no longer pink inside and carrot is tender-crisp. Stir cornstarch mixture. Add to chicken mixture. Heat and stir for about 1 minute until boiling and thickened. Serves 4.

1 serving: 229 Calories; 9.1 g Total Fat (3.6 g Mono, 2.3 g Poly, 2.2 g Sat); 76 mg Cholesterol; 14 g Carbohydrate; 1 g Fibre; 22 g Protein; 191 mg Sodium

Pictured on page 233.

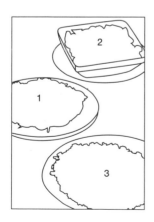

1. Apricot Chicken Pasta, page 168
2. Chicken Hotpot, page 77
3. Lemon Ginger Chicken, page 183

Chicken Vegetable Fried Rice

With veggies, chicken and ham, this great mix can be served as a side or dinner's star attraction. Can you think of a better way to use leftover rice?

Cooking oil	1 tbsp.	15 mL
Boneless, skinless chicken breast halves, thinly sliced	3/4 lb.	340 g
Chopped green pepper	1 cup	250 mL
Chopped red pepper	1 cup	250 mL
Frozen peas	1 cup	250 mL
Can of sliced water chestnuts (8 oz., 227 mL), drained	1	1
Thinly sliced green onion	1/2 cup	125 mL
Chopped low-fat deli ham	1/2 cup	125 mL
Low-sodium soy sauce	1 1/2 tbsp.	25 mL
Hoisin sauce	1 tbsp.	15 mL
Sweet (or regular) chili sauce	1 tbsp.	15 mL
Cold cooked long grain white rice (about 2/3 cup, 150 mL, uncooked)	2 cups	500 mL

Heat wok or large frying pan on medium-high until very hot. Add cooking oil. Add chicken. Stir-fry for 3 to 5 minutes until no longer pink.

Add next 6 ingredients. Stir-fry for 2 to 3 minutes until peppers are tender-crisp.

Combine next 3 ingredients in small bowl. Add to chicken mixture. Stir.

Add rice. Stir-fry for about 5 minutes until heated through and liquid is almost evaporated. Serves 6.

1 serving: 228 Calories; 4.0 g Total Fat (1.8 g Mono, 1.1 g Poly, 0.6 g Sat); 38 mg Cholesterol; 29 g Carbohydrate; 3 g Fibre; 19 g Protein; 450 mg Sodium

Trendy Tacos

A good do-it-yourself meal.

Lean ground raw chicken	1 lb.	454 g
Cooking oil	1 tbsp.	15 mL
Chili powder	1 1/2 tsp.	7 mL
Salt	1/2 tsp.	2 mL
Pepper	1/8 tsp.	0.5 mL
Dried oregano	1/4 tsp.	1 mL
Garlic powder	1/4 tsp.	1 mL
Paprika	1 tsp.	5 mL

(continued on next page)

Taco shells	10	10
Diced tomatoes	2	2
Shredded lettuce	1 1/2 cups	375 mL
Onion slivers (optional)	1/3 cup	75 mL
Grated medium or sharp Cheddar cheese	3/4 cup	175 mL
Sliced pitted ripe olives (optional)	10	10
Sour cream	2/3 cup	150 mL

Scramble-fry chicken in cooking oil until browned. Add next 6 ingredients. Stir.

Spoon about 2 tbsp. (30 mL) chicken in each taco shell. Add remaining ingredients in layers dividing among the 10 taco shells. Makes 10 tacos.

1 taco: 220 Calories; 16 g Total Fat (2.5 g Mono, 0.5 g Poly, 4.5 g Sat); 50 mg Cholesterol; 9 g Carbohydrate; <1 g Fibre; 11 g Protein; 160 mg Sodium

Pictured on page 288.

Chicken Vegetable Fry

Serve this stir-fry with steamed rice to round off the meal.

Cooking oil	2 tbsp.	30 mL
Water	2 tbsp.	30 mL
Red wine vinegar	2 1/2 tbsp.	37 mL
Dried oregano	1/2 tsp.	2 mL
Salt	1/4 tsp.	1 mL
Garlic powder	1/8 tsp.	0.5 mL
Small short thin carrot sticks	1 cup	250 mL
Large chicken breast (about 6 oz., 170 g,) halved, skinned and boned, cut into bite-sized pieces	1	1
Broccoli florets	1 cup	250 mL
Cauliflower florets	1 cup	250 mL
Sliced green onion	1/3 cup	75 mL
Soy sauce	4 tsp.	20 mL
Cornstarch	1/4 tsp.	1 mL
Ground ginger	1/2 tsp.	2 mL

Combine first 6 ingredients in wok or frying pan. Add carrot sticks. Stir-fry on medium-high about 4 minutes until tender crisp.

Add chicken. Stir-fry for 3 to 4 minutes until no pink remains.

Add broccoli, cauliflower and onion. Stir. Cover. Cook on lower heat, stirring occasionally, for 5 minutes.

Mix remaining ingredients in small cup. Add to chicken and vegetable mixture, stirring until it bubbles. Serves 2.

1 serving: 260 Calories; 16 g Total Fat (8 g Mono, 4 g Poly, 1.5 g Sat); 40 mg Cholesterol; 14 g Carbohydrate; 3 g Fibre; 19 g Protein; 1380 mg Sodium

Orange Chicken Stir-fry

One bite and you will be hooked! Sweet orange and tangy mustard combine in this citrusy stir-fry. Serve over brown rice.

Low-sodium prepared chicken broth	3/4 cup	175 mL
Liquid honey	2 tbsp.	30 mL
Dijon mustard	2 tbsp.	30 mL
Cornstarch	2 tsp.	10 mL
White vinegar	1 tsp.	5 mL
Grated orange zest	1/2 tsp.	2 mL
Canola oil	1 tsp.	5 mL
Boneless, skinless chicken breast halves, cut into 1/4 inch (6 mm) slices	3/4 lb.	340 g
Canola oil	1 tsp.	5 mL
Thinly sliced onion	1/2 cup	125 mL
Broccoli slaw (or shredded cabbage with carrot)	4 1/2 cups	1.1 L
Chopped broccoli	2 cups	500 mL
Can of mandarin orange segments (10 oz., 284 mL), drained	1	1

Combine first 6 ingredients in small bowl. Set aside.

Heat wok or large frying pan on medium-high until very hot. Add first amount of canola oil. Add chicken. Stir-fry for about 3 minutes until no longer pink inside. Remove to plate. Set aside.

Add second amount of canola oil to hot wok. Add onion. Stir-fry for 1 to 2 minutes until onion is tender-crisp.

Add broccoli slaw, broccoli and chicken. Stir-fry for 3 to 4 minutes until broccoli is tender-crisp. Stir broth mixture. Add to wok. Heat and stir for 1 to 2 minutes until sauce is boiling and thickened. Remove from heat.

Add mandarin oranges. Toss gently. Serves 4.

1 serving: 224 Calories; 4.2 g Total Fat (1.8 g Mono, 1.2 g Poly, 0.6 g Sat); 49 mg Cholesterol; 25 g Carbohydrate; 4 g Fibre; 23 g Protein; 197 mg Sodium

Walnut Chicken Stir-fry

Colourful, nutty, chewy and crispy. What a treat!

Cooking oil	2 tbsp.	30 mL
Chopped onion	1 1/2 cups	350 mL
Thinly sliced celery	1 1/2 cups	350 mL
Small red pepper, seeded and slivered	1	1
Cooking oil	2 tbsp.	30 mL
Chicken breasts, halved, skin and bones removed, slivered	2	2
Chopped walnuts	1 cup	250 mL
Slivered Chinese cabbage	3 cups	750 mL
Sliced water chestnuts (10 oz., 284 mL), drained	1	1
Bamboo shoots (10 oz., 284 mL), drained and sliced	1	1
Soy sauce	3 tbsp.	45 mL
Sherry (or alcohol-free sherry)	2 tbsp.	30 mL
Granulated sugar	1 tsp.	5 mL
Salt	1/2 tsp.	2 mL
Garlic powder	1/4 tsp.	1 mL
Ground ginger	1/4 tsp.	1 mL
Cornstarch	4 tsp.	20 mL
Water	1/4 cup	60 mL

Heat first amount of cooking oil in wok or frying pan. Add onion, celery and red pepper. Stir-fry until soft. Turn into bowl.

Add second amount of cooking oil to wok. Add chicken. Stir-fry until no pink remains in meat.

Add walnuts and cabbage. Stir-fry 4 minutes to wilt cabbage.

Add next 8 ingredients along with onion mixture. Stir-fry for 5 minutes.

Mix cornstarch with water in small cup. Add and stir until thickened and glazed. Makes 6 1/2 cups (1.5 L).

1 cup (250 mL): 390 Calories; 24 g Total Fat (7 g Mono, 12 g Poly, 2.5 g Sat); 55 mg Cholesterol; 21 g Carbohydrate; 5 g Fibre; 26 g Protein; 1240 mg Sodium

Chicken Stir-fry

Serve this colourful dish with noodles or rice for a full meal.

Cooking oil	2 tbsp.	30 mL
Chicken breasts, halved, skin and bones removed, slivered or cubed	2	2
Medium onion, sliced in thin rings	1	1
Thinly sliced carrot coins	1 cup	250 mL
Thinly sliced celery	1/2 cup	125 mL
Coarsely chopped fresh mushrooms	1 cup	250 mL
Medium zucchini, with peel, slivered or cubed	2	2
Water	2 tbsp.	30 mL
Snow peas, fresh or frozen, thawed	6 oz.	170 g
Green pepper, seeded and slivered	1	1
Fresh grated ginger (or 1/4 tsp., 1 mL, powdered)	1 tsp.	5 mL
Green onions, sliced	2	2
Cornstarch	2 tsp.	10 mL
Soy sauce	2 tsp.	10 mL
Sherry (or alcohol-free sherry)	2 tbsp.	30 mL
Salt	1/2 tsp.	2 mL
Cayenne pepper	1/8 tsp.	0.5 mL

Heat cooking oil in wok or large frying pan. Add chicken. Stir-fry until no pink remains. Turn into bowl.

Add next 6 ingredients to wok. Cover. Steam about 5 minutes until tender crisp.

Add peas, green pepper, ginger and onions. Stir-fry about 5 minutes to soften. Add chicken. Heat through.

Mix cornstarch, soy sauce, sherry, salt and cayenne pepper together. Stir into chicken and vegetable mixture to thicken and coat. Makes 6 1/2 cups (1.5 L).

1 cup (250 mL): 200 Calories; 7 g Total Fat (3 g Mono, 1.5 g Poly, 1 g Sat); 55 mg Cholesterol; 12 g Carbohydrate; 2 g Fibre; 22 g Protein; 860 mg Sodium

 tip If you don't have a mortar and pestle, crush aniseed or caraway on a cutting board using the flat side of a chef's knife.

Chicken Risotto

This risotto makes leftovers sublime!

Prepared chicken broth	5 cups	1.25 L
Cooking oil	2 tbsp.	30 mL
Chopped onion	1 cup	250 mL
Garlic clove, minced (or 1/4 tsp., 1 mL, powder)	1	1
Mild Italian sausage, casing removed, cut into 1/2 inch (12 mm) pieces	1	1
Bay leaf	1	1
Dried thyme	1/2 tsp.	2 mL
Arborio rice	1 1/4 cups	300 mL
Dry (or alcohol-free) white wine	1/2 cup	125 mL
Chopped cooked chicken (see Tip, page 58)	2 cups	500 mL
Frozen Brussels sprouts, thawed and halved	1 1/2 cups	375 mL
Grated Parmesan cheese	1/3 cup	75 mL
Butter (or hard margarine)	2 tbsp.	30 mL

Measure broth into medium saucepan. Bring to a boil. Reduce heat to low. Cover to keep hot.

Heat cooking oil in large saucepan on medium. Add onion and garlic. Cook, uncovered, for about 2 minutes, stirring often, until onion starts to soften.

Add next 3 ingredients. Scramble-fry (see Note) for 5 to 10 minutes until onion is softened and sausage is no longer pink.

Add rice to sausage mixture. Cook and stir for about 2 minutes until rice is transparent. Add wine. Cook, stirring constantly, until wine is almost absorbed. Add 1 cup (250 mL) hot broth, stirring constantly, until broth is absorbed. Repeat with remaining broth, 1 cup (250 mL) at a time, until broth is absorbed and rice is tender. Entire process will take about 25 minutes. Discard bay leaf.

Add remaining 4 ingredients. Cook and stir for about 2 minutes until heated through. Serve immediately. Makes about 6 cups (1.5 L).

1 cup (250 mL): 359 Calories; 16.7 g Total Fat (6.9 g Mono, 2.7 g Poly, 6.0 g Sat); 73 mg Cholesterol; 21 g Carbohydrate; 2 g Fibre; 26 g Protein; 968 mg Sodium

Note: While stirring be careful not to break up the bay leaf.

Shrimpy Chicken and Rice

This combination is excellent over rice and equally good over noodles.

Long grain rice	1 1/2 cups	375 mL
Boiling water	3 cups	750 mL
Salt	1/2 tsp.	2 mL
SHRIMP SAUCE		
Butter (or hard margarine)	4 tbsp.	60 mL
Sliced fresh mushrooms	2 cups	500 mL
Finely chopped onion	3 tbsp.	45 mL
All-purpose flour	1/4 cup	60 mL
Evaporated skim milk (or half and half)	13 1/2 oz.	385 mL
Milk	2/3 cup	150 mL
Cooked shrimp (or 4 oz., 114 g, can)	1 cup	250 mL
Coarsely chopped cooked chicken (see Tip, page 58)	2 cups	500 mL
Chopped chives	2 tbsp.	30 mL
Sherry (or alcohol-free sherry)	2 tbsp.	30 mL
Chopped pimiento	2 tbsp.	30 mL

Cook rice in boiling water and salt about 15 minutes until tender and water is absorbed.

Shrimp Sauce: Melt butter in frying pan. Add mushrooms and onion. Sauté until soft.

Mix in flour. Stir in both milks until it boils and thickens.

Add shrimp, chicken and chives. Stir. Heat through.

Stir in sherry and pimiento. Serve over rice. Makes 4 cups (1 L).

1 cup (250 mL): 430 Calories; 13 g Total Fat (3.5 g Mono, 1.5 g Poly, 6 g Sat); 93 mg Cholesterol; 52 g Carbohydrate; <1 g Fibre; 23 g Protein; 240 mg Sodium

Sesame Chicken Stir-fry

When your family comes home to roost, serve them this impressive-looking dish. The subtle sesame sauce will really give them something to crow about!

Prepared chicken broth	1/3 cup	75 mL
Cornstarch	2 tsp.	10 mL
Soy sauce	1 tbsp.	15 mL
Sesame seeds, toasted (see Tip, page 22)	1 tbsp.	15 mL
Brown sugar, packed	2 tsp.	10 mL
Sesame oil (optional)	1/2 tsp.	2 mL

(continued on next page)

Peanut (or cooking) oil	2 tbsp.	30 mL
Boneless, skinless chicken thighs, cut into 3/4 inch (2 cm) pieces	1 lb.	454 g
Sliced leek (white part only)	2 cups	500 mL
Julienned carrot (see Tip, page 86)	1 cup	250 mL
Garlic cloves, minced (or 1/2 tsp., 2 mL, powder)	2	2

Stir broth into cornstarch in small cup. Add next 4 ingredients. Stir. Set aside.

Heat wok or large frying pan on medium-high until very hot. Add peanut oil. Add chicken. Stir-fry for about 4 minutes until no longer pink. Remove with slotted spoon to plate, leaving any excess oil in wok. Cover to keep warm.

Add remaining 3 ingredients to hot wok. Stir-fry for 2 to 3 minutes until tender-crisp. Add chicken. Stir cornstarch mixture. Add to chicken mixture. Heat and stir for 1 to 2 minutes until boiling and thickened. Serves 4.

1 serving: 301 Calories; 16.5 g Total Fat (6.7 g Mono, 4.8 g Poly, 3.5 g Sat); 76 mg Cholesterol; 15 g Carbohydrate; 2 g Fibre; 23 g Protein; 492 mg Sodium

Pictured on page 233.

Pineapple Chicken Bliss

Find your bliss in this saucy pineapple and coconut treat that has just enough heat to keep you reaching for the water glass. Serve over a bed of hot jasmine rice.

Cooking oil	1 tsp.	5 mL
Boneless, skinless chicken breast halves, cut into 2 inch (5 cm) pieces	1 1/2 lbs.	680 g
Can of coconut milk (14 oz., 398 mL)	1	1
Can of crushed pineapple (14 oz., 398 mL), drained	1	1
Chili sauce	1/2 cup	125 mL
Finely diced Thai hot chili pepper, (see Tip, page 166), or 1/8 tsp., 0.5 mL, cayenne pepper	1/4 tsp.	1 mL
Salt	1/4 tsp.	1 mL
Chopped fresh cilantro or parsley	3 tbsp.	45 mL

Heat cooking oil in large frying pan on medium-high. Add chicken. Cook for about 5 minutes, stirring occasionally, until browned.

Add next 5 ingredients. Stir. Reduce heat to medium. Boil gently, uncovered, for about 15 minutes, stirring occasionally, until sauce is thickened and chicken is no longer pink inside. Sprinkle with cilantro. Makes about 4 cups (1 L).

1 cup (250 mL): 468 Calories; 25.4 g Total Fat (2.3 g Mono, 1.3 g Poly, 19.6 g Sat); 99 mg Cholesterol; 21 g Carbohydrate; 2 g Fibre; 42 g Protein; 265 mg Sodium

Pictured on page 143.

Kung Pao Chicken

Kung-Pow! This spicy Szechuan dish will hit your taste buds where it counts. Want a little less wow in your pow? Adjust the number of chilies to your preferred heat level.

Water	2 tbsp.	30 mL
Cornstarch	1 tbsp.	15 mL
Hoisin sauce	1 tbsp.	15 mL
Soy sauce	1 tbsp.	15 mL
Chili paste (sambal oelek)	1 tsp.	2 mL
Soy sauce	1 tbsp.	15 mL
Cornstarch	1 tbsp.	15 mL
Boneless, skinless chicken breast halves (or thighs), diced	1 lb.	454 g
Sesame oil	1 tsp.	5 mL
Egg white (large), fork-beaten	1	1
Garlic clove, minced (or 1/4 tsp., 1 mL, powder)	1	1
Cooking oil	1 tbsp.	15 mL
Small carrots, thinly sliced	2	2
Garlic clove, minced (or 1/4 tsp., 1 mL, powder)	1	1
Finely grated ginger root (or 1/8 tsp., 0.5 mL, ground ginger)	1/2 tsp.	2 mL
Diced green pepper	1/2 cup	125 mL
Diced red pepper	1/2 cup	125 mL
Green onions, cut into 1 inch (2.5 cm) pieces	3	3
Fresh small red chilies (see Tip, page 166), optional	3	3
Cooking oil	1 tbsp.	15 mL

Chopped salted peanuts, for garnish

Combine first 5 ingredients in small cup. Set aside.

Stir second amount of soy sauce into second amount of cornstarch in medium bowl.

Add next 4 ingredients. Stir well. Set aside.

Heat wok or large frying pan on medium-high until very hot. Add first amount of cooking oil. Add next 3 ingredients. Stir-fry for 1 minute.

Add next 4 ingredients. Stir-fry for 1 to 2 minutes until peppers are tender-crisp. Transfer to separate medium bowl. Cover to keep warm.

(continued on next page)

Add second amount of cooking oil to hot wok. Add chicken mixture. Stir-fry for about 3 minutes until chicken is no longer pink. Stir hoisin sauce mixture. Add to chicken mixture. Heat and stir until boiling and thickened. Add pepper mixture. Heat and stir until peppers are coated and heated through.

Garnish with peanuts. Serves 4.

1 serving: 249 Calories; 10.1 g Total Fat (4.9 g Mono, 3.0 g Poly, 1.2 g Sat); 66 mg Cholesterol; 11 g Carbohydrate; 1 g Fibre; 28 g Protein; 811 mg Sodium

------

Chicken Marrakesh

Experience a taste of Morocco with this earthy and warm chicken and couscous dinner.

Olive (or cooking) oil	1 tbsp.	15 mL
Boneless, skinless chicken breast halves, cut into 1/4 inch (6 mm) slices	1 lb.	454 g
Salt	1/2 tsp.	2 mL
Pepper	1/8 tsp.	0.5 mL
Chopped red pepper	1 1/2 cups	375 mL
Sliced green onion	1/4 cup	60 mL
Ground cumin	1 1/2 tsp.	7 mL
Ground cinnamon	1/2 tsp.	2 mL
Ground ginger	1/2 tsp.	2 mL
Salt	1/2 tsp.	2 mL
Cayenne pepper	1/8 tsp.	0.5 mL
Water	1 3/4 cups	425 mL
Dried apricots, chopped	1/2 cup	125 mL
Orange juice	1/2 cup	125 mL
Couscous	1 cup	250 mL
Sliced almonds, toasted (see Tip, page 22)	1/4 cup	60 mL

Heat large frying pan or wok on medium-high until very hot. Add olive oil. Add chicken. Sprinkle with first amount of salt and pepper. Stir-fry for about 5 minutes until chicken is no longer pink inside. Transfer to plate. Cover to keep warm.

Add next 7 ingredients to same frying pan. Stir-fry for about 2 minutes until red pepper starts to soften.

Add next 3 ingredients. Stir. Bring to a boil.

Add couscous. Stir. Remove from heat. Let stand, covered, for 5 minutes. Fluff with fork. Add chicken. Stir.

Sprinkle with almonds. Makes about 5 1/2 cups (1.4 L).

1 cup (250 mL): 266 Calories; 6.8 g Total Fat (3.7 g Mono, 1.3 g Poly, 0.9 g Sat); 48 mg Cholesterol; 30 g Carbohydrate; 3 g Fibre; 24 g Protein; 487 mg Sodium

Pictured on page 269.

Uptown Asparagus Chicken

We know you can forget all your troubles, forget all your cares downtown, but when it comes to chicken, things will be great uptown. The delightful presentation and the combination of havarti, asparagus and ham over lemon-peppered chicken is well worth the change of location.

Fresh asparagus, trimmed of tough ends	1 lb.	454 g
Boneless, skinless chicken breast halves (about 4 oz., 113 g, each)	4	4
Cooking oil	1 tbsp.	15 mL
Lemon pepper	1/2 tsp.	2 mL
Thin deli ham slices (about 4 oz., 113 g)	4	4
Roasted red peppers, drained and blotted dry, cut into strips	1/2 cup	125 mL
Slices of havarti cheese, cut diagonally into triangles (about 4 oz., 113 g)	4	4

Blanch asparagus in boiling salted water in medium frying pan for about 2 minutes until bright green. Drain. Immediately plunge into ice water in large bowl. Let stand for 5 minutes. Drain well.

Place 1 chicken breast between 2 sheets of plastic wrap. Pound with mallet or rolling pin to 1/2 inch (12 mm) thickness. Transfer to greased baking sheet with sides. Repeat with remaining chicken. Brush chicken with cooking oil. Sprinkle with lemon pepper. Broil on top rack in oven for about 7 minutes until golden brown and internal temperature reaches 170°F (77°C).

Place 1 slice of ham, folding if necessary, on each chicken breast. Place 3 or 4 asparagus spears over ham. Arrange red pepper strips over asparagus. Overlap 2 triangles of cheese over red pepper. Broil for about 2 minutes until cheese is melted and bubbling. Serves 4.

1 serving: 362 Calories; 14.9 g Total Fat (2.5 g Mono, 1.5 g Poly, 6.9 g Sat); 104 mg Cholesterol; 12 g Carbohydrate; 2 g Fibre; 42 g Protein; 973 mg Sodium

Pictured on page 90.

 tip To make dry bread crumbs, remove the crusts from slices of stale or two-day-old bread. Leave the bread on the counter for a day or two until it's dry, or, if you're in a hurry, set the bread slices on a baking sheet and bake in a 200°F (95°C) oven, turning occasionally, until dry. Break the bread into pieces and process until crumbs reach the desired fineness. One slice of bread will make about 1/4 cup (60 mL) fine dry bread crumbs. Freeze extra bread crumbs in an airtight container or in a resealable freezer bag.

Spring Chicken Pot Pie

Using only a top crust for this hearty pot pie cuts way back on fat and calories.
To make this recipe gluten-free, use gluten-free chicken broth.

Canola oil	2 tsp.	10 mL
Boneless, skinless chicken breast halves, cut into 3/4 inch (2 cm) pieces	3/4 lb.	340 g
Sliced leek (white part only)	1 1/2 cups	375 mL
Diced unpeeled potato	1 cup	250 mL
Garlic cloves, minced (or 1/2 tsp., 2 mL, powder)	2	2
Salt	1/8 tsp.	0.5 mL
Pepper	1/4 tsp.	1 mL
Prepared chicken broth	1 1/2 cups	375 mL
Cornstarch	2 tbsp.	30 mL
Chopped trimmed asparagus	1 cup	250 mL
Frozen peas, thawed	1 cup	250 mL
Prepared chicken broth	3 cups	750 mL
Yellow cornmeal	1 cup	250 mL
Chopped green onion (green part only)	1 tbsp.	15 mL
Chopped fresh dill (or 3/4 tsp., 4 mL, dried)	1 tbsp.	15 mL

Heat canola oil in large saucepan on medium. Add next 6 ingredients. Cook for about 10 minutes, stirring often, until chicken is no longer pink and potato is tender.

Stir first amount of broth into cornstarch in small bowl. Add to chicken mixture. Bring to a boil. Cook for 2 minutes, stirring occasionally.

Add asparagus and peas. Stir. Transfer to greased 8 x 8 inch (20 x 20 cm) baking dish.

Bring second amount of broth to a boil in medium saucepan. Add cornmeal. Heat and stir for about 5 minutes until mixture thickens and pulls away from side of pan. Stir in green onion and dill. Pour evenly over chicken mixture. Bake in 375°F (190°C) oven for about 35 minutes until bubbling and topping is set. Serves 4.

1 serving: 378 Calories; 3.5 g Total Fat (1.5 g Mono, 1 g Poly, 0.5 g Sat); 49 mg Cholesterol; 57 g Carbohydrate; 5 g Fibre; 26 g Protein; 806 mg Sodium

Lemon Basil Chicken Rolls

Roll out the red carpet in honour of these exquisite chicken rolls. Your guests will think you've been slaving in the kitchen all day—even though the rolls are actually quite simple to make!

Fine dry bread crumbs	1/4 cup	60 mL
Basil pesto	2 tbsp.	30 mL
Grated lemon zest	1 tsp.	5 mL
Boneless, skinless chicken breast halves (about 4 oz., 113 g, each)	4	4
Large egg	1	1
Water	1 tbsp.	15 mL
Fine dry bread crumbs	3/4 cup	175 mL
Paprika	1 tsp.	5 mL
Salt	1/2 tsp.	2 mL
Pepper	1/4 tsp.	1 mL

Chopped fresh basil, for garnish

Combine first 3 ingredients in small cup.

Place 1 chicken breast between 2 sheets of plastic wrap. Pound with mallet or rolling pin to 1/2 inch (12 mm) thickness. Spread pesto mixture over chicken, leaving about 1/2 inch (12 mm) edge. Roll up tightly, jelly-roll style. Secure with wooden pick. Repeat with remaining chicken and pesto mixture.

Beat egg and water with fork in small bowl.

Combine next 4 ingredients in small shallow dish. Dip chicken rolls into egg mixture. Press into crumb mixture until coated. Place on greased baking sheet with sides. Discard any remaining egg and crumb mixtures. Bake in 400°F (200°C) oven for 25 to 30 minutes until fully cooked and internal temperature reaches 170°F (77°C). Remove wooden picks. Slice rolls in half diagonally to serve.

Garnish with basil. Makes 4 rolls.

1 roll: 268 Calories; 7.9 g Total Fat (1.4 g Mono, 0.8 g Poly, 1.7 g Sat); 103 mg Cholesterol; 16 g Carbohydrate; 1 g Fibre; 31 g Protein; 506 mg Sodium

Pictured on page 90.

Chicken Spinach Rolls

Presentation is everything, and these divine rolls are perfect for serving to company. Plus, they're delicious.

MARINARA SAUCE

Olive oil	2 tbsp.	30 mL
Chopped onion	1 cup	250 mL
Garlic clove, minced	2	2
Canned tomatoes (28 oz., 796 mL), with juice, broken up	1	1
Sugar	1 tbsp.	15 mL
Tomato paste	5 tbsp.	75 mL
Fresh parsley, chopped	2 tbsp.	30 mL
Fresh basil, chopped	1 tbsp.	15 mL
Fresh oregano, chopped	2 tbsp.	30 mL
Salt	1/2 tsp	2 mL
Chicken breasts (about 6 oz., 170 g, each)	4	4
Baby spinach leaves, chopped	2 cups	500 mL
Mozzarella cheese, grated	1/2 cup	125 mL
Parmesan cheese, grated	4 tbsp.	60 mL

Marinara Sauce: Heat olive oil in frying pan. Add onion and garlic. Sauté until soft, about 5 minutes.

Add the next 7 ingredients. Mix together. Bring to a boil. Stir occasionally as it simmers, uncovered, for about 15 minutes. Makes about 2 2/3 cups (650 mL) sauce.

Put 1 cup of marinara sauce on the bottom of a 2 quart (2 L) baking dish. Place chicken breast in between 2 sheets of plastic wrap on cutting board. Pound with meat mallet or rolling pin until chicken is about 1/4 inch (0.6 cm) thick. Repeat with remaining chicken breasts. Mix spinach and mozzarella together. Press 1/2 cup (125 mL) of spinach mixture on each breast. Roll up tightly. Place rolls seam side down in baking dish. Cover with remaining sauce.

Cover with foil. Bake for 35 minutes in 400°F (200°C) oven. Remove foil and bake for another 10 minutes. Garnish each roll with 1 Tbsp (15 mL) parmesan. Serves 4.

1 serving: 440 Calories; 14 g Total Fat (7 g Mono, 1.5 g Poly, 4.5 g Sat); 115 mg Cholesterol; 27 g Carbohydrate; 8 g Fibre; 51 g Protein; 1270 g Sodium

Pictured on page 161.

Cordon Spinach Roll variation: Omit Marinara Sauce. Combine spinach with 1/3 cup (75 mL) grated carrot, 1/4 cup (60 mL) chopped celery and 1/4 cup (60 mL) crushed seasoned croutons. Layer chicken breasts with deli ham slices and Swiss cheese, and spread with spinach mixture. Roll up tightly. Brush with egg and roll in crushed seasoned croutons. Cook as above.

Macaroni Sausage Frittata

There's no need to give up pasta or Parmesan cheese when you use whole wheat macaroni and lighter ingredients.

Water	4 cups	1 L
Salt	1/2 tsp.	2 mL
Whole wheat elbow macaroni	1 cup	250 mL
Canola oil	1 tsp.	5 mL
Chicken sausages, cut into 1/2 inch (12 mm) pieces	4	4
Chopped onion	1/2 cup	125 mL
Cajun seasoning	1 tsp.	5 mL
Egg whites (large)	3	3
Large eggs	2	2
1% buttermilk	1/2 cup	125 mL
Grated Parmesan cheese	1/4 cup	60 mL

Combine water and salt in large saucepan. Bring to a boil. Add pasta. Boil, uncovered, for 8 to 10 minutes, stirring occasionally, until tender but firm. Drain. Return to same pot. Cover to keep warm.

Heat canola oil in large frying pan on medium. Add next 3 ingredients. Cook for about 5 minutes, stirring often, until sausage is browned. Drain. Add pasta. Stir. Spread evenly in pan.

Whisk next 3 ingredients in medium bowl. Pour over sausage mixture. Heat and stir for 5 seconds. Reduce heat to medium-low. Cook, covered, for about 5 minutes until bottom is set.

Sprinkle cheese over top. Broil on centre rack in oven for about 5 minutes until top is set and golden (see Tip, page 279). Cuts into 4 wedges.

1 wedge: 400 Calories; 21 g Total Fat (9 g Mono, 3.5 g Poly, 7 g Sat); 205 mg Cholesterol; 24 g Carbohydrate; 2 g Fibre; 28 g Protein; 1080 mg Sodium

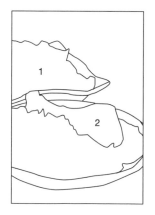

1. Chicken Divan, page 254
2. Arroz con Pollo, page 250

Chicken Tourtière

An excellent variation of this French Canadian pie.

Ground raw chicken	1 1/2 lbs.	680 g
Finely chopped onion	1 cup	250 mL
Salt	1 tsp.	5 mL
Pepper	1/4 tsp.	1 mL
Garlic powder	1/4 tsp.	1 mL
Ground sage	1/4 tsp.	1 mL
Ground allspice	1/4 tsp.	1 mL
Ground cloves	1/16 tsp.	0.5 mL
Water	1/3 cup	75 mL
Medium potatoes	3	3
Pastry for 2 crust pie		

Put first 9 ingredients into saucepan. Cook, stirring occasionally until no pink remains in meat, about 10 to 15 minutes.

Peel and quarter potatoes. Cook in boiling water until tender. Drain. Mash. Add to chicken mixture. Cool.

Roll 1/2 pastry and line 9 inch (23 cm) pie plate. Fill with chicken mixture. Roll top crust. Dampen edges and cover with crust. Crimp and trim edges. Cut slits in top. Bake in 400°F (200°C) oven for about 30 minutes until browned. Serves 6.

1 serving: 540 Calories; 27 g Total Fat (9 g Mono, 5 g Poly, 7 g Sat); 100 mg Cholesterol; 49 g Carbohydrate; 4 g Fibre; 26 g Protein; 790 mg Sodium

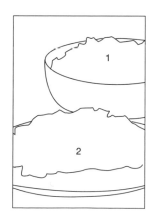

1. Chicken Supreme, page 186
2. Chicken and Greens, page 178

Savoury Chicken Pie

Each wedge is a colourful mix of cheese and vegetables.

Cooking oil	1 tbsp.	15 mL
Ground raw chicken	1/2 lb.	250 g
Salt	1/2 tsp.	2 mL
Pepper	1/4 tsp.	1 mL
Ground thyme, pinch		
Ground sage, pinch		
Cayenne pepper	1/8 tsp.	0.5 mL
Garlic powder	1/4 tsp.	1 mL
Dried oregano	1/2 tsp.	2 mL
Large eggs	2	2
Ricotta cheese	1 1/2 cups	375 mL
Grated Parmesan cheese	3/4 cup	175 mL
Package of frozen chopped spinach	1	1
(10 oz., 284 g), thawed		
and squeezed dry		
Chopped red pepper	1/4 cup	60 mL

Pastry, regular or puff, for 2 crust pie

Heat cooking oil in frying pan. Add next 8 ingredients. Scramble-fry until chicken is cooked. Remove from heat.

Combine next 5 ingredients in bowl. Mix with chicken mixture.

Roll pastry and line 9 inch (23 cm) pie plate. Pour chicken mixture into shell. Roll top crust. Dampen edges. Cover with top crust. Trim and crimp to seal. Cut slits in top. Bake on bottom rack in 400°F (200°C) oven for about 45 minutes until browned. Makes 8 servings.

1 serving: 410 Calories; 26 g Total Fat (10 g Mono, 4.5 g Poly, 9 g Sat); 100 mg Cholesterol; 23 g Carbohydrate; 3 g Fibre; 19 g Protein; 630 mg Sodium

Chicken Burritos

A big, chubby burrito loaded with chicken, beans, cheese and vegetables.

Chopped onion	1/2 cup	125 mL
Ripe tomtoes, scalded, peeled and chopped	2	2
Canned whole jalapeño pepper, finely chopped	1 tbsp.	15 mL
Ketchup	1 tbsp.	15 mL
Lemon juice	1 tbsp.	15 mL
Granulated sugar	1 tbsp.	15 mL
Diced cooked chicken (see Tip, page 58)	1 1/2 cups	375 mL
Flour tortillas (8 inch, 20 cm, diameter)	6	6
Canned refried beans	1 cup	250 mL
Grated Monterey Jack cheese	1 cup	250 mL
Grated Monterey cheese	1 cup	250 mL
Sour cream	1/2 cup	125 mL

Put first 6 ingredients into saucepan. Heat, stirring often, until it comes to a boil. Simmer, uncovered, for about 15 minutes until onion is soft and sauce thickens.

Add chicken. Stir. Cook until heated through.

Spoon beans down centre of each tortilla. Spoon chicken mixture over beans, followed by first amount of cheese. Roll up, tucking in sides as you roll. Place seam side down in 9 x 13 inch (23 x 33 cm) baking dish.

Sprinkle with second amount of cheese. Spoon sour cream accross centre. Bake, uncovered, in 350°F (175°C) oven for 30 to 45 minutes. Makes 6 servings.

1 serving: 460 Calories; 20 g Total Fat (3.5 g Mono, 1 g Poly, 10 g Sat); 70 mg Cholesterol; 41 g Carbohydrate; 4 g Fibre; 26 g Protein; 790 mg Sodium

Pictured on page 288.

Chicken Mushroom Pie

Savoury chicken filling in a flaky pastry crust. Real comfort food.

Bacon slices, diced	6	6
Chopped onion	1 1/4 cups	300 mL
Canned whole mushrooms (10 oz., 284 mL), drained	1	1
Diced cooked chicken (see Tip, page 58)	3 cups	675 mL
Parsley flakes	1 tsp.	5 mL
All-purpose flour	1 tbsp.	15 mL
Salt	1/2 tsp.	2 mL
Pepper	1/4 tsp.	1 mL
Hot water	1 cup	250 mL
Vegetable bouillon powder	1 tsp.	5 mL
Chicken bouillon powder	1 tsp.	5 mL
Package of frozen puff pastry (14 oz., 397 g), thawed	1/2	1/2

In large frying pan, stir-fry bacon and onion over medium-high heat until onion is soft. Remove to large bowl. Add next 6 ingredients. Stir well.

Mix water and bouillon powders together. Pour over contents in bowl. Stir well. Turn into 3 quart (3 L) casserole.

Roll pastry about 1 inch (2.5 cm) wider than casserole dish. Fit over chicken mixture allowing it to come up sides. Cut slits in top. Use extra bits of pastry to put cutouts on top. Bake in 400°F (200°C) oven for 35 to 40 minutes until browned. Makes 6 servings.

1 serving: 570 Calories; 44 g Total Fat (13 g Mono, 3.5 g Poly, 9 g Sat); 85 mg Cholesterol; 20 g Carbohydrate; 1 g Fibre; 21 g Protein; 600 mg Sodium

Mexican Chicken Bundles

Serve these wonderful burritos with sour cream for dipping.

Cooking oil	2 tbsp.	30 mL
Chicken breasts, halved, skin and bones removed, cut in strips	2	2
Green pepper, seeded and chopped	1	1
Red pepper, seeded and chopped	1	1
Green onions, sliced	4	4
Very finely chopped canned jalapeño pepper	1 tbsp.	15 mL

(continued on next page)

Ground coriander	1 tbsp.	15 mL
Garlic powder (or 1 clove, minced)	1/4 tsp.	1 mL
Flour tortillas	8	8
Medium tomatoes, seeded and diced	2	2
Grated medium Cheddar cheese	1 cup	250 mL
Grated medium Cheddar cheese	3/4 cup	175 mL

Heat cooking oil in large frying pan. Add next 7 ingredients. Stir-fry until no pink remains in chicken and peppers soften.

On each tortilla, spoon 1/8 mixture in a row off centre. Divide tomatoes and first amount of cheese evenly on top of chicken mixture. Roll tortillas like a jelly roll, tucking sides in as you roll. Lay seam side down on 9 x 13 inch (23 33 cm) pan.

Sprinkle with remaining cheese. Cover. Cook in 350°F (175°C) oven for 25 to 40 minutes to heat through. Serves 4.

1 serving: 680 Calories; 32 g Total Fat (13 g Mono, 3.3 g Poly, 13 g Sat); 90 mg Cholesterol; 62 g Carbohydrate; 5 g Fibre; 37 g Protein; 1180 mg Sodium

Pictured on page 288.

Chicken Quiche

An excellent way to use up leftover chicken.

Chopped cooked chicken (see Tip, page 58)	2 cups	500 mL
Unbaked 9 inch (23 cm) pie shell	1	1
Dry bread crumbs	1/4 cup	60 mL
Onion flakes	1 tbsp.	15 mL
Parsley flakes	1/2 tsp.	2 mL
Poultry seasoning	1/2 tsp.	2 mL
Celery flakes	1/4 tsp.	1 mL
Salt	1/2 tsp.	2 mL
Large eggs	2	2
All-purpose flour	3 tbsp.	45 mL
Milk	1 1/4 cups	300 mL

Scatter chicken in pie shell.

Mix next 6 ingredients in small bowl. Sprinkle over chicken.

Beat eggs until frothy. Beat in flour. Add milk. Stir. Pour over chicken. Bake on bottom rack in 350°F (175°C) oven for about 40 to 50 minutes until set. Serves 6.

1 serving: 340 Calories; 15 g Total Fat (6 g Mono, 3.5 g Poly, 4 g Sat); 110 mg Cholesterol; 27 g Carbohydrate; 2 g Fibre; 23 g Protein; 310 mg Sodium

Chicken Enchiladas

Corn tortillas are not as readily available as their wheat flour counterpart, but they are well worth seeking out.

Cooking oil	2 tbsp.	30 mL
Chicken breasts, halved, skin and bones removed, diced	4	4
Chopped onion	1 cup	250 mL
Garlic clove, minced (or 1/4 tsp., 1 mL, garlic powder)	1	1
Canned sliced mushrooms (10 oz., 284 mL), drained	1	1
Canned chopped green chilies (4 oz., 114 mL), drained	1	1
Sour cream	1 cup	250 mL
Chili powder	1 tsp.	5 mL
Ground cumin	1 tsp.	5 mL
Salt	1/2 tsp.	2 mL
Pepper	1/4 tsp.	1 mL
Cooking oil	1/2 cup	125 mL
Corn tortillas	16	16
Grated medium Cheddar cheese or Monterey Jack	2 cups	500 mL
Sour cream	2 cups	500 mL
Grated medium Cheddar cheese or Monterey Jack	2 cups	500 mL

Heat cooking oil in frying pan. Add chicken, onion and garlic. Stir-fry until no pink remains in meat.

Stir next 7 ingredients together well in bowl. Add chicken mixture.

Heat second amount of cooking oil in frying pan. Using tongs, dip each tortilla into cooking oil to soften for 3 to 5 seconds per side. Add more cooking oil if needed. Drain on paper towels. Place scant 1/4 cup (60 mL) chicken mixture in centre of each tortilla.

Add 2 tbsp. (30 mL) cheese. Roll tortilla tightly around filling. Arrange seam side down in 1 or 2 greased pans. Bake, uncovered, in 350°F (175°C) oven for 15 minutes until hot.

Spread sour cream over top. Sprinkle with cheese. Return to oven for about 5 minutes. Makes 16 enchiladas.

1 enchilada: 370 Calories; 24 g Total Fat (8 g Mono, 2 g Poly, 12 g Sat); 90 mg Cholesterol; 16 g Carbohydrate; 2 g Fibre; 25 g Protein; 710 mg Sodium

Pictured on page 288.

Fajitas

Delicious, nutritous and fun for the whole family.

Cooking oil	1 tbsp.	15 mL
Chicken breast halves, skin and bones removed, sliced in long thin strips	4	4
Spanish onion, sliced in rings	1	1
Green pepper, seeded and cut in strips (see Note)	1	1
Red pepper, seeded and cut in strips (see Note)	1	1
Salt, sprinkle		
Pepper, sprinkle		
Lemon juice	1 tbsp.	15 mL
Flour tortillas (7 inch, 18 cm), heated in covered bowl	8	8
Grated medium or sharp Cheddar cheese	1 cup	250 mL
Sour cream	1 cup	250 mL
Salsa	1 cup	250 mL
Guacamole	1 cup	250 mL

Heat cooking oil in frying pan. Add chicken. Stir-fry until cooked. Remove to bowl.

To same frying pan, add onion, green pepper, red pepper and more cooking oil, if needed. Sauté until browned. Spread on warm platter.

Return chicken to pan to heat. Sprinkle with salt and pepper. Drizzle with lemon juice. Heat quickly. Place over onion mixture.

Lay 1 tortilla on plate. Place some onion mixture down centre, then a few chicken strips on top. Top with cheese, sour cream, salsa and guacamole. Roll. Makes 8 fajitas.

Note: To make without peppers, use 2 onions.

1 fajita: 450 Calories; 22 g Total Fat (6 g Mono, 1.5 g Poly, 11 g Sat); 65 mg Cholesterol; 39 g Carbohydrate; 3 g Fibre; 25 g Protein; 1230 mg Sodium

Pictured on page 288.

Chicken Shortcake

Showy and as good as it is different.

BISCUIT LAYERS		
All-purpose flour	4 cups	900 mL
Baking powder	4 tsp.	20 mL
Salt	2 tsp.	10 mL
Cold butter (or hard margarine)	3/4 cup	175 mL
Milk	1 1/2 cups	350 mL
Butter (or hard margarine), softened	1 tbsp.	15 mL
FILLING		
Butter (or hard margarine)	2 tbsp.	30 mL
Chopped onion	3/4 cup	175 mL
Finely chopped celery	1/3 cup	75 mL
Grated carrot	1 cup	250 mL
All-purpose flour	1/3 cup	75 mL
Beef bouillon powder	1 tbsp.	15 mL
Milk	3 1/4 cups	725 mL
Chopped cooked chicken (see Tip, page 58)		
Salt	1/2 tsp.	2 mL
Pepper	1/8 tsp.	0.5 mL

Biscuit Layers: Stir flour, baking powder and salt in bowl. Cut in butter until mixture is crumbly.

Add milk. Stir to form a soft ball. Turn out onto lightly floured surface. Divide dough into 2 equal parts. Roll each part into an 8 x 8 inch (20 x 20 cm) square.

Place 1 square on ungreased baking sheet. Spread with butter. Lay second square over first square. Bake as one unit in 400°F (200°C) oven for about 20 minutes.

Filling: Melt butter in frying pan. Add onion, celery and carrot. Sauté until soft.

Mix in flour and bouillon powder. Stir in milk until it boils and thickens.

Add remaining ingredients. Stir. Heat through. Carefully split shortcake into layers. Spread about 2/3 filling over bottom layer. Cover with other layer. Spoon remaining 1/3 filling over top. Cuts into 6 pieces. Serves 6.

1 serving: 820 Calories; 36 g Total Fat (9 g Mono, 2.5 g Poly, 21 g Sat); 135 mg Cholesterol; 85 g Carbohydrate; 3 g Fibre; 36 g Protein; 2020 mg Sodium

Nacho Chicken Squares

Think of this dish as lazy tacos. Serve with your favourite salsa.

Large eggs, fork-beaten	2	2
Coarsely crushed nacho chips	1 cup	250 mL
Grated sharp Cheddar (or mozzarella) cheese	1 cup	250 mL
Can of tomato sauce (7 1/2 oz., 213 mL)	1	1
Fine dry bread crumbs	1/2 cup	125 mL
Finely chopped onion	1/2 cup	125 mL
Finely chopped jalapeño pepper (see Tip, page 166)	1 tbsp.	15 mL
Ground cumin	1 tsp.	5 mL
Salt	1 tsp.	5 mL
Pepper	1/2 tsp.	2 mL
Lean ground chicken	2 lbs.	900 g
Sour cream	1 cup	250 mL
Chopped fresh chives (or green onion)	1/3 cup	75 mL

Combine first 10 ingredients in large bowl. Add chicken. Mix well. Spread evenly in greased 9 x 13 inch (23 x 33 cm) baking pan. Bake in 375°F (190°C) oven for about 40 minutes until lightly browned and internal temperature reaches 175°F (80°C). Cut into 8 squares.

Combine sour cream and chives in small bowl. Spoon over squares. Serves 8.

1 serving: 460 Calories; 29.9 g Total Fat (3.9 g Mono, 0.9 g Poly, 7.6 g Sat); 82 mg Cholesterol; 17 g Carbohydrate; 2 g Fibre; 28 g Protein; 783 mg Sodium

 To bruise cardamom, pound the pods with a mallet, or press them with the flat side of a wide knife to "bruise," or crack them open slightly.

Chicken Sweet Potato Pie

This picadillo-inspired pie will warm you on a cool evening—the topping hides a rich layer of chicken chili and green olives. Try it with a spinach side salad.

Cooking oil	2 tsp.	10 mL
Lean ground chicken	1 lb.	454 g
Chopped fresh white mushrooms	1 cup	250 mL
Chopped onion	1 cup	250 mL
Chili powder	2 tsp.	10 mL
Garlic cloves, minced	2	2
Dried oregano	1 tsp.	5 mL
Can of tomato sauce (14 oz., 398 mL)	1	1
Chopped pecans, toasted (see Tip, page 22)	1 cup	250 mL
Sliced green olives	1 cup	250 mL
Chili sauce	1/4 cup	60 mL
Chopped peeled orange-fleshed sweet potato	1 1/2 cups	375 mL
Chopped peeled potato	1 1/2 cups	375 mL
Large egg, fork-beaten	1	1
Butter (or hard margarine)	2 tbsp.	30 mL
Ground cumin	1/4 tsp.	1 mL
Salt	1/4 tsp.	1 mL
Pepper	1/4 tsp.	1 mL
Finely chopped pecans, toasted (see Tip, page 22)	1/2 cup	125 mL

Heat cooking oil in large frying pan on medium-high. Add chicken. Scramble-fry for about 5 minutes until no longer pink. Reduce heat to medium.

Add next 5 ingredients. Cook for about 5 minutes, stirring often, until onion is softened and liquid is evaporated.

Add next 4 ingredients. Stir. Spread in greased 9 inch (23 cm) deep dish pie plate.

Pour water into large saucepan until about 1 inch (2.5 cm) deep. Add sweet potato and potato. Bring to a boil. Reduce heat to medium. Boil gently, covered, for 12 to 15 minutes until tender. Drain. Return to same pot.

Add next 5 ingredients. Mash. Add pecans. Stir. Spread over chicken mixture. Using fork, score decorative pattern on top. Bake in 375°F (190°C) oven for about 30 minutes until sweet potato mixture is firm. Cuts into 6 wedges.

1 wedge: 550 Calories; 38.3 g Total Fat (17.6 g Mono, 7.7 g Poly, 6.9 g Sat); 95 mg Cholesterol; 39 g Carbohydrate; 8 g Fibre; 19 g Protein; 1486 mg Sodium

Pictured on page 197.

Honey Garlic Crostata

Sweet and saucy chicken and vegetables crowned with golden puff pastry.

Liquid honey	1/4 cup	60 mL
Dry sherry	2 tbsp.	30 mL
Soy sauce	2 tbsp.	30 mL
Garlic cloves, minced	4	4
Dijon mustard	1 tbsp.	15 mL
Pepper	1/2 tsp.	2 mL
Sesame oil (optional)	1 tsp.	5 mL
Cooking oil	2 tsp.	10 mL
Boneless, skinless chicken breast halves, cut into 1 inch (2.5 cm) cubes	1/2 lb.	225 g
Cooking oil	2 tsp.	10 mL
Chopped onion	1 cup	250 mL
Chopped red pepper	1 cup	250 mL
Frozen mixed vegetables	1 cup	250 mL
Package of puff pastry (14 oz., 397 g), thawed according to package directions	1/2	1/2

Combine first 7 ingredients in small bowl. Set aside.

Heat first amount of cooking oil in large frying pan on medium-high. Add chicken. Cook for 2 to 3 minutes, stirring occasionally, until browned. Remove to plate. Reduce heat to medium.

Add second amount of cooking oil to same frying pan. Add onion and red pepper. Cook for 5 to 10 minutes, stirring often, until onion is golden. Add chicken and honey mixture. Stir. Cook for 3 minutes. Add frozen vegetables. Stir. Transfer to large bowl. Cool.

Roll out puff pastry on lightly floured surface to 11 inch (28 cm) diameter circle. Place on baking sheet. Spoon chicken mixture onto centre of pastry, leaving 2 inch (5 cm) edge. Fold a section of edge up and over edge of filling. Repeat with next section, allowing pastry to overlap so that a fold is created. Repeat until pastry border is completely folded around filling. Bake in 375°F (190°C) oven for 25 to 30 minutes until pastry is puffed and golden. Let stand for 5 minutes before serving. Serves 4.

1 serving: 640 Calories; 32.2 g Total Fat (17.4 g Mono, 4.0 g Poly, 7.9 g Sat); 33 mg Cholesterol; 62 g Carbohydrate; 4 g Fibre; 22 g Protein; 1272 mg Sodium

Pictured on page 72.

Fiesta Torta

A fiesta of chicken, beans, cheese and salsa sandwiched between layers of tortilla.

Cooking oil	2 tsp.	10 mL
Lean ground chicken	1 lb.	454 g
Chopped onion	1/2 cup	125 mL
Lime juice	1 tbsp.	15 mL
Ground cumin	1 tsp.	5 mL
Garlic clove, minced (or 1/4 tsp., 1 mL, powder)	1	1
Can of red kidney beans (19 oz., 540 mL), rinsed and drained	1	1
Salsa	1 cup	250 mL
Roasted red peppers, drained and blotted dry, cut into strips	1/2 cup	125 mL
Can of diced green chilies (4 oz., 113 g)	1	1
Chili powder	1 tsp.	5 mL
Flour tortillas (9 inch, 23 cm, diameter)	5	5
Grated Mexican cheese blend	3 cups	750 mL

Heat cooking oil in large frying pan on medium-high. Add chicken. Scramble-fry for about 5 minutes until no longer pink.

Add next 4 ingredients. Cook for about 5 minutes, stirring often, until onion is softened. Set aside.

Mash beans in medium bowl. Add next 4 ingredients. Stir.

To assemble, layer ingredients in greased 3 quart (3 L) round casserole as follows:

1. 1 tortilla (fold edge if necessary to fit casserole)

2. 1/2 of chicken mixture

3. 3/4 cup (175 mL) cheese

4. 1 tortilla

5. 1/2 of bean mixture

6. 1 tortilla

7. Remaining chicken mixture

8. 3/4 cup (175 mL) cheese

(continued on next page)

9. 1 tortilla

10. Remaining bean mixture

11. 1 tortilla

12. Remaining cheese

Bake, covered, in 375°F (190°C) oven for 45 minutes. Bake, uncovered, for another 20 minutes until cheese is golden. Let stand for 15 minutes before serving. Cut into wedges. Serves 8.

1 serving: 641 Calories; 49.7 g Total Fat (19.2 g Mono, 8.8 g Poly, 17.3 g Sat); 198 mg Cholesterol; 2 g Carbohydrate; trace Fibre; 44 g Protein; 1268 mg Sodium

---

Chicken Stuffing Pie

A crustless herb-flavoured pie that makes for a good lunch. Add a salad and dinner rolls.

Diced cooked chicken (see Tip, page 58)	2 cups	500 mL
Chopped green onion	1/4 cup	60 mL
Finely chopped celery	1/4 cup	60 mL
Small seasoned croutons	1 cup	250 mL
Pepper, sprinkle		
Biscuit mix	3/4 cup	175 mL
Salt	1/2 tsp.	2 mL
Ground thyme	1/4 tsp.	1 mL
Ground sage	1/4 tsp.	1 mL
Milk	1 1/4 cups	275 mL

Spread chicken in bottom of greased 9 inch (23 cm) pie plate. Sprinkle with onion, celery, croutons and pepper.

Stir biscuit mix, salt, thyme and sage together in bowl. Stir in milk. Pour over chicken mixture. Bake in 350°F (175°C) oven for 30 to 35 minutes until browned. Serves 4.

1 serving: 410 Calories; 21 g Total Fat (1 g Mono, 0 g Poly, 2 g Sat); 65 mg Cholesterol; 33 g Carbohydrate; 2 g Fibre; 21 g Protein; 980 mg Sodium

Italian Rice Cups

Let your cup runneth over—with chicken, sausage, herbs and bubbly melted cheese. Invert the cups onto a plate so you and your guests can see the luscious, golden-brown Parmesan cheese crust.

Large eggs, fork-beaten	2	2
Cooked wild rice and brown rice blend	2 cups	500 mL
Cooked millet	1 cup	250 mL
Grated Parmesan cheese	1/2 cup	125 mL
Canola oil	2 tsp.	10 mL
Lean ground chicken	3/4 lb.	340 g
Hot Italian sausage, casing removed (about 3 oz., 85 g)	1	1
Finely chopped onion	1 cup	250 mL
Finely chopped celery	1/2 cup	125 mL
Finely chopped red pepper	1/2 cup	125 mL
Tomato sauce	1/2 cup	125 mL
Chili sauce	1 tbsp.	15 mL
Garlic cloves, minced (or 1/2 tsp., 2 mL, powder)	2	2
Dried basil	1/2 tsp.	2 mL
Dried oregano	1/2 tsp.	2 mL
Grated mozzarella cheese	1 cup	250 mL

Combine first 4 ingredients in medium bowl. Set aside.

Heat canola oil in large frying pan on medium-high. Add chicken and sausage. Scramble-fry for about 5 minutes until no longer pink.

Add onion and celery. Cook for about 3 minutes, stirring often, until onion starts to soften.

Add next 6 ingredients. Stir. Cook for 1 minute. Press 1/3 cup (75 mL) rice mixture firmly into bottom and up sides of 6 well-greased 6 oz. (170 mL) custard cups or ramekins. Place about 1/2 cup (125 mL) chicken mixture in centre of each cup. Press remaining rice mixture on top of chicken mixture.

Sprinkle mozzarella cheese over top. Pour 1/2 inch (12 mm) hot water into 9 x 13 inch (23 x 33 cm) pan. Place cups in pan. Bake in 375°F (190°C) oven for 30 minutes. Transfer cups from pan to wire rack. Let stand for 5 minutes. Run knife around edges of cups to loosen. Makes 6 rice cups.

1 rice cup: 358 Calories; 22.5 g Total Fat (5.7 g Mono, 1.7 g Poly, 6.5 g Sat); 95 mg Cholesterol; 15 g Carbohydrate; 2 g Fibre; 23 g Protein; 530 mg Sodium

Pictured on page 287.

Picadillo Pastries

Packets of poultry poetry—feel free to reheat in the microwave.

Cooking oil	1 tbsp.	15 mL
Lean ground chicken	3/4 lb.	340 g
Salt	1/4 tsp.	1 mL
Chopped onion	2 cups	500 mL
Garlic clove, minced (or 1/4 tsp., 1 mL, powder)	1	1
Can of tomato sauce (7 1/2 oz., 213 mL)	1	1
Chopped pimiento-stuffed olives	1/4 cup	60 mL
Chopped raisins	1/4 cup	60 mL
Lime juice	2 tbsp.	30 mL
Finely chopped chipotle pepper in adobo sauce (see Tip, page 78)	2 tsp.	10 mL
Chili powder	1 tsp.	5 mL
Dried oregano	1/2 tsp.	2 mL
Ground cinnamon	1/4 tsp.	1 mL
PASTRY		
Biscuit mix	4 1/2 cups	1.1 L
Finely chopped black olives (optional)	1/4 cup	60 mL
Boiling water	1 1/4 cups	300 mL
Milk	2 tbsp.	30 mL

Heat cooking oil in large frying pan on medium. Add chicken and salt. Scramble fry for about 5 minutes until chicken is no longer pink.

Add onion and garlic. Cook for about 15 minutes, stirring often, until onion is browned.

Add next 8 ingredients. Cook for 1 minute, stirring constantly, to blend flavours. Remove from heat. Cool to room temperature.

Pastry: Combine biscuit mix and olives in medium bowl. Add boiling water. Stir until soft dough forms. Turn dough out onto lightly floured surface. Knead about 20 times until dough is smooth. Divide into 6 equal portions. Roll out 1 portion to form a 7 inch (18 cm) diameter circle. Place about 1/2 cup (125 mL) chicken mixture on half of circle, leaving 1/2 inch (12 mm) edge. Dampen edges of dough with water. Fold dough in half over filling. Crimp edges with fork to seal. Carefully transfer to greased baking sheet. Cut 2 small slits in top to allow steam to escape. Repeat with remaining dough portions and chicken mixture. Brush milk over pastries. Bake in 400°F (200°C) oven for about 30 minutes until golden brown. Makes 6 pastries.

1 pastry: 585 Calories; 25.0 g Total Fat (9.8 g Mono, 2.7 g Poly, 3.9 g Sat); 2 mg Cholesterol; 72 g Carbohydrate; 4 g Fibre; 19 g Protein; 1676 mg Sodium

Picture on page 72.

Chicken Chèvre Spirals

Put a whole new spin on dinner with these attractive chicken pinwheels. Make them early in the day and serve at your next dinner party.

Coarsely chopped fresh basil	1/2 cup	125 mL
Goat (chèvre) cheese	3 oz.	85 g
Sun-dried tomato pesto	1/4 cup	60 mL
Chicken breasts	4	4
Thin deli ham slices (about 3 oz., 85 g)	4	4
Balsamic vinegar	1 tbsp.	15 mL
Olive oil	1 tbsp.	15 mL

Combine first 3 ingredients in small bowl.

Place chicken breasts between 2 sheets of plastic wrap. Pound with mallet or rolling pin until flattened.

Spread pesto mixture evenly over chicken. Arrange ham slices over pesto, trimming to fit if necessary. Roll up tightly, jelly-roll style. Arrange, seam-side down, on greased baking sheet with sides.

Combine vinegar and olive oil in small cup. Brush over rolls. Bake in 350°F (175°C) oven for about 25 minutes until internal temperature reaches 70°F (77°C). Let stand for about 30 minutes until cool. Wrap in plastic wrap. Chill for at least 4 hours or overnight. Cut each roll into 1/2 inch 12 mm) slices. Makes about 24 spirals.

1 spiral: 50 Calories; 2.5 g Total Fat (0.5 g Mono, 0 g Poly, 0.7 g Sat); 15 mg Cholesterol; <1 g Carbohydrate; 0 g Fibre; 6 g Protein; 170 mg Sodium

1. Sesame Chicken Stir-fry, page 206
2. Sweet Orange Chicken, page 199

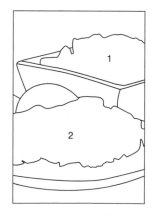

Bruschetta Chicken

An appetizer of fussy tomato-topped toasts transforms into a hearty casserole.

Chopped Roma (plum) tomato	4 cups	1 L
Chopped green onion	1 1/4 cups	300 mL
Chopped fresh basil	1/4 cup	60 mL
Garlic cloves, minced	4	4
Olive oil	1 tbsp.	15 mL
Red wine vinegar	1 1/2 tsp.	7 mL
Salt	1/2 tsp.	2 mL
Water	8 cups	2 L
Salt	1 tsp.	5 mL
Penne pasta	2 cups	500 mL
Boneless, skinless chicken thighs (about 3 oz., 85 g, each)	8	8
Box of chicken stove-top stuffing mix (4 1/4 oz., 120 g)	1	1
Grated Italian cheese blend	1 cup	250 mL

Combine first 7 ingredients in large bowl. Let stand, covered, for 30 minutes.

Combine water and salt in large saucepan. Bring to a boil. Add pasta. Boil, uncovered, for 10 minutes, stirring occasionally. Drain. Transfer to greased 9 x 13 inch (23 x 33 cm) baking dish.

Arrange chicken thighs over pasta in single layer.

Add stuffing mix to tomato mixture. Stir until moistened. Scatter over chicken. Sprinkle with cheese. Bake, covered, in 375°F (190°C) oven for 30 minutes. Bake, uncovered, for about 30 minutes until browned. Serves 4.

1 serving: 760 Calories; 28.0 g Total Fat (7.5 g Mono, 3.7 g Poly, 8.2 g Sat); 132 mg Cholesterol; 75 g Carbohydrate; 6 g Fibre; 50 g Protein; 1101 mg Sodium

Pictured on page 179.

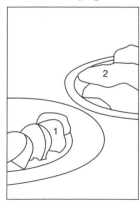

1. Stuffed Breasts of Chicken, page 282
2. Chicken Parmesan, page 279

Spinach Chicken Lasagna

With lots of sauce, rich flavours and a tempting appearance,
this dish is sure to best its beef brother.

Water	16 cups	4 L
Salt	2 tsp.	10 mL
Spinach lasagna noodles	12	12
Cooking oil	1 1/2 tbsp.	25 mL
Boneless, skinless chicken breast halves, chopped	1 3/4 lbs.	790 g
Sliced fresh white mushrooms	2 cups	500 mL
Chopped onion	1 1/2 cups	375 mL
Chopped red pepper	1 1/2 cups	375 mL
Garlic cloves, minced (or 1/2 tsp., 2 mL, powder)	2	2
Tomato pasta sauce	4 cups	1 L
Chopped fresh spinach leaves, lightly packed	2 cups	500 mL
Can of diced tomatoes (14 oz., 398 mL), with juice	1	1
Dried oregano	2 tsp.	10 mL
Dried basil	1 tsp.	5 mL
Salt	1/4 tsp.	1 mL
Pepper	1/8 tsp.	0.5 mL
Cayenne pepper (optional)	1/4 tsp.	1 mL
2% cottage cheese	1 1/2 cups	375 mL
Crumbled feta cheese	1/2 cup	125 mL
Grated Parmesan cheese	1/3 cup	75 mL
Dried thyme	1/2 tsp.	2 mL
Pepper	1/2 tsp.	2 mL
Dried rosemary, crushed	1/4 tsp.	1 mL
Grated mozzarella and Cheddar cheese blend	2 cups	500 mL
Parsley flakes	2 tsp.	10 mL

Combine water and salt in Dutch oven or large pot. Bring to a boil. Add noodles. Boil, uncovered, for 12 to 14 minutes, stirring occasionally, until tender but firm. Drain. Rinse with cold water. Drain well. Set aside.

(continued on next page)

Oven Ovations

Heat cooking oil in same pot on medium-high. Add chicken. Cook for 8 to 10 minutes, stirring occasionally, until no longer pink. Remove to plate. Reduce heat to medium.

Add next 4 ingredients to same pot. Cook for about 10 minutes, stirring often, until onion is softened.

Add next 8 ingredients and chicken. Stir. Simmer, covered, for 10 minutes, stirring occasionally, to blend flavours. Remove from heat. Set aside.

Combine next 6 ingredients in medium bowl.

To assemble, layer ingredients in greased 9 x 13 inch (23 x 33 cm) baking pan as follows:

1. 1 cup (250 mL) chicken mixture

2. 3 lasagna noodles

3. 3 cups (750 mL) chicken mixture

4. 3 lasagna noodles

5. Cottage cheese mixture

6. 3 lasagna noodles

7. 3 cups (750 mL) chicken mixture

8. 3 lasagna noodles

9. Remaining chicken mixture

Combine cheese blend and parsley in medium bowl. Sprinkle over top. Cover with greased foil. Bake in 350°F (175°F) oven for 60 minutes. Remove foil. Bake for another 30 minutes until cheese is bubbling and starting to turn golden. Let stand for 10 minutes before serving. Serves 8.

1 serving: 574 Calories; 22.8 g Total Fat (5.2 g Mono, 1.6 g Poly, 9.8 g Sat); 99 mg Cholesterol; 46.9 g Carbohydrate; 11 g Fibre; 48 g Protein; 1325 mg Sodium

Pictured on page 89.

Chicken Feta Pizzas

Go ultra-thin for this pizza by using a tortilla as a base. Serve as a light meal or slice into wedges for a great starter.

Olive (or cooking) oil	1 tsp.	5 mL
Lean ground chicken	1/2 lb.	225 g
Garlic clove, minced	1	1
(or 1/4 tsp., 1 mL, powder)		
Dried oregano	1/4 tsp.	1 mL
Ground cinnamon, just a pinch		
Salt	1/8 tsp.	0.5 mL
Pepper, just a pinch		
Flour tortillas (9 inch, 23 cm, diameter)	2	2
Tomato sauce	1/4 cup	60 mL
Small green pepper, cut into thin rings	1	1
Crumbled feta cheese	1/2 cup	125 mL

Preheat oven to 475°F (240°C). Heat olive oil in large frying pan on medium-high. Add next 6 ingredients. Scramble-fry for about 6 minutes until chicken is browned and no longer pink.

Arrange tortillas on greased baking sheet with sides. Spread tomato sauce over each tortilla, almost to edge. Scatter chicken mixture over top. Arrange green pepper over chicken. Sprinkle with cheese. Cook on bottom rack in oven for about 7 minutes until edges are browned. Makes 2 pizzas.

1 pizza: 520 Calories; 23 g Total Fat (6 g Mono, 1.5 g Poly, 9 g Sat); 135 mg Cholesterol; 46 g Carbohydrate; 3 g Fibre; 32 g Protein; 1030 mg Sodium

Chicken Porcini Risotto

Risotto is so delicious, but really, who has time for all that stirring? This recipe uses an easy oven method that makes it possible to enjoy a delicious risotto any time. Serve with a squeeze of lemon for a fresh burst of flavour.

Prepared chicken broth	2 1/2 cups	625 mL
Dry (or alcohol-free) white wine	1/2 cup	125 mL
Package of dried porcini mushrooms	1	1
(1/2 oz., 14 g)		
Arborio rice	1 cup	250 mL
Finely chopped onion	1/2 cup	125 mL
Garlic cloves, minced (or 1/2 tsp., 2 mL, powder)	2	2
Olive oil	2 tsp.	10 mL
Pepper	1/4 tsp.	1 mL

(continued on next page)

Oven Ovations

Chopped cooked chicken (see Tip, page 58)	2 cups	500 mL
Finely chopped red pepper	1/2 cup	125 mL
Grated Parmesan cheese	1/2 cup	125 mL
Chopped fresh parsley (or 3/4 tsp., 4 mL, flakes)	1 tbsp.	15 mL

Bring broth and wine to a boil in medium saucepan. Add mushrooms. Stir. Remove from heat. Let stand, covered, for 10 minutes. Remove mushrooms to cutting board with slotted spoon. Chop. Strain liquid through fine sieve into small bowl. Discard solids.

Combine next 5 ingredients in greased shallow 2 quart (2 L) casserole. Add broth mixture. Stir. Bake, covered, in 400°F (200°C) oven for about 30 minutes until rice is tender and liquid is almost absorbed.

Add chicken, red pepper and mushrooms. Stir. Bake, covered, for about 5 minutes until peppers are tender-crisp and mixture is heated through.

Add cheese and parsley. Stir. Makes about 8 cups (2 L).

1 cup (250 mL): 210 Calories; 5.0 g Total Fat (2.0 g Mono, 1.0 g Poly, 1.5 g Sat); 35 mg Cholesterol; 22 g Carbohydrate; 1 g Fibre; 14 g Protein; 280 mg Sodium

---

Springtime Chicken Pizza

This cheesy chicken pizza, topped with lots of veggies, is destined to become a year-round favourite.

Prebaked pizza crust (12 inch, 30 cm, diameter)	1	1
Pizza sauce	1/3 cup	75 mL
Grated Parmesan cheese	1/2 cup	125 mL
Chopped cooked chicken	1 1/2 cups	375 mL
Roasted red peppers, drained, blotted dry, cut into strips	1/3 cup	75 mL
Fresh asparagus spears, trimmed of tough ends	8	8
Goat (chèvre) cheese, cut up	2/3 cup	150 mL

Preheat oven to 475°F (240°C). Place pizza crust on greased 12 inch (30 cm) pizza pan. Spread pizza sauce evenly on crust. Sprinkle with Parmesan cheese.

Scatter chicken and red pepper over Parmesan cheese.

Arrange asparagus spears in spoke pattern on top of red pepper. Scatter goat cheese over top. Bake for about 15 minutes until crust is crisp and golden. Cuts into 8 wedges.

1 wedge: 246 Calories; 10.5 g Total Fat (2.7 g Mono, 0.8 g Poly, 5.2 g Sat); 43 mg Cholesterol; 19 g Carbohydrate; 1 g Fibre; 18 g Protein; 455 mg Sodium

Chicken Paella

Saffron, though a tad pricey, gives this dish an authentic taste and look.

Cooking oil	1 tsp.	5 mL
Boneless, skinless chicken thighs (about 3 oz., 85 g, each)	8	8
Chicken (or turkey) sausages, halved (about 6 1/2 oz., 184 g)	6	6
Chopped onion	1 cup	250 mL
Sliced red pepper	3/4 cup	175 mL
Sliced green pepper	1/2 cup	125 mL
Jalapeño pepper, finely diced (see Tip, page 166)	1	1
Garlic clove, minced (or 1/4 tsp., 1 mL, powder)	1	1
Can of diced tomatoes (14 oz., 398 mL), with juice	1	1
Dry (or alcohol-free) white wine	1/2 cup	125 mL
Dried thyme	1 tsp.	5 mL
Paprika	1/2 tsp.	2 mL
Long grain white rice	1 1/4 cups	300 mL
Saffron threads (or turmeric)	1/8 tsp.	0.5 mL
Prepared chicken broth	1 1/2 cups	375 mL
Frozen peas	2 cups	500 mL
Can of artichoke hearts (14 oz., 398 mL), drained and quartered	1	1
Frozen, uncooked large shrimp (peeled and deveined), thawed	1/2 lb.	225 g

Heat cooking oil in large frying pan on medium. Add chicken. Cook for 3 to 4 minutes per side until browned. Transfer to 4 quart (4 L) casserole.

Add sausage to same frying pan. Cook for 5 to 10 minutes, turning occasionally, until browned on all sides. Transfer to casserole. Arrange chicken and sausage evenly in bottom of casserole. Drain and discard all but 2 tsp. (10 mL) drippings from frying pan.

Add next 5 ingredients. Cook for about 5 minutes, stirring occasionally, until vegetables are tender-crisp.

(continued on next page)

Add next 4 ingredients. Bring to a boil. Reduce heat to medium. Cook for about 5 minutes, stirring occasionally and scraping any brown bits from bottom of pan, until thickened.

Add rice and saffron. Stir until rice is coated. Add broth. Bring to a boil. Remove from heat. Spoon rice mixture around chicken and sausage in casserole. Bake, covered, in 375°F (190°C) oven for 45 minutes.

Scatter remaining 3 ingredients over rice mixture. Bake, covered, for another 15 minutes until artichokes and peas are heated through and shrimp are pink and curled. Serves 8.

1 serving: 398 Calories; 11.5 g Total Fat (4.1 g Mono, 2.5 g Poly, 3.8 g Sat); 116 mg Cholesterol; 39 g Carbohydrate; 5 g Fibre; 33 g Protein; 480 mg Sodium

Pictured on page 71.

Mushroom Swiss Strata

A smart Swiss miss will tell you that grated Swiss cheese gives a chicken casserole an unexpected flavour twist.

Cooking oil	1 tbsp.	15 mL
Lean ground chicken	1 lb.	454 g
Sliced fresh white mushrooms	4 cups	1 L
Chopped onion	1 cup	250 mL
Diced whole wheat (or white) bread	6 cups	1.5 L
Large eggs	6	6
Milk	2 cups	500 mL
Dijon mustard	1 tbsp.	15 mL
Parsley flakes	1 tbsp.	15 mL
Salt	1/4 tsp.	1 mL
Pepper	1/4 tsp.	1 mL
Grated Swiss cheese	2 cups	500 mL

Heat cooking oil in large frying pan on medium-high. Add chicken. Scramble-fry for 5 minutes.

Add mushrooms and onion. Cook for about 10 minutes, stirring often, until onion is softened and mushrooms are lightly browned.

Place 2 cups (500 mL) diced bread in greased 3 quart (3 L) round casserole. Spread 1 cup (250 mL) chicken mixture over top. Repeat layers with remaining bread and chicken mixture.

Whisk next 6 ingredients in medium bowl until smooth. Pour over top.

Sprinkle with cheese. Press down lightly. Bake, uncovered, in 350°F (175°C) oven for about 50 minutes until puffed and golden. Let stand for 10 minutes before serving. Cut into wedges. Serves 8.

1 serving: 389 Calories; 22.4 g Total Fat (5.2 g Mono, 1.7 g Poly, 6.7 g Sat); 167 mg Cholesterol; 20 g Carbohydrate; 2 g Fibre; 28 g Protein; 402 mg Sodium

Coconut Curry Casserole

Creamy, dreamy and loaded with sweet coconut and curry flavours, consider this dish to be la crème de la crème *of casseroles.*

Large egg, fork-beaten	1	1
Cooked long grain white rice (about 1 cup, 250 mL, uncooked), see Note	3 cups	750 mL
Crushed unsalted peanuts	1/4 cup	60 mL
Salt	1/2 tsp.	2 mL
Pepper	1/2 tsp.	2 mL
Brown sugar, packed	3 tbsp.	45 mL
All-purpose flour	1 tbsp.	15 mL
Can of coconut milk (14 oz., 398 mL)	1	1
Soy sauce	3 tbsp.	45 mL
Lime juice	2 tbsp.	30 mL
Red curry paste	1/2 tsp.	2 mL
Cooking oil	1 tbsp.	15 mL
Boneless, skinless chicken breast halves, cut into 1 inch (2.5 cm) cubes	1 lb.	454 g
Can of cut baby corn (14 oz., 398 mL), drained	1	1
Chopped fresh asparagus, trimmed of tough ends	1 cup	250 mL
Chopped red pepper	1 cup	250 mL

Combine first 5 ingredients in large bowl. Press rice mixture evenly into bottom of greased 2 quart (2 L) shallow baking dish. Bake in 350°F (175°C) oven for about 15 minutes until golden. Set aside.

Combine brown sugar and flour in medium bowl. Add next 4 ingredients. Stir until smooth.

Heat cooking oil in large frying pan on medium-high. Add chicken. Cook for about 5 minutes, stirring occasionally, until browned. Remove to small bowl. Reduce heat to medium. Add coconut milk mixture. Heat and stir for about 3 minutes until boiling and thickened.

Add remaining 3 ingredients and chicken. Stir. Spoon over rice mixture in baking dish. Bake, uncovered, in 350°F (175°C) oven for about 25 minutes until chicken is tender and vegetables are tender-crisp. Let stand for 5 minutes before serving. Serves 4.

1 serving: 757 Calories; 34.1 g Total Fat (6.6 g Mono, 4.0 g Poly, 20.9 g Sat); 112 mg Cholesterol; 80 g Carbohydrate; 5.2 g Fibre; 40 g Protein; 1426 mg Sodium

Note: For best results, use rice that is cooled to room temperature.

Pictured on page 71.

Thai Pizza on a Garlic Crust

*A thin crust pizza with lots of colour and crunch from the fresh vegetables.
Although not a traditional dish in Thailand, it is North America's favourite
kind of food—pizza—with a Thai kick.*

All-purpose flour, approximately	1 1/3 cups	325 mL
Instant yeast	1 tsp.	5 mL
Salt	1/2 tsp.	2 mL
Garlic powder	1/4 tsp.	1 mL
Hot water	1/2 cup	125 mL
Cooking oil	1 tbsp.	15 mL
Peanut sauce	1/4 cup	60 mL
Grated part-skim mozzarella cheese	3/4 cup	175 mL
Cooking (or chili-flavoured) oil	1 tbsp.	15 mL
Boneless, skinless chicken breast half, cut into 1/8 inch (3 mm) slices	5 oz.	140 g
Medium carrot, cut julienne	1	1
Cayenne pepper	1/8 tsp.	0.5 mL
Large red pepper, cut into 8 rings	1	1
Fresh bean sprouts	1 cup	250 mL
Green onions, thinly sliced	3	3
Sesame seeds, toasted (see Tip, page 22)	1 tsp.	5 mL

Food Processor Method: Measure first 4 ingredients into food processor fitted with dough blade. With motor running, pour hot water and first amount of cooking oil through food chute. Process for 1 minute. If dough seems sticky, turn out onto lightly floured surface. Knead for about 5 minutes, adding more flour as needed, until smooth and elastic. Cover with tea towel. Let dough rest for 15 minutes.

Hand Method: Combine first 4 ingredients in medium bowl. Add hot water and first amount of cooking oil. Mix well until dough pulls away from side of bowl. Turn out onto lightly floured surface. Knead for 5 to 8 minutes until smooth and elastic. Cover with tea towel. Let dough rest for 15 minutes.

To Complete: Roll out and press dough into greased 12 inch (30 cm) pizza pan, forming rim around edge. Spread with peanut sauce. Sprinkle with cheese.

Heat second amount of cooking oil in frying pan on medium. Add chicken, carrot and cayenne pepper. Cook for about 5 minutes, stirring often, until chicken is no longer pink. Arrange over cheese.

Place red pepper around outside edge. Bake on bottom rack in 425°F (220°C) oven for about 15 minutes until cheese is melted and crust is golden. Remove from oven.

Sprinkle with bean sprouts, green onion and sesame seeds. Cuts into 8 wedges.

1 wedge: 204 Calories; 8.2 g Total Fat (3.7 g Mono, 2 g Poly, 2 g Sat); 17 mg Cholesterol; 22 g Carbohydrate; 2 g Fibre; 11 g Protein; 359 mg Sodium

Hungarian Chicken

The attractive, zesty colour is the result of an abundance of paprika.

Chicken parts	3 lbs.	1.36 kg
All-purpose flour	1/4 cup	60 mL
Hard margarine (butter browns too fast)	2 tbsp.	30 mL
Salt, sprinkle		
Pepper, sprinkle		
Hard margarine (butter browns too fast)	2 tbsp.	30 mL
Chopped onion	1 1/2 cups	350 mL
All-purpose flour	2 tbsp.	30 mL
Paprika	1 1/2 tbsp.	25 mL
Chicken bouillon powder	2 tsp.	10 mL
Water	1 cup	250 mL
Ketchup	1 tbsp.	15 mL
Sour cream	1 cup	250 mL

Skin may be removed or left on chicken. Roll damp chicken in flour. Brown in first amount of margarine in frying pan. Sprinkle with salt and pepper. Transfer to small roaster.

Add second amount of margarine and onion to frying pan. Scramble-fry until soft.

Mix in flour, paprika and bouillon powder. Stir in water and ketchup until it boils and thickens a bit. Scrape all bits from bottom. Pour over chicken. Cover. Bake in 350°F (175°C) oven for 1 to 1 1/2 hours until tender. Use tongs to remove chicken to serving dish.

Add sour cream to roaster. Stir. Spoon over chicken or pour into small bowl or gravy boat to serve. A bit of milk may be added to make 2 cups (500 mL). Serves 6 to 8.

1 serving: 400 Calories; 23 g Total Fat (8 g Mono, 4.5 g Poly, 8 g Sat); 120 mg Cholesterol; 9 g Carbohydrate; <1 g Fibre; 38 g Protein; 470 mg Sodium

Creamy Chicken Casserole

A classic chicken, broccoli and rice casserole that skips high-sodium canned soup in favour of a homemade creamy vegetable mixture.

All-purpose flour	3 tbsp.	45 mL
Milk	1 1/2 cups	375 mL
Boneless, skinless chicken breast halves, cut into 3/4 inch (2 cm) pieces	1 lb.	454 g
Sliced fresh white mushrooms	2 cups	500 mL
Chopped onion	1 cup	250 mL
Long-grain brown rice	1 cup	250 mL
Prepared chicken broth	1 cup	250 mL
Sliced celery	1 cup	250 mL

(continued on next page)

Dried rosemary, crushed	1/4 tsp.	1 mL
Dried thyme	1/4 tsp.	1 mL
Salt	1/4 tsp.	1 mL
Pepper	1/2 tsp.	2 mL
Small broccoli florets	2 cups	500 mL
Fine dry bread crumbs	1/2 cup	125 mL
Grated Parmesan cheese	1/2 cup	125 mL
Canola oil	1 tbsp.	15 mL

Whisk flour into milk in large bowl until smooth.

Add next 10 ingredients. Stir. Transfer to greased 9 x 13 inch (23 x 33 cm) baking dish. Cook, covered, in 375°F (190°C) oven for 45 minutes.

Add broccoli. Stir well. Cook, covered, for about 35 minutes until rice is tender.

Combine remaining 3 ingredients in small bowl. Sprinkle over top. Broil on centre rack for about 3 minutes until golden. Let stand, covered, for 10 minutes. Serves 6.

1 serving: 340 Calories; 7 g Total Fat (2.5 g Mono, 1 g Poly, 2 g Sat); 53 mg Cholesterol; 42 g Carbohydrate; 3 g Fibre; 27 g Protein; 454 mg Sodium

Flamenco Chicken

A traditional, colourful, tasty dish.

Chicken parts	3 lbs.	1.36 kg
Hard margarine (butter browns too fast)	2 tbsp.	30 mL
Chopped onion	2 1/2 cups	525 mL
Green pepper, seeded and chopped	1	1
Canned tomatoes (14 oz., 398 mL), broken up	1	1
Long grain rice, uncooked	1 1/2 cups	350 mL
Water	2 cups	450 mL
Chicken bouillon powder	1 tbsp.	15 mL
Canned mushroom pieces (10 oz., 284 mL), drained	1	1
Salt	1 tsp.	5 mL
Pepper	1/4 tsp.	1 mL
Garlic powder	1/4 tsp.	1 mL
Turmeric or saffron	1/8 tsp.	0.5 mL

Brown chicken in margarine in frying pan. Add more margarine if needed. Transfer to plate.

Sauté onion and green pepper in same pan until soft. Add remaining ingredients to onion mixture. Bring to a boil. Pour into small roaster. Arrange chicken over top. Cover. Bake in 350°F (175°C) oven for about 1 1/4 to 1 1/2 hours until chicken and rice are tender. Serves 4 to 6.

1 serving: 510 Calories; 10 g Total Fat (3.5 g Mono, 3 g Poly, 2.5 g Sat); 145 mg Cholesterol; 49 g Carbohydrate; 3 g Fibre; 5 g Protein; 1200 mg Sodium

Chicken Shepherd's Pie

Although shepherds usually mind their sheep, this rebel shepherd minds a flock of chickens!
Join the rebellion and enjoy this take on a classic favourite.

Peeled potatoes, cut into 2 inch (5 cm) pieces (about 3 medium)	1 1/2 lbs.	680 g
Large egg, fork-beaten	1	1
Grated sharp Cheddar cheese	2/3 cup	150 mL
Milk	2 tbsp.	30 mL
Salt	1/2 tsp.	2 mL
Pepper	1/4 tsp.	1 mL
Cooking oil	1 tbsp.	15 mL
Lean ground chicken	1 1/2 lbs.	680 g
Garlic clove, minced (or 1/4 tsp., 1 mL, powder)	1	1
Chopped onion	2 cups	500 mL
Frozen peas and carrots	4 cups	1 L
Can of condensed cream of chicken soup (10 oz., 284 mL)	1	1
Dried sage	1 tsp.	5 mL
Salt	1/4 tsp.	1 mL
Pepper	1/2 tsp.	2 mL

Pour about 1 inch (2.5 cm) of water into large saucepan. Add potato. Cover. Bring to a boil. Reduce heat to medium. Boil gently for 12 to 15 minutes until tender. Drain. Return to same pot.

Add next 5 ingredients. Mash. Cover to keep warm.

Heat cooking oil in large frying pan on medium. Add chicken and garlic. Scramble-fry for 5 minutes.

Add onion. Cook for about 5 minutes, stirring occasionally, until onion is softened and chicken is no longer pink.

Add remaining 5 ingredients. Heat and stir for about 5 minutes until boiling. Transfer to greased 3 quart (3 L) shallow baking dish. Spoon potato mixture over top. Spread evenly. Using fork, score decorative pattern on potato mixture. Bake, uncovered, in 350°F (175°C) oven for 30 to 40 minutes until bubbling and golden. Serves 6.

1 serving: 521 Calories; 26.1 g Total Fat (2.9 g Mono, 1.2 g Poly, 4.1 g Sat); 48 mg Cholesterol; 43 g Carbohydrate; 6 g Fibre; 31 g Protein; 824 mg Sodium

Savoury Bread Pudding

If stuffing sends you sailing over the moon with delight, this delicious strata will send you clear to another galaxy. Truly out of this world!

White (or whole wheat) bread cubes	3 cups	750 mL
Diced onion	1 cup	250 mL
Chicken sausages, cut into 1/2 inch (12 mm) pieces (about 3 oz., 85 g)	3	3
Bacon slices, diced	3	3
Boneless, skinless chicken breast halves, cut into 3/4 inch (2 cm) cubes	1/2 lb.	225 g
Large eggs	6	6
Milk	1 1/4 cups	300 mL
Italian seasoning	1 1/2 tsp	7 mL
Salt	1/2 tsp	2 mL
Pepper	1/2 tsp	2 mL
Grated medium Cheddar cheese	1 1/2 cups	375 mL
Grated Parmesan cheese	1/2 cup	125 mL

Arrange bread cubes in single layer on ungreased baking sheet with sides. Bake in 350°F (175°C) oven for 10 to 12 minutes until toasted. Cool.

Cook next 3 ingredients in large frying pan on medium for about 15 minutes, stirring often, until bacon is crisp and onion and sausage are browned. Transfer with slotted spoon to plate lined with paper towel to drain. Increase heat to medium-high.

Add chicken to same frying pan. Cook for 1 minute, stirring constantly. Remove to separate plate.

Whisk next 5 ingredients in large bowl until smooth. Add bread cubes. Stir. Let stand for 10 minutes to allow bread to absorb egg mixture. Add chicken and bacon mixture. Stir. Spread evenly in greased 2 quart (2 L) shallow baking dish.

Sprinkle with both cheeses. Bake, uncovered, in 350°F (175°C) oven for about 40 minutes until top is browned and knife inserted in centre comes out clean. Serves 4.

1 serving: 586 Calories; 32.3 g Total Fat (10.4 g Mono, 2.7 g Poly, 16.6 g Sat); 390 mg Cholesterol; 23 g Carbohydrate; 1 g Fibre; 49 g Protein; 1277 mg Sodium

Fried Chicken in Cream

Rich and wonderful.

Chicken parts	3 lbs.	1.36 kg
All-purpose flour	1/4 cup	60 mL
Hard margarine (butter browns too fast)	2 tbsp.	30 mL
Salt, sprinkle		
Pepper, sprinkle		
Sliced onion	1 cup	250 mL
Thinly sliced carrots	1 cup	250 mL
Water	2 cups	500 mL
Salt	1/2 tsp.	2 mL
Sliced fresh mushrooms	2 cups	500 mL
Whipping cream	1 1/2 cups	350 mL

Coat chicken with flour. Brown well in margarine in frying pan. Sprinkle with salt and pepper. Arrange in small roaster.

Put onion, carrots, water and salt into frying pan. Cover. Simmer slowly until tender crisp. Add to chicken.

Add mushrooms. Pour cream over top. Cover. Bake in 350°F (175°C) oven for about 1 1/2 hours until tender. Serves 4 to 6.

1 serving: 600 Calories; 44 g Total Fat (18 g Mono, 9 g Poly, 13 g Sat); 180 mg Cholesterol; 9 g Carbohydrate; 1 g Fibre; 41 g Protein; 410 mg Sodium

Simple Corn Flake Chicken

Crunchy and succulent.

Chicken, cut up, or chicken parts	3 lbs.	1.36 kg
Butter (or hard margarine)	1/4 cup	60 mL
Salt	1/2 tsp.	2 mL
Pepper	1/8 tsp.	0.5 mL
Coarsely crushed corn flakes	1 cup	250 mL

Remove skin or leave on. Pat dry with paper towels.

Melt butter in small saucepan. Mix in salt and pepper.

Brush chicken with butter mixture. Coat with corn flake crumbs. Arrange skin side up on greased baking sheet with sides. Bake in 375°F (190°C) oven for 1 to 1 1/4 hours until tender. Drizzle with remaining melted butter half way through baking. Serves 4 to 6.

1 serving: 620 Calories; 44 g Total Fat (17 g Mono, 8 g Poly, 15 g Sat); 185 mg Cholesterol; 14 g Carbohydrate; trace Fibre; 40 g Protein; 520 mg Sodium

Foiled Chicken

Tarragon adds an extra flavour. Easy to prepare and extra easy cleanup.

Boneless chicken breast halves	6	6
Condensed cream of mushroom soup	2/3 cup	150 mL
Sherry (or alcohol-free sherry)	1 tbsp.	15 mL
Chopped green onion	1/4 cup	60 mL
Garlic powder	1/4 tsp.	1 mL
Ground thyme	1/4 tsp.	1 mL
Dried tarragon	1/4 tsp.	1 mL
Salt	1/4 tsp.	1 mL
Pepper	1/8 tsp.	0.5 mL
Paprika, sprinkle		

Line small roaster with a piece of foil long enough to fold over top of chicken. Place chicken breasts on greased foil.

In small bowl, mix remaining ingredients. Spoon over chicken being sure to put some on each piece. Fold foil over chicken. Bake in 350°F (175°C) oven for about 1 1/2 hours until tender. Makes 6 servings.

1 serving: 180 Calories; 4.5 g Total Fat (0 g Mono, 0 g Poly, 1.5 g Sat); 80 mg Cholesterol; 4 g Carbohydrate; 0 g Fibre; 30 g Protein; 1050 mg Sodium

Chicken in Mock Wine

Excellent. Easy to prepare with a gourmet touch.

Red wine vinegar	1/2 cup	125 mL
Prepared orange juice	1/2 cup	125 mL
Salt	1 tsp.	5 mL
Pepper	1/4 tsp.	1 mL
Garlic powder	1/4 tsp.	1 mL
Chicken parts	3 lbs.	1.36 kg
Sliced fresh mushrooms	2 cups	500 mL

Measure first 5 ingredients into bowl that has a tight fitting cover. Stir well. Add chicken. Cover tightly. Marinate in refrigerator for 4 to 6 hours, shaking bowl every 30 minutes or so. Arrange chicken, skin side down, in small roaster. Reserve marinade. Bake, uncovered, in 375°F (190°C) oven for 30 minutes.

Turn chicken skin side up. Add mushrooms around chicken. Pour reserved marinade over top. Cover. Lower heat to 350°F (175°C). Bake for 1 hour more until tender. Baste 2 or 3 times during last hour. Serves 4 to 6.

1 serving: 350 Calories; 14 g Total Fat (4.5 g Mono, 3.5 g Poly, 3.3 g Sat); 145 mg Cholesterol; 3 g Carbohydrate; 0 g Fibre; 49 g Protein; 580 mg Sodium

Arroz con Pollo

Literally "rice with chicken," Arroz Con Pollo (ah-ROHS con POH-yoh) is a Latin American dish your family will ask for often. Saffron may be a bit more expensive than other spices but it adds a special touch.

Bone-in chicken parts, skin removed	3 1/2 lbs.	1.6 kg
Boiling water	3 cups	750 mL
Frozen peas	2 cups	500 mL
Can of diced tomatoes (14 oz., 398 mL), with juice	1	1
Long grain white rice	1 1/2 cups	375 mL
Finely chopped onion	1/2 cup	125 mL
Jar of pimiento (2 oz., 57 mL), well drained and chopped	1	1
Chicken bouillon powder	1 tbsp.	15 mL
Dried basil	1/2 tsp.	2 mL
Salt	1 tsp.	5 mL
Pepper	1/4 tsp.	1 mL
Saffron threads (or turmeric)	1/4 tsp.	1 mL
Garlic powder	1/4 tsp.	1 mL

Arrange chicken in greased 9 x 13 inch (23 33 cm) pan. Bake, uncovered, in 350°F (175°C) oven for 30 minutes. Transfer to large plate.

Combine remaining 12 ingredients in same pan. Arrange chicken on rice mixture. Cover with greased foil. Bake for another 35 to 45 minutes until chicken is no longer pink inside, rice is tender and liquid is absorbed. Serves 6.

1 serving: 396 Calories; 4.9 g Total Fat (1.4 g Mono, 1.3 g Poly, 1.2 g Sat); 90 mg Cholesterol; 51 g Carbohydrate; 4 g Fibre; 35 g Protein; 990 mg Sodium

Pictured on page 215.

1. Elegant Chicken, page 142
2. Chicken Mole, page 145

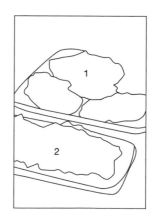

Chicken Angelo

This not-quite-so-common cheese makes this a great dish for company.

Large eggs	2	2
Fine dry bread crumbs	1 cup	250 mL
Italian seasoning	1 tsp.	5 mL
Hard margarine (butter browns too fast)	2 tbsp.	30 mL
Chicken breasts, halved, skin and bones removed	4	4
Sliced fresh mushrooms	1 cup	250 mL
Muenster cheese, sliced	3/4 lb.	375 g
Sliced fresh mushrooms	1 cup	250 mL
Hot water	1 1/2 cups	375 mL
Chicken bouillon powder	2 tsp.	10 mL

Beat eggs with fork in small bowl until smooth.

Stir bread crumbs and Italian seasoning together in a separate bowl.

Melt margarine in frying pan. Dip chicken in egg, coat with crumb mixture and brown both sides well. Arrange in 9 x 13 inch (23 33 cm) baking dish.

Sprinkle with first amount of mushrooms. Lay cheese slices over top. Sprinkle with remaining mushrooms.

Mix water with bouillon powder. Pour over all. Bake, uncovered, in 350°F (175°C) oven for 40 to 45 minutes until chicken is tender. Makes 8 servings.

1 serving: 430 Calories; 22 g Total Fat (6 g Mono, 1.5 g Poly, 11 g Sat); 180 mg Cholesterol; 13 g Carbohydrate; <1 g Fibre; 44 g Protein; 1520 mg Sodium

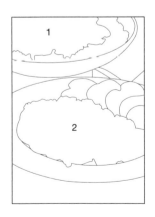

1. Polynesian Apricot Chicken, page 152
2. Mango Salsa Chicken, page 131

Chicken Divan

This Divan is simply divine! You'll love the delicate curry flavour.

Water	2 cups	500 mL
Vegetable bouillon powder	2 tsp.	10 mL
Boneless, skinless chicken breast halves	1 1/2 lbs.	680 g
Water	2 1/2 cups	625 mL
Long grain white rice	1 1/4 cups	300 mL
Frozen chopped broccoli, chopped smaller	1 lb.	454 g
Can of condensed cream of chicken soup (10 oz., 284 mL)	1	1
Light sour cream (see Tip, page 132)	1/2 cup	125 mL
Grated medium Cheddar cheese	1/2 cup	125 mL
Water	1/2 cup	125 mL
Light salad dressing (or mayonnaise)	1/3 cup	75 mL
Curry powder	1 tsp.	5 mL

Combine first amount of water and bouillon powder in medium saucepan. Bring to a boil.

Add chicken. Reduce heat to medium-low. Simmer, partially covered, for about 35 minutes until no longer pink inside. Drain. Let chicken stand until cool enough to handle. Cut into cubes. Set aside.

Combine second amount of water and rice in same saucepan. Bring to a boil. Reduce heat to medium-low. Simmer, covered, for about 20 minutes until rice is tender and water is absorbed. Transfer to ungreased 3 quart (3 L) casserole.

Layer broccoli and chicken on rice.

Combine remaining 6 ingredients in medium bowl. Pour over chicken. Bake, uncovered, in 350°F (175°C) oven for about 1 hour until heated through. Serves 6.

1 serving: 470 Calories; 14.1 g Total Fat (5.8 g Mono, 2.5 g Poly, 5.6 g Sat); 100 mg Cholesterol; 43 g Carbohydrate; 2 g Fibre; 41 g Protein; 598 mg Sodium

Pictured on page 215.

Cordon Bleu Bake

We've made this blue-ribbon favourite fuss-free. No fiddly prep is required to achieve this fine French flavour. Serve with steamed veggies and bon appétit!

Water	10 cups	2.5 L
Salt	1 1/4 tsp.	6 mL
Medium egg noodles	6 cups	1.5 L
Cooking oil	1 tbsp.	15 mL
Boneless, skinless chicken breast halves, cut into 1/2 inch (12 mm) strips	1 1/2 lbs.	680 g
Butter (or hard margarine)	2 tbsp.	30 mL
Fine dry bread crumbs	1/2 cup	125 mL
Butter (or hard margarine)	3 tbsp.	45 mL
All-purpose flour	1/4 cup	60 mL
Milk	3 3/4 cups	925 mL
Grated Gruyère (or Swiss) cheese	2 cups	500 mL
Deli (or Black Forest) ham, chopped	6 oz.	170 mL

Combine water and salt in Dutch oven or large pot. Bring to a boil. Add noodles. Boil, uncovered, for about 4 minutes, stirring occasionally, until tender but firm. Drain. Return to same pot. Cover to keep warm.

Heat cooking oil in large frying pan on medium. Add chicken. Cook for about 10 minutes, stirring occasionally, until browned. Remove to plate.

Melt first amount of butter in medium saucepan on medium. Add bread crumbs. Stir well. Transfer to small bowl. Wipe saucepan clean.

Melt second amount of butter in same saucepan on medium. Add flour. Heat and stir for 1 minute.

Slowly add milk, stirring constantly with whisk, until smooth. Heat and stir for about 5 minutes until boiling and thickened. Remove from heat.

Add cheese. Stir until smooth. Add to noodles.

Add chicken and ham. Stir until coated. Spread evenly in 9 x 13 inch (23 x 33 cm) baking dish. Sprinkle bread crumb mixture over top. Bake in 375°F (190°C) oven for about 25 minutes until bubbling and edges are starting to brown. Let stand for 10 minutes before serving. Serves 6.

1 serving: 701 Calories; 29.5 g Total Fat (8.5 g Mono, 2.8 g Poly, 15.1 g Sat); 197 mg Cholesterol; 52 g Carbohydrate; 2 g Fibre; 55 g Protein; 800 mg Sodium

Tropical Delight

If you want something really different, look no further. Bananas are roasted with the chicken during the last few minutes of cooking.

Skim milk powder	1 cup	250 mL
Granulated sugar	2/3 cup	150 mL
Water	2/3 cup	150 mL
Lemon juice	1/4 cup	60 mL
Butter (or hard margarine)	1/4 cup	60 mL
Flaked (or medium) coconut	1/2 cup	125 mL
Ground cardamom	1/8 tsp.	0.5 mL
Green tipped bananas, halved lengthwise, then crosswise	6	6
Corn flake crumbs	3 cups	750 mL
Chicken parts	5 lbs.	2.27 kg
Butter (or hard margarine), melted	3/4 cup	175 mL

Put first 7 ingredients in blender. Process until smooth. Pour into bowl.

Dip bananas in milk mixture, roll in crumbs and set aside on tray.

Dip chicken in milk mixture, roll in crumbs and arrange in greased 11 x 17 inch (28 x 43 cm) pan or use 2 smaller pans. Drizzle with about 1/2 cup (125 mL) butter saving rest for bananas. Bake in 350°F (175°C) oven for 1 1/2 hours until tender. Arrange 1 or 2 pieces of banana over each piece of chicken. Drizzle with remaining butter. Bake for 10 to 15 minutes more. Serves 7 to 10.

1 serving: 860 Calories; 39 g Total Fat (13 g Mono, 4.5 g Poly, 18 g Sat); 215 mg Cholesterol; 60 g Carbohydrate; 2 g Fibre; 52 g Protein; 540 mg Sodium

Cajun Chicken Strips

Don't feel the least bit cagey about serving these baked bites for a main dish or appetizer. Serve with ranch or blue cheese salad dressing as a cooling dip.

Cornflake crumbs	3/4 cup	175 mL
Paprika	1 tbsp.	15 mL
Dried basil	2 tsp.	10 mL
Dried oregano	2 tsp.	10 mL
Garlic powder	1 tsp.	5 mL
Seasoned salt	1 tsp.	5 mL
Cayenne pepper	1 tsp.	5 mL
Large eggs	2	2
Chicken breast cutlets, cut lengthwise into 12 strips	1 lb.	454 g

(continued on next page)

Combine first 7 ingredients in small shallow bowl.

Beat eggs with a fork in separate small shallow bowl.

Dip 1 chicken strip into egg. Press both sides into crumb mixture until evenly coated. Place on greased baking sheet with sides. Repeat with remaining chicken, egg and crumb mixture. Discard any remaining egg and crumb mixture. Spray strips with cooking spray. Bake in 425°F (220°C) oven for 15 to 20 minutes until no longer pink inside. Makes 12 strips.

1 strip: 71 Calories; 1.5 g Total Fat (0.5 g Mono, 0.3 g Poly, 0.4 g Sat); 45 mg Cholesterol; 4 g Carbohydrate; trace Fibre; 10 g Protein; 146 mg Sodium

---

Chipotle Chicken Loaf

By using convenient pre-shredded cheese, jarred salsa and bagged bread crumbs, this family-friendly meatloaf will give you more time to loaf around!

Large egg, fork-beaten	1	1
Finely chopped onion	1 1/2 cups	375 mL
Grated Mexican cheese blend	1 cup	250 mL
Fine dry bread crumbs	1/2 cup	125 mL
Salsa	1/2 cup	125 mL
Garlic cloves, minced (or 1/2 tsp., 2 mL, powder)	2	2
Chili powder	1 tsp.	5 mL
Finely chopped chipotle pepper in adobo sauce (see Tip, page 78)	1 tsp.	5 mL
Salt	1/2 tsp.	2 mL
Pepper	1/4 tsp	1 mL
Lean ground chicken	2 lbs.	900 g
Grated Mexican cheese blend	1/2 cup	125 mL

Lime wedges, for garnish

Combine first 10 ingredients in large bowl. Add chicken. Mix well. Press into greased 9 x 5 x 3 inch (22 x 12.5 x 7.5 cm) loaf pan. Bake, uncovered, in 350°F (175°C) oven for 30 minutes.

Sprinkle second amount of cheese evenly over loaf. Bake for another 45 to 50 minutes until fully cooked and internal temperature reaches 175°F (80°C). Let stand for 10 minutes. Cut into slices.

Garnish individual servings with lime wedges. Serves 8.

1 serving: 359 Calories; 23.1 g Total Fat (0.5 g Mono, 0.2 g Poly, 4.8 g Sat); 42 mg Cholesterol; 10 g Carbohydrate; 1 g Fibre; 26 g Protein; 499 mg Sodium

Pictured on page 54.

Sun-dried Tomato Chicken Roll

*The colourful filling creates a striking red-orange pinwheel
design once the roll is cut into slices.*

Boneless, skinless chicken breast halves	2	2
Sun-dried tomatoes in oil, blotted dry and chopped	1/2 cup	125 mL
Grated Parmesan cheese	3 tbsp.	45 mL
Olive (or cooking) oil	2 tbsp.	30 mL
Garlic cloves, minced (or 1/2 tsp., 2 mL, powder)	2	2
Chopped fresh rosemary	2 tsp.	10 mL
Dried crushed chilies	1/4 tsp.	1 mL
Salt	1/4 tsp.	1 mL
Pepper	1/2 tsp.	2 mL
Bacon slices	4	4
Sprigs of fresh rosemary, for garnish		

To butterfly chicken, cut breasts horizontally lengthwise almost, but not quite through, to other side. Open flat. Place between 2 sheets of plastic wrap. Pound with mallet or rolling pin to 1/2 inch (12 mm) thickness.

Combine next 8 ingredients in small bowl. Spread evenly on cut side of chicken. Roll up tightly, jelly-roll style, starting from long edge. Tie with butcher's string. Place on greased wire rack set in baking sheet with sides or small roasting pan.

Lay bacon slices over rolls. Bake in 350°F (175°C) oven for about 1 1/2 hours until internal temperature reaches 170°F (77°C). Remove to platter. Cover with foil. Let stand for 10 minutes. Remove and discard butcher's string. Cut each roll into 3 slices.

Garnish individual servings with rosemary sprigs. Serves 6.

1 serving: 300 Calories; 20 g Total Fat (9 g Mono, 2 g Poly, 6 g Sat); 75 mg Cholesterol; 4 g Carbohydrate; <1 g Fibre; 25 g Protein; 940 mg Sodium

Pictured on page 144.

Sunday Fried Chicken

For those who prefer to wade rather than sink when they're frying, we've "shallow fried" then baked this crispy chicken delight just for you. Start marinating on Saturday for dinner on Sunday—and don't forget a side of coleslaw.

Bone-in chicken thighs (about 5 oz., 140 g, each)	6	6
Chicken drumsticks (about 3 oz., 85 g, each)	6	6
Buttermilk	1 1/2 cups	375 mL
Water	1 1/2 cups	375 mL
Louisiana hot sauce	1 tbsp.	15 mL
Soy sauce	1 tbsp.	15 mL
Worcestershire sauce	1 tsp.	5 mL
Garlic powder	1/2 tsp.	2 mL
All-purpose flour	1 cup	250 mL
Onion powder	1 tsp.	5 mL
Salt	1 tsp.	5 mL
Pepper	1/2 tsp.	2 mL
Baking powder	1/2 tsp.	2 mL
Cayenne pepper	1/2 tsp.	2 mL
Poultry seasoning	1/2 tsp.	2 mL
Seasoned salt	1 tsp.	5 mL
Cooking oil, approximately	3 cups	750 mL

Put chicken into large resealable freezer bag.

Combine next 6 ingredients in small bowl. Pour over chicken. Seal bag. Turn until coated. Let stand in refrigerator for 12 to 24 hours, turning occasionally. Remove chicken. Do not pat dry. Discard any remaining buttermilk mixture.

Combine next 7 ingredients in separate large resealable freezer bag.
Add chicken in batches. Toss until coated. Discard any remaining flour mixture. Place chicken on baking sheet. Let stand for 10 minutes.

Sprinkle chicken with seasoned salt.

Heat 1/2 inch (12 mm) cooking oil in large frying pan or large pot on medium-high until hot. Add half of chicken pieces. Cook for about 3 minutes per side until golden. Transfer to wire rack set in baking sheet with sides. Repeat with remaining chicken. Bake chicken in 375°F (190°C) oven for 20 to 30 minutes until fully cooked and internal temperature reaches 170°F (77°C). Serves 6.

1 serving: 336 Calories; 15.7 g Total Fat (7.2 g Mono, 4.1 g Poly, 3.0 g Sat); 98 mg Cholesterol; 17 g Carbohydrate; 1 g Fibre; 29 g Protein; 836 mg Sodium

Pictured on page 53.

Pizza-style Meatloaf

Turn your dining experience upside down and inside out with this unique meatloaf that looks like a pizza! Instead of a traditional crust, the toppings sit over a thin, round meatloaf!

Cooking oil	2 tsp.	10 mL
Lean ground chicken	1 1/2 lbs.	680 g
Large eggs, fork-beaten	2	2
Grated havarti cheese	1/2 cup	125 mL
Fine dry bread crumbs	1/4 cup	60 mL
Lemon pepper	1 tsp.	5 mL
Dried tarragon	1/2 tsp.	2 mL
Tomato sauce	1/3 cup	75 mL
Basil pesto	2 tbsp.	30 mL
Grated havarti cheese	2/3 cup	150 mL
Thinly sliced red onion	1/2 cup	125 mL
Thinly sliced red pepper	1 cup	250 mL
Thinly sliced green pepper	1 cup	250 mL
Grated jalapeño Monterey Jack cheese	2/3 cup	150 mL

Heat cooking oil in large frying pan on medium-high. Add chicken. Scramble-fry for 5 to 10 minutes until no longer pink. Drain. Transfer to large bowl. Cool.

Add next 5 ingredients. Stir well. Press chicken mixture into bottom and halfway up sides of greased 12 inch (30 cm) deep dish pizza pan. Bake in 400°F (200°C) oven for about 5 minutes until firm and cheese is melted. Let stand for 5 minutes.

Combine tomato sauce and pesto in small cup. Spread evenly over chicken mixture.

Sprinkle second amount of havarti cheese over top. Layer next 3 ingredients, in order given, over cheese. Sprinkle with Monterey Jack cheese. Bake for another for 15 to 20 minutes until cheese is melted and golden. Cut into wedges. Serves 6.

1 serving: 467 Calories; 31.4 g Total Fat (2.8 g Mono, 0.9 g Poly, 8.7 g Sat); 93 mg Cholesterol; 8 g Carbohydrate; 1 g Fibre; 35 g Protein; 459 mg Sodium

Pictured on page 72.

Pecan-crusted Chicken

Seasoned with honey mustard and coated with pecans,
this easy-to-make chicken is special enough for company.

Dijon mustard	3 tbsp.	45 mL
Liquid honey	2 tbsp.	30 mL
Boneless, skinless chicken breast halves (4 oz., 113 g, each)	4	4
Ground pecans	3/4 cup	175 mL
Fine dry bread crumbs	1/4 cup	60 mL
Hard margarine (or butter), melted	2 tbsp.	30 mL
Dried basil	1 tsp.	5 mL
Salt	1/4 tsp.	1 mL

Combine mustard and honey in small bowl. Brush on both sides of each chicken breast half.

Combine remaining 5 ingredients in medium shallow dish. Press both sides of each chicken breast half into crumb mixture until coated. Place on greased baking sheet with sides. Bake in 425°F (220°C) oven for 15 to 20 minutes until chicken is no longer pink inside and crumb mixture is golden. Serves 4.

1 serving: 399 Calories; 21.9 g Total Fat (12.5 g Mono, 4.8 g Poly, 3 g Sat); 77 mg Cholesterol; 18 g Carbohydrate; 2 g Fibre; 34 g Protein; 510 mg Sodium

Chicken Marengo

A reddish sauce covers pieces of chicken that cook to perfection.

Grated medium or sharp Cheddar cheese	1 cup	250 mL
Cream cheese, softened	4 oz.	125 g
Chili sauce	1/2 cup	125 mL
Salt	1/2 tsp.	2 mL
Pepper	1/8 tsp.	0.5 mL
Boneless chicken breast halves, skin removed	8	8

Combine first 5 ingredients in bowl. Beat until smooth.

Arrange breast halves in pan large enough to hold in single layer. Spread cheese mixture over top. Cover. Bake in 350°F (175°C) oven for about 1 1/2 hours until tender. Makes 8 servings.

1 serving: 290 Calories; 13 g Total Fat (1.5 g Mono, 0 g Poly, 7 g Sat); 110 mg Cholesterol; 10 g Carbohydrate; trace Fibre; 34 g Protein; 1170 mg Sodium

Fennel Roast Chicken

Not your everyday roast chicken. Take the usual Sunday night fare up a notch with this dressy and flavourful fennel, sausage and wild rice stuffing.

SAUSAGE FENNEL STUFFING

Water	2 1/4 cups	550 mL
Package of long grain and wild rice mix (6 1/4 oz., 180 g)	1	1
Chopped sun-dried tomatoes	1/2 cup	125 mL
Fennel seed	1 tsp.	5 mL
Mild Italian sausages, casing removed and chopped	2	2
Olive oil	1 tsp.	5 mL
Chopped onion	1 cup	250 mL
Finely chopped fennel bulb (white part only)	1 cup	250 mL
Whole chicken	5 lbs.	2.3 kg
Olive oil	1 tbsp.	15 mL
Dried sage	2 tsp.	10 mL
Dried thyme	2 tsp.	10 mL
Lemon pepper	1 1/2 tsp.	7 mL
Fennel seed, crushed (see Tip, page 204)	1 tsp.	5 mL
Olive oil	1 tbsp.	15 mL
Thickly sliced fennel bulb (white part only)	5 cups	1.25 L
Garlic cloves, minced	4	4
Dry (or alcohol-free) white wine	1/2 cup	125 mL
Prepared chicken broth	1/2 cup	125 mL

Chopped fresh sage, for garnish
Chopped fresh thyme, for garnish

Sausage Fennel Stuffing: Combine first 4 ingredients in medium saucepan. Bring to a boil. Reduce heat to medium-low. Cook, covered, for 20 to 25 minutes, without stirring, until rice is tender. Transfer to large bowl. Cool slightly. Fluff with fork.

Put sausage into medium frying pan. Scramble-fry on medium for about 5 minutes until no longer pink. Transfer sausage with slotted spoon to plate lined with paper towel to drain. Drain and discard drippings from pan.

Heat first amount of olive oil in same frying pan on medium. Add onion and first amount of fennel. Cook for about 5 minutes, stirring occasionally, until fennel is tender-crisp. Add to rice mixture. Add sausage. Stir. Makes about 5 cups (1.25 L) stuffing.

(continued on next page)

Loosely till body cavity of chicken with stuffing. Secure with wooden picks or small metal skewers. Tie wings with butcher's string close to body. Tie legs to tail. Transfer to medium roasting pan.

Rub second amount of olive oil over surface of chicken. Combine next 4 ingredients in small cup. Sprinkle half of seasoning mixture over chicken. Bake, covered, in 400°F (200°C) oven for 20 minutes. Reduce heat to 350°F (175°C).

Combine next 3 ingredients and remaining seasoning mixture in large bowl. Arrange around chicken in roasting pan. Bake, uncovered, for 1 hour.

Pour wine and broth over chicken. Bake, uncovered, for another 30 to 40 minutes until meat thermometer inserted into thickest part of breast reads 185°F (85°C). Temperature of stuffing should reach at least 165°F (74°C). Remove chicken from oven. Remove stuffing to serving dish. Cover to keep warm. Cover chicken with foil. Let stand for 10 minutes before carving. Spoon vegetables and skimmed pan juices over chicken.

Garnish with sage and thyme. Serves 8.

1 serving: 762 Calories; 28 g Total Fat (12.2 g Mono, 5.3 g Poly, 7.3 g Sat); 226 mg Cholesterol; 43 g Carbohydrate; 10.4 g Fibre; 81 g Protein; 962 mg Sodium

Pictured on page 108.

Cordon Bleu Chicken

Rich and decadent, this is perfect for entertaining! Splitting the chicken breasts makes for much healthier portion sizes than classic Cordon Bleu recipes.

Boneless, skinless chicken breast halves (about 4 oz., 113 g, each)	4	4
Garlic powder	1/2 tsp.	2 mL
Pepper	1/4 tsp.	1 mL
Shaved lean deli ham	5 oz.	140 g
Grated Swiss cheese	1 cup	250 mL
Panko (or fine dry) bread crumbs	1/2 cup	125 mL
Canola oil	1 tbsp.	15 mL
Chopped fresh parsley	1 tbsp.	15 mL

Cut each chicken breast in half horizontally. Place 1 chicken piece between 2 sheets of plastic wrap. Pound with mallet or rolling pin to 1/4 inch (6 mm) thickness. Repeat with remaining chicken.

Sprinkle garlic powder and pepper on both sides of chicken. Arrange on greased baking sheet with sides. Arrange ham over chicken. Sprinkle with cheese.

Combine remaining 3 ingredients in small bowl. Sprinkle over cheese. Cook in 375°F (190°C) oven for about 25 minutes until internal temperature reaches 170°F (77°C). Makes 8 pieces.

1 piece: 210 Calories; 8 g Total Fat (1.5 g Mono, 0.5 g Poly, 3.5 g Sat); 75 mg Cholesterol; 4 g Carbohydrate; 0 g Fibre; 28 g Protein; 321 mg Sodium

Pictured on page 180.

Maple Glazed Chicken

The sweet maple glaze is complimented the favours of orange and cranberry.

Boneless, skinless chicken breasts (about 1 1/2 lbs., 680 g)	2	2
Maple (or maple-flavoured) syrup	1/3 cup	75 mL
Salt	1/4 tsp.	1 mL
Pepper	1/4 tsp.	1 mL
Medium oranges, sliced	2	2
ORANGE CRANBERRY COMPOTE		
Brown sugar, packed	1/3 cup	75 mL
Balsamic vinegar	1 tbsp.	15 mL
Fresh (or frozen) cranberries	1 cup	250 mL
Orange juice	3/4 cup	175 mL
Grated orange zest	1 tsp.	5 mL
Star anise	2	2

Place chicken in greased foil-lined 9 x 9 inch (23 x 23 cm) baking dish. Brush with half of syrup. Sprinkle with salt and pepper. Arrange orange slices over chicken. Bake in 400°F (200°C) oven for 30 minutes. Remove and discard orange slices. Brush with syrup. Bake for another 15 minutes, brushing with syrup every 5 minutes, until browned and internal temperature reaches 170°F (77°C). Cover with foil. Let stand for 10 minutes. Cut chicken crosswise into 1/4 inch (6 mm) slices.

Orange Cranberry Compote: Combine brown sugar and vinegar in small saucepan. Heat and stir on medium until brown sugar is dissolved.

Add remaining 4 ingredients. Stir. Bring to a boil. Reduce heat to medium-low. Simmer, uncovered, for about 10 minutes until cranberries split and sauce is thickened. Remove from heat. Discard anise. Makes about 1 cup (250 mL) compote. Serve with chicken. Serves 6.

1 serving: 236 Calories; 2.2 g Total Fat (0.9 g Mono, 0.5 g Poly, 0.7 g Sat); 58 mg Cholesterol; 28 g Carbohydrate; 1 g Fibre; 26 g Protein; 181 mg Sodium

Festive Chicken Bake

Enjoy the festive flavours of cranberry, orange, and cinnamon—any time of year! And be sure to make merry with all the time you save on prep. The sauce goes great with rice or noodles.

All-purpose flour	3 tbsp.	45 mL
Salt	1/4 tsp.	1 mL
Pepper	1/8 tsp.	0.5 mL
Paprika	1/8 tsp.	0.5 mL
Boneless, skinless chicken breast halves (about 4 oz., 113 g, each)	6	6
Cooking oil	1 tbsp.	15 mL
Prepared chicken broth	1/2 cup	125 mL
Frozen (or fresh) cranberries	1 cup	250 mL
Frozen concentrated orange juice, thawed	1/3 cup	75 mL
Diced onion	1/4 cup	60 mL
Ground cinnamon	1/4 tsp.	1 mL
Ground ginger	1/4 tsp.	1 mL

Combine first 4 ingredients in large resealable freezer bag. Add chicken. Toss until coated. Remove chicken. Reserve remaining flour mixture.

Heat cooking oil in large frying pan on medium-high. Add chicken. Cook for 2 to 3 minutes per side until browned. Arrange in single layer in greased 2 quart (2 L) shallow baking dish.

Stir broth into reserved flour mixture in small bowl until smooth.

Add remaining 5 ingredients. Stir. Pour over chicken. Bake, covered, in 350°F (175°C) oven for about 45 minutes until fully cooked and internal temperature of chicken reaches 170°F (77°C). Serves 6.

1 serving: 199 Calories; 4.3 g Total Fat (1.9 g Mono, 1.2 g Poly, 0.7 g Sat); 66 mg Cholesterol; 12 g Carbohydrate; 1 g Fibre; 27 g Protein; 226 mg Sodium

Pictured on page 90.

Millet Pecan Roast Chicken

Take your everyday roast chicken, baste it in a delectable sauce, and stuff it with whole-grain bread, millet and pecans. A familiar meal with a healthy, yet sinfully tasty, twist!

MILLET PECAN STUFFING

Whole-grain (or whole wheat) bread cubes	3 cups	750 mL
Cooked millet	1/2 cup	125 mL
Finely chopped pecans, toasted (see Tip, page 22)	1/4 cup	60 mL
Bacon slices, cooked crisp and crumbled	2	2
Parsley flakes	2 tsp.	10 mL
Dried rosemary, crushed	1/2 tsp.	2 mL
Dried sage	1/4 tsp.	1 mL
Salt	1/4 tsp.	1 mL
Pepper	1/8 tsp.	0.5 mL
Olive (or canola) oil	2 tsp.	10 mL
Chopped onion	1/2 cup	125 mL
Grated peeled cooking apple (such as McIntosh)	1/2 cup	125 mL
Apple juice	1/4 cup	60 mL
Whole chicken	3 lbs.	1.4 kg
Olive (or canola) oil	1 tbsp.	15 mL
Salt	1/4 tsp.	1 mL
Pepper	1/4 tsp.	1 mL
Dijon mustard	2 tbsp.	30 mL
Maple syrup	2 tbsp.	30 mL

Millet Pecan Stuffing: Arrange bread cubes in single layer on greased baking sheet with sides. Bake in 350°F (175°C) oven for 10 to 12 minutes until toasted. Cool. Transfer to large bowl.

Add next 8 ingredients. Toss.

Heat olive oil in medium frying pan on medium. Add onion and apple. Cook for about 10 minutes, stirring often, until onion starts to turn golden. Remove from heat. Add to millet mixture.

Add apple juice. Toss. Makes about 2 cups (500 mL) stuffing.

Loosely fill body cavity of chicken with stuffing. Secure with wooden picks or small metal skewers. Tie wings with butcher's string close to body. Tie legs and tail. Transfer to greased wire rack set in medium roasting pan.

(continued on next page)

Brush olive oil over surface of chicken. Sprinkle with second amount of salt and pepper. Bake, covered, in 400°F (200°C) oven for 15 minutes. Reduce heat to 325°F (160°C). Bake for 1 hour.

Combine mustard and syrup in small cup. Brush mustard mixture over chicken. Bake, covered, for another 30 minutes until meat thermometer inserted into thickest part of breast reads 185°F (85°C). Temperature of stuffing should reach at least 165°F (74°C). Remove chicken from oven. Remove stuffing to serving dish. Cover to keep warm. Cover chicken with foil. Let stand for 10 minutes before carving. Serves 4.

1 serving: 989 Calories; 64.9 g Total Fat (29.5 g Mono, 13.6 g Poly, 16.6 g Sat); 259 mg Cholesterol; 31 g Carbohydrate; 3 g Fibre; 69 g Protein; 815 mg Sodium

---

Pesto-stuffed Chicken

Play hide and seek with this spectacular chicken dish! Your guests will be delighted to discover a layer of creamy pesto hidden just beneath the skin of these tender chicken breasts. Decadent and delicious!

Herb and garlic cream cheese	6 tbsp.	90 mL
Finely diced red pepper	1/4 cup	60 mL
Basil pesto	2 tbsp.	30 mL
Salt	1/4 tsp.	1 mL
Pepper	1/4 tsp.	1 mL
Bone-in chicken breast halves (about 10 oz., 285 g, each)	4	4

Combine first 5 ingredients in small bowl.

Carefully loosen chicken skin but do not remove (see Tip, page 134). Stuff cream cheese mixture between meat and skin, spreading mixture as evenly as possible. Secure skin with wooden picks. Place chicken, skin-side up, on greased baking sheet with sides. Bake in 350°F (175°C) oven for about 50 minutes until fully cooked and internal temperature reaches 170°F (77°C). Remove wooden picks. Serves 4.

1 serving: 298 Calories; 11.4 g Total Fat (0.6 g Mono, 0.5 g Poly, 4.6 g Sat); 132 mg Cholesterol; 1 g Carbohydrate; trace Fibre; 44 g Protein; 434 mg Sodium

Chili-rubbed Chicken

Is a friend or a family member's love of spicy food rubbing off on you? Return the favour by giving chicken a rub down with this spicy mixture. Serve with a crisp, cool salad and a baked potato.

Brown sugar, packed	2 tbsp.	30 mL
Chili powder	2 tbsp.	30 mL
Paprika	2 tsp.	10 mL
Garlic powder	1 tsp.	5 mL
Cayenne pepper	1/2 tsp.	2 mL
Bone-in chicken thighs (about 5 oz., 140 g, each)	8	8
Worcestershire sauce	2 tbsp.	30 mL

Combine first 5 ingredients in small cup.

Brush chicken with Worcestershire sauce. Rub spice mixture on chicken. Place on greased wire rack set in foil-lined baking sheet with sides. Bake in 375°F (190°C) oven for about 45 minutes until chicken is crispy and internal temperature reaches 170°F (77°C). Makes 8 thighs.

1 thigh: 157 Calories; 7.3 g Total Fat (2.7 g Mono, 1.8 g Poly, 2.0 g Sat); 60 mg Cholesterol; 5 g Carbohydrate; 1 g Fibre; 17 g Protein; 123 mg Sodium

Pictured on page 54.

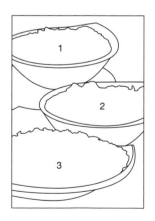

1. Curried Chicken and Peaches, page 141
2. West Indian Chicken Curry, page 149
3. Chicken Marrakesh, page 209

Oven-fried Chicken

Crisp on the outside and deliciously moist and tender on the inside. Use gluten-free cereal to make this chicken dish gluten-free.

Crisp rice cereal	4 cups	1 L
Sesame seeds	2 tbsp.	30 mL
Egg white (large), fork beaten	1	1
1% buttermilk	1/3 cup	75 mL
Dijon mustard	2 tsp.	10 mL
Garlic powder	1/4 tsp.	1 mL
Paprika	1/4 tsp.	1 mL
Salt	1/2 tsp	2 mL
Pepper	1/4 tsp.	1 mL
Boneless, skinless chicken breast halves (about 4 oz., 113 g, each)	6	6
Cornstarch	3 tbsp.	45 mL

Process cereal and sesame seeds in food processor until mixture resembles coarse crumbs. Transfer to large shallow dish.

Whisk next 7 ingredients in medium bowl until smooth.

Press chicken in cornstarch on large plate until coated on both sides. Lightly brush off any excess. Dip into buttermilk mixture. Press in cereal mixture until coated. Place on well-greased rack set in foil-lined baking sheet. Discard any excess cornstarch, egg mixture and cereal mixture. Spray chicken with cooking spray. Cook in 425°F (220°C) oven for about 30 minutes until golden and internal temperature reaches 170°F (77°C). Makes 6 pieces.

1 piece: 220 Calories; 2 g Total Fat (0 g Mono, 0 g Poly, 0.5 g Sat); 97 mg Cholesterol; 7 g Carbohydrate; 1 g Fibre; 40 g Protein; 280 mg Sodium

1. Crumby Chicken Strips, page 276
2. Hurry Chimichurri Patties, page 109

Cantonese Chicken

The chicken cooks right in the marinade. A fantastic glaze.

Chicken parts	3 lbs.	1.36 kg
Ketchup	1/2 cup	125 mL
Soy sauce	3 tbsp.	45 mL
Liquid honey	3 tbsp.	45 mL
Lemon juice	2 tbsp.	30 mL
Water	2 tbsp.	30 mL

Arrange chicken skin side down in small roaster or 9 x 13 inch (23 x 33 cm) pan.

Mix remaining ingredients well. Spoon over chicken. Cover. Marinate in refrigerator for at least 1 hour. Turn chicken over. Cover and marinate at least 1 hour more. Bake, covered, in 375°F (190°C) oven for 30 minutes. Baste chicken. Bake, uncovered, for 30 minutes or more until tender. Serves 4 to 6.

1 serving: 530 Calories; 36 g Total Fat (13 g Mono, 8 g Poly, 10 g Sat); 165 mg Cholesterol; 14 g Carbohydrate; trace Fibre; 40 g Protein; 870 mg Sodium

Sesame Chicken

The little sesame seeds cling well while chicken is cooking. A very attractive dish.

Fine soda cracker crumbs	1 cup	250 mL
Sesame seeds, toasted (see Tip, page 22)	1/2 cup	125 mL
Paprika	1 tsp.	5 mL
Onion salt	1/2 tsp.	2 mL
Salt	3/4 tsp.	4 mL
Pepper	1/4 tsp.	1 mL
Bone-in chicken parts (see Note)	3 lbs.	1.4 kg
Milk	1/2 cup	125 mL

Combine first 6 ingredients in shallow dish.

Dip chicken in milk, then coat with crumb mixture. Arrange chicken, skin side up, in single layer on greased baking sheet with sides. Bake in 375°F (190°C) oven for 30 minutes. Turn chicken. Bake for about 30 minutes until tender. Serves 4 to 6.

1 serving: 718 Calories; 47.3 g Total Fat (19.5 g Mono, 12.1 g Poly, 12 g Sat); 175 mg Cholesterol; 22 g Carbohydrate; 4 g Fibre; 50 g Protein; 1056 mg Sodium

Note: If desired, remove skin from chicken before dipping, to reduce fat.

Sherried Chicken

Rich looking and very tasty.

Hard margarine (butter browns too fast)	2 tbsp.	30 mL
Chicken parts	3 lbs.	1.36 kg
Sliced fresh mushrooms	3 cups	750 mL
All-purpose flour	1/4 cup	60 mL
Chicken bouillon powder	1 tbsp.	15 mL
Water	11/2 cups	350 mL
Sherry (or alcohol-free sherry)	1/4 cup	60 mL
Ground rosemary	1/4 tsp.	1 mL

Melt margarine in frying pan. Add chicken. Brown well. Transfer to small roaster.

Add mushrooms to frying pan, adding more margarine if necessary. Scramble-fry until soft.

Mix in flour and bouillon powder. Stir in water, sherry and rosemary until it boils and thickens. Pour over chicken. Cover. Bake in 350°F (175°C) oven for about 1 hour until tender. Serves 4 to 6.

1 serving: 560 Calories; 40 g Total Fat (17 g Mono, 9 g Poly, 11 g Sat); 165 mg Cholesterol; 6 g Carbohydrate; trace Fibre; 41 g Protein; 650 mg Sodium

Chinese Chicken

This flavourful dish can be prepared early in the day or at the last minute. Just transfer from refrigerator to oven when needed.

Chicken, cut up	3 lbs.	1.36 kg
Soy sauce	1/3 cup	75 mL
Water	2 tbsp.	30 mL
Granulated sugar	1/4 cup	60 mL
Ground ginger	1/2 tsp.	2 mL
Garlic powder	1/4 tsp.	1 mL
Onion salt	1/4 tsp.	1 mL
Dry mustard powder	1/4 tsp.	1 mL
Pepper	1/8 tsp.	0.5 mL

Arrange chicken in single layer in small roaster.

Combine remaining 8 ingredients in small bowl. Stir well. Pour over chicken. Cover. May be refrigerated at this point or placed in 350°F (175°C) oven. Cook for 30 minutes. Allow an extra 20 minutes if refrigerated. Remove cover. Baste. Cook, uncovered, for about 1 hour or until tender. Serves 4 to 6.

1 serving: 530 Calories; 36 g Total Fat (15 g Mono, 8 g Poly, 10 g Sat); 165 mg Cholesterol; 9 g Carbohydrate; trace Fibre; 41 g Protein; 970 mg Sodium

Chicken Puffs

Two recipes in one. The puffs have a smooth golden coating while the nuggets are crumbed and ready for dipping. Serve as an appetizer or main course.

BATTER

All-purpose flour	1 cup	250 mL
Baking powder	2 tsp.	10 mL
Salt	1 tsp.	5 mL
Granulated sugar	1/2 tsp.	2 mL
Large egg	1	1
Cooking oil	2 tbsp.	30 mL
Club soda	1 cup	250 mL
Chicken breasts, halved, skin and bones removed	3	3
All-purpose flour	1/2 cup	125 mL

Cooking oil for deep-frying

Batter: Combine flour, baking powder, salt and sugar in bowl. Stir. Make a well in centre.

Beat egg with a fork in small bowl. Mix in cooking oil and club soda. Pour into well. Stir to moisten.

Cut each chicken breast half into 6 to 8 pieces. Dip chicken into water to moisten. Drain well. Roll in flour. Dip in batter.

Deep-fry in hot 375°F (190°C) cooking oil for 3 to 5 minutes, turning to brown second side. Remove a piece to check now and then to see if it is cooked through. Do not crowd deep-fryer. Remove with slotted spoon to drain on pan lined with paper towel. Put pan in 175°F (80°C) oven to keep warm while finishing cooking. Makes 36 to 48 pieces.

1 piece: 60 Calories; 4.5 g Total Fat (2.5 g Mono, 1 g Poly, 0 g Sat); 10 mg Cholesterol; 3 g Carbohydrate; trace Fibre; 3 g Protein; 130 mg Sodium

CHICKEN NUGGETS

Fine dry bread crumbs	1 cup	250 mL
Paprika	2 tsp.	10 mL
Seasoned salt	2 tsp.	10 mL
Salt	1 1/2 tsp.	7 mL
Pepper	1/2 tsp.	2 mL

Mix all ingredients in small bowl. After dipping chicken pieces in batter, coat with crumb mixture, then deep-fry. Makes 36 to 48 pieces.

1 piece: 90 Calories; 4.5 g Total Fat (2.5 g Mono, 1 g Poly, 0 g Sat); 15 mg Cholesterol; 6 g Carbohydrate; trace Fibre; 5 g Protein; 400 mg Sodium

Zippy Anise Drumsticks

Anise, anise, we've got a crush on you! For those of you who haven't experimented with aniseed yet, join the love train and give the subtle licorice flavour a go.

Brown sugar, packed	3 tbsp.	45 mL
Aniseed, crushed (see Tip, page 204)	1 tbsp.	15 mL
Dried crushed chilies	3/4 tsp.	4 mL
Salt	1/2 tsp.	2 mL
Chicken drumsticks (about 3 oz., 85 g, each)	12	12
Olive oil	3 tbsp.	45 mL

Combine first 4 ingredients in small cup.

Brush chicken with olive oil. Rub aniseed mixture over chicken. Place on greased wire rack set in foil-lined baking sheet with sides. Bake in 400°F (200°C) oven for about 40 minutes, turning at halftime, until fully cooked and internal temperature reaches 170°F (77°C). Makes 12 drumsticks.

1 drumstick: 153 Calories; 7.8 g Total Fat (3.9 g Mono, 1.4 g Poly, 1.6 g Sat); 65 mg Cholesterol; 4 g Carbohydrate; trace Fibre; 16 g Protein; 174 mg Sodium

Ginger Meatballs

These tasty little meatballs are great over rice for dinner or served with wooden picks as cocktail-party fare.

Large egg, fork-beaten	1	1
Fine dry bread crumbs	1/2 cup	125 mL
Finely chopped pickled ginger slices	3 tbsp.	45 mL
Finely chopped canned water chestnuts	2 tbsp.	30 mL
Finely chopped green onion	2 tbsp.	30 mL
Sweet and sour sauce	2 tbsp.	30 mL
Soy sauce	1 tbsp.	15 mL
Salt	1/4 tsp.	1 mL
Extra-lean ground chicken	1 lb.	454 g
Sweet and sour sauce	1/2 cup	125 mL

Combine first 8 ingredients in large bowl. Add chicken. Mix well. Roll into 1 1/2 inch (3.8 cm) balls. Arrange on greased baking sheet with sides. Bake in 400°F (200°C) oven for about 20 minutes until fully cooked and internal temperature reaches 175°F (80°C).

Heat second amount of sweet and sour sauce in medium saucepan on medium. Add meatballs. Stir gently until coated. Makes about 22 meatballs.

1 meatball: 44 Calories; 0.6 g Total Fat (0.2 g Mono, 0.1 g Poly, 0.1 g Sat); 17 mg Cholesterol; 4 g Carbohydrate; trace Fibre; 6 g Protein; 171 mg Sodium (need new NI)

Crispy Chicken

A coating flavoured with thyme. Crispy like its name.

All-purpose flour	3/4 cup	175 mL
Paprika	1 tsp.	5 mL
Salt	1 tsp.	5 mL
Pepper	1/4 tsp.	1 mL
Ground thyme	1 tsp.	5 mL
Large egg	1	1
Milk	2 tbsp.	30 mL
Lemon juice	2 tsp.	10 mL
Chicken parts	3 lbs.	1.36 kg
Butter (or hard margarine), melted	1/4 cup	60 mL

Measure first 5 ingredients into bowl. Mix.

Beat egg in separate dish. Add milk and lemon juice. Stir.

Dip chicken into flour mixture. Dip into egg mixture and again into flour. Arrange skin side up on greased baking sheet. Let stand 30 minutes.

Drizzle with butter. Bake in 350°F (175°C) oven for 1 to 1 1/4 hours until tender. Serves 4 to 6.

1 serving: 630 Calories; 43 g Total Fat (16 g Mono, 8 g Poly, 15 g Sat); 225 mg Cholesterol; 13 g Carbohydrate; trace Fibre; 45 g Protein; 620 mg Sodium

Crumby Chicken Strips

Serve these golden-crumbed chicken strips with plum or honey mustard dipping sauce.

Large eggs	2	2
Cornflake crumbs	1 cup	250 mL
Grated Parmesan cheese	1/2 cup	125 mL
Lemon pepper	1 tbsp.	15 mL
Chicken breast cutlets (about 1 lb., 454 g), each cut into 3 equal pieces	4	4

Beat eggs with fork in small shallow dish. Combine next 3 ingredients in shallow medium dish.

Dip each chicken piece in egg. Press both sides of each piece into crumb mixture until coated. Place on greased baking sheet with sides. Spray top of chicken pieces with cooking spray. Bake in 425°F (220°C) oven for about 15 minutes until no longer pink inside. Makes 12 chicken strips. Serves 4.

1 serving: 322 Calories; 8.5 g Total Fat (2.6 g Mono, 0.9 g Poly, 3.8 g Sat); 184 mg Cholesterol; 23 g Carbohydrate; 1 g Fibre; 36 g Protein; 966 mg Sodium

Pictured on page 270.

Chicken Rolls

Instead of frying, the skin is removed, rolls are crumbed then baked in the oven. Rolled with ham, cheese and tomato.

Large chicken breasts, halved, skin and bones removed	3	3
Thin ham slices	6	6
Mozzarella, Swiss or Cheddar cheese slices, halved	3	3
Medium tomato, halved, seeded and diced	1	1
Fine dry bread crumbs	1/3 cup	75 mL
Grated Parmesan cheese	2 tbsp.	30 mL
Parsley flakes	1 tsp.	5 mL
Ground sage	1/2 tsp.	2 mL
Butter (or hard margarine), melted	1/4 cup	60 mL

Pound chicken breast halves between 2 sheets of plastic wrap to make even thickness.

Lay ham slice, 1/2 cheese slice and 1/6 diced tomato on top. Roll, tucking in sides. Tie with string. Fasten ends with wooden picks.

Stir next 4 ingredients together in small dish.

Brush chicken with butter. Coat with crumb mixture. Place seam side down in 9 x 13 inch (23 x 33 cm) pan. Bake, uncovered, in 350°F (175°C) oven for 45 to 55 minutes until tender. Makes 6 rolls.

1 roll: 290 Calories; 14 g Total Fat (2 g Mono, 0 g Poly, 8 g Sat); 110 mg Cholesterol; 8 g Carbohydrate; trace Fibre; 35 g Protein; 1070 mg Sodium

Tarragon Butter Chicken

Butter up the guests at your next dinner party with this juicy roast chicken. The herb butter is applied underneath the skin for extra flavour and moistness.

Butter (or hard margarine), softened	1/4 cup	60 mL
Dijon mustard (with whole seeds)	2 tbsp.	30 mL
Finely chopped green onion	2 tbsp.	30 mL
Chopped fresh tarragon (or 3/4 tsp., 4 mL, dried)	1 tbsp.	15 mL
Garlic clove, minced (or 1/4 tsp., 1 mL, powder)	1	1
Whole chicken	3 lbs.	1.4 kg
Cooking oil	1 tbsp.	15 mL
Salt	1 tsp.	5 mL
Pepper	1/2 tsp.	2 mL
Prepared chicken broth	1 1/2 cups	375 mL

Combine first 5 ingredients in small bowl.

Carefully loosen chicken skin but do not remove (see Tip, page 134). Stuff butter mixture between meat and skin, spreading mixture as evenly as possible.

Rub cooking oil over surface of chicken. Sprinkle with salt and pepper. Tie wings with butcher's string close to body. Tie legs to tail. Place on greased wire rack set in small roasting pan.

Bake, uncovered, in 350°F (175°C) oven for 1 1/2 to 2 hours, basting with broth every 30 minutes, until meat thermometer inserted in thickest part of breast reads 185°F (85°C). Remove chicken from oven. Cover with foil. Let stand for 10 minutes before carving. Serves 4.

1 serving: 641 Calories; 49.7 g Total Fat (19.2 g Mono, 8.8 g Poly, 17.3 g Sat); 198 mg Cholesterol; 2 g Carbohydrate; trace Fibre; 44 g Protein; 1268 mg Sodium

Chicken Parmesan

Tasty and quick to prepare. The addition of oregano gives a faint comparison to the flavour of pizza.

Grated Parmesan cheese	3/4 cup	175 mL
Fine dry bread crumbs	1/2 cup	125 mL
Dried whole oregano (optional)	1/2 tsp.	2 mL
Garlic powder	1/4 tsp.	1 mL
Salt	1 tsp.	5 mL
Pepper	1/4 tsp.	1 mL
Bone-in chicken parts (see Note)	3 lbs.	1.4 kg
Hard margarine (or butter), melted	1/2 cup	125 mL

Combine first 6 ingredients in small bowl.

Dip each chicken part into melted margarine. Roll in crumb mixture until coated. Arrange in single layer in greased 9 x 13 inch (23 x 33 cm) baking pan. Cover. Bake in 350°F (175°C) oven for 1 to 1 1/4 hours until tender. Serves 4 to 6.

1 serving: 646 Calories; 41.6 g Total Fat (16.5 g Mono, 7.8 g Poly, 14 g Sat); 189 mg Cholesterol; 11 g Carbohydrate; trace Fibre; 53 g Protein; 1248 mg Sodium

Note: If desired, remove skin from chicken before dipping, to reduce fat.

Pictured on page 234.

 tip When baking or broiling food in a frying pan with a handle that isn't ovenproof, wrap the handle in foil and keep it to the front of the oven, away from the element.

Roast Chicken

Have an old-fashioned Sunday dinner.

STUFFING

Butter (or hard margarine)	1 tbsp.	15 mL
Chopped onion	1/2 cup	125 mL
Chopped celery (optional)	2 tbsp.	30 mL
Dry bread crumbs	3 cups	750 mL
Chopped fresh parsley	2 tbsp.	30 mL
Poultry seasoning	1 tsp.	5 mL
Salt	1/2 tsp.	2 mL
Pepper	1/8 tsp.	0.5 mL
Butter (or hard margarine)	2 tbsp.	30 mL
Chicken bouillon powder	1/2 tsp.	2 mL
Hot water	3/4 cups	175 mL
Roasting chicken	5 lbs.	2.27 kg

Stuffing: Melt first amount of butter in large Dutch oven. Add onion and celery. Sauté until soft.

Stir in next 5 ingredients.

Mix second amount of butter, bouillon powder and hot water in small bowl until butter melts. Pour over crumb mixture. Toss. When a handful is squeezed, mixture should hold shape. Makes about 5 cups (1.25 L).

Tie wings with string to hold close to body. Pack stuffing lightly into neck and body cavities. Skewer skin together to hold in stuffing. Tie legs to tail. Place in roaster. Cover. Roast in 400°F (200°C) oven for 20 minutes. Reduce heat. Roast in 325°F (160°C) oven for 2 1/2 to 3 hours. Meat thermometer should read 190°F (90°C). Leg joints should move easily. Remove cover last few minutes to brown. If you prefer to cook uncovered, brush skin with softened butter and baste several times during cooking. Serves 6 to 8.

1 serving: 570 Calories; 33 g Total Fat (13 g Mono, 7 g Poly, 11 g Sat); 135 mg Cholesterol; 30 g Carbohydrate; 2 g Fibre; 34 g Protein; 650 mg Sodium

Forty Clove Chicken

Turn the fan on the kitchen vent to high, then put this in the oven. Baked garlic imparts a sweet flavour to this delectable chicken. Serve with warmed French bread slices spread with the soft garlic cloves.

Cooking oil	1/4 cup	60 mL
Salt	1 1/2 tsp.	7 mL
Pepper	1/4 tsp.	1 mL
Parsley flakes	1 tsp.	5 mL
Ground rosemary	1/2 tsp.	2 mL
Dried tarragon	1/2 tsp.	2 mL
Ground thyme	1/2 tsp.	2 mL
Celery flakes	1/2 tsp.	2 mL
Small onion, quartered	1	1
Roasting chicken, about 4 to 4 1/4 lbs. (1.81 to 2 kg)	1	1
Garlic cloves, unpeeled	40	40

Measure cooking oil in cup. Stir in next 7 ingredients.

Place onion in chicken cavity. Tie wings to body. Tie legs to tail. Brush bottom of roaster with cooking oil mixture. Place chicken in centre.

Add garlic cloves. Brush chicken and dab garlic with cooking oil mixture. Cover. Roast in 350°F (175°C) oven for about 1 1/2 to 2 hours until tender. Serves 6.

1 serving: 600 Calories; 45 g Total Fat (18 g Mono, 13 g Poly, 10 g Sat); 165 mg Cholesterol; 8 g Carbohydrate; <1 g Fibre; 40 g Protein; 740 mg Sodium

Stuffed Breasts of Chicken

Gourmet-style chicken, yet easy to do and so attractive to serve.

STUFFING

Hard margarine (or butter)	2 tbsp.	30 mL
Finely chopped onion	2 tbsp.	30 mL
Finely chopped celery	2 tbsp.	30 mL
Coarse dry bread crumbs	1 cup	250 mL
Dried chives	1 tbsp.	15 mL
Poultry seasoning	1/4 tsp.	1 mL
Salt, sprinkle		
Pepper, sprinkle		
Milk, approximately	1 1/2 tbsp.	25 mL
Boneless, skinless chicken breast halves (about 4 oz., 113 g, each)	4	4

MARMALADE ORANGE SAUCE

Orange marmalade	1/2 cup	125 mL
Frozen concentrated orange juice	1 tbsp.	15 mL

Stuffing: Melt margarine in medium saucepan or frying pan on medium. Add onion and celery. Cook for 5 to 10 minutes, stirring often, until onion is softened. Remove from heat.

Add next 6 ingredients. Stir well. Add more milk, if needed, until stuffing is moist and holds together when squeezed.

Pound chicken with mallet to 1/4 inch (6 mm) thickness. Divide and spoon stuffing on half of each piece. Fold over crosswise to cover stuffing. Secure with wooden picks. Transfer to 1 1/2 quart (1.5 L) dish.

Marmalade Orange Sauce: Heat marmalade and concentrated orange juice in small saucepan on low, stirring often, until smooth. Spoon some over chicken. Bake, uncovered, in 325°F (160°C) oven for about 45 minutes until tender. Cut into 1/2 inch (12 mm) slices. Arrange on individual plates. Spoon more sauce over top. Serves 4.

1 serving: 359 Calories; 8.7 g Total Fat (2.6 g Mono, 0.9 g Poly, 4.4 g Sat); 57 mg Cholesterol; 51 g Carbohydrate; 1 g Fibre; 20 g Protein; 374 mg Sodium

Pictured on page 234.

Rosemary Tomato Sauce

Subtle spices make this dish a simple delight. Serve on pasta.

All-purpose flour	2 tbsp.	30 mL
Boneless, skinless chicken thighs, halved	1 lb.	454 g
Chopped tomato	2 1/4 cups	550 mL
Chopped onion	1 cup	250 mL
Chopped yellow pepper	1 cup	250 mL
Dry (or alcohol-free) white wine	1 cup	250 mL
Tomato paste (see Tip, page 136)	1/3 cup	75 mL
Finely chopped fresh rosemary, (or 3/4 tsp., 4 mL, dried, crushed)	1 tbsp.	15 mL
Garlic cloves, minced (or 1/2 tsp., 2 mL, powder)	2	2
Bay leaf	1	1
Granulated sugar	1 tsp.	5 mL
Salt	1/4 tsp.	1 mL
Pepper	1/2 tsp.	2 mL

Measure flour into large resealable freezer bag. Add chicken. Seal bag. Toss until coated. Transfer chicken to 3 1/2 to 4 quart (3.5 to 4 L) slow cooker. Discard any remaining flour.

Combine remaining 11 ingredients in large bowl. Pour over chicken. Cook, covered, on Low for 8 to 10 hours or on High for 4 to 5 hours. Discard bay leaf. Makes about 5 cups (1.25 L).

1 cup (250 mL): 240 Calories; 7.3 g Total Fat (2.7 g Mono, 1.8 g Poly, 2.0 g Sat); 59 mg Cholesterol; 17 g Carbohydrate; 3 g Fibre; 19 g Protein; 201 mg Sodium

Chicken and Lentils

The apple and raisins add a touch of sweetness.

All-purpose flour	2 tbsp.	30 mL
Salt	1/2 tsp.	2 mL
Pepper	1/2 tsp.	2 mL
Bone-in chicken thighs, skin removed (about 5 oz., 140 g, each)	8	8
Cooking oil	1 tbsp.	15 mL
Chopped carrot	1 cup	250 mL
Chopped onion	1 cup	250 mL
Sliced peeled tart apple (such as Granny Smith)	2 cups	500 mL
Apple juice	1 cup	250 mL
Dried green lentils	1/2 cup	125 mL
Dry (or alcohol-free) red wine	1/2 cup	125 mL
Raisins	1/2 cup	125 mL
Grated orange zest	1 tsp.	5 mL
Ground cinnamon	1/2 tsp.	2 mL
Bay leaf	1	1
Chopped fresh parsley	3 tbsp.	45 mL
Salt	1/4 tsp.	1 mL

Combine first 3 ingredients in large resealable freezer bag. Add chicken. Seal bag. Toss until coated. Remove chicken. Discard any remaining flour mixture.

Heat cooking oil in large frying pan on medium. Add chicken. Cook for about 10 minutes, turning occasionally, until browned on all sides. Transfer with slotted spoon to plate. Set aside.

Add carrot and onion to same frying pan. Cook for 5 to 10 minutes, stirring often, until onion is softened. Transfer to 3 1/2 to 4 quart (3.5 to 4 L) slow cooker. Arrange chicken over top.

Combine next 8 ingredients in large bowl. Pour over chicken. Cook, covered, on Low for 8 to 10 hours or on High for 4 to 5 hours. Discard bay leaf.

Add parsley and salt. Stir gently. Serves 4.

1 serving: 693 Calories; 20.9 g Total Fat (8.3 g Mono, 4.9 g Poly, 4.9 g Sat); 143 mg Cholesterol; 76 g Carbohydrate; 7 g Fibre; 46 g Protein; 504 mg Sodium

Tangy Pineapple Chicken

*Let your taste buds be fickle tonight. Sweet? Sour? Let them
have it all—in one delightfully tangy dish!*

Chopped onion	1 cup	250 mL
Sliced carrots	1 cup	250 mL
Sliced celery	1 cup	250 mL
Finely grated ginger root (or 1/2 tsp., 2 mL, ground ginger)	2 tsp.	10 mL
All-purpose flour	1/4 cup	60 mL
Curry powder	2 tsp.	10 mL
Salt	1/2 tsp.	2 mL
Pepper	1/4 tsp.	1 mL
Boneless, skinless chicken thighs (about 3 oz., 85 g, each)	8	8
Can of diced tomatoes (14 oz., 398 mL), with juice	1	1
Can of pineapple tidbits (14 oz., 398 mL), with juice	1	1
Ketchup	1/4 cup	60 mL

Put first 4 ingredients into 4 quart (4 L) slow cooker.

Combine next 4 ingredients in large resealable freezer bag. Add chicken. Seal bag. Toss
until coated. Arrange chicken over vegetables. Sprinkle with any remaining flour mixture.

Combine remaining 3 ingredients in medium bowl. Pour over chicken. Cook, covered, on
Low for 5 to 6 hours or on High for 2 1/2 to 3 hours. Stir. Serves 4.

*1 serving: 392 Calories; 13.2 g Total Fat (5.0 g Mono, 3.1 g Poly, 3.6 g Sat); 112 mg Cholesterol; 35 g Carbohydrate;
3 g Fibre; 33 g Protein; 899 mg Sodium*

Pictured on page 107.

Pulled Tex Chicken

Got a hankerin' for some good, old southwestern sandwich flavour? Then, yee doggies, this is the meal for you! Sweet and tangy with an authentic flavour. Don't forget the napkins!

Sliced onion	1 1/2 cups	375 mL
Barbecue sauce	1 cup	250 mL
Can of tomato sauce (7 1/2 oz., 213 mL)	1	1
Can of diced green chilies (4 oz., 113 g)	1	1
Chili powder	1 tbsp.	15 mL
Dried oregano	1 tsp.	5 mL
Ground cumin	1/2 tsp.	2 mL
Ground cinnamon	1/4 tsp.	1 mL
Boneless, skinless chicken thighs	1 3/4 lbs.	790 g
Kaiser rolls, split	6	6

Combine first 8 ingredients in 3 1/2 to 4 quart (3.5 to 4 L) slow cooker.

Add chicken. Spoon barbecue sauce mixture over chicken to cover. Cook, covered, on Low for 7 to 8 hours or on High for 3 1/2 to 4 hours until chicken is tender. Remove chicken to cutting board using tongs. Shred chicken using 2 forks. Add to sauce mixture. Stir.

Serve chicken mixture in rolls. Makes 6 sandwiches.

1 sandwich: 390 Calories; 7 g Total Fat (2 g Mono, 1.5 g Poly, 2 g Sat); 110 mg Cholesterol; 51 g Carbohydrate; 5 g Fibre; 34 g Protein; 1350 mg Sodium

1. Chicken Couscous Cakes, page 163
2. Barley Bean Rolls, page 92
3. Italian Rice Cups, page 230

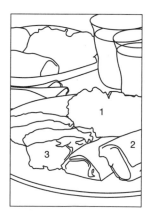

Raspberry Chicken

Rah, rah raspberry! Three cheers for this MVI (most valuable ingredient). Sweet yet tangy, all the stats agree—this dish is a sure winner!

Raspberry jam	1/2 cup	125 mL
Dry (or alcohol-free) white wine	1/3 cup	75 mL
Raspberry red wine vinegar	1/4 cup	60 mL
Soy sauce	1 tbsp.	15 mL
Dijon mustard	1 tsp.	5 mL
Garlic clove, minced (or 1/4 tsp., 1 mL, powder)	1	1
Chicken legs, back attached (about 11 oz., 310 g, each), skin removed	4	4
Water	2 tbsp.	30 mL
Cornstarch	1 tbsp.	15 mL

Chopped fresh parsley, for garnish

Combine first 6 ingredients in small bowl. Transfer to large resealable freezer bag. Add chicken. Seal bag. Turn until coated. Let stand in refrigerator for at least 4 hours or overnight, turning occasionally. Transfer chicken with raspberry mixture to 1 1/2 to 2 quart (1.5 to 2 L) slow cooker. Cook, covered, on Low for 6 to 8 hours or High for 3 to 4 hours. Remove chicken to serving dish with slotted spoon or tongs. Cover to keep warm. Skim fat from sauce.

Stir water into cornstarch in small cup. Add to slow cooker. Stir. Cook, covered, on High for about 5 minutes until boiling and thickened. Pour over chicken.

Garnish with parsley. Serves 4.

1 serving: 525 Calories; 15 g Total Fat (4.7 g Mono, 3.8 g Poly, 3.9 g Sat); 250 mg Cholesterol; 29 g Carbohydrate; trace Fibre; 62 g Protein; 607 mg Sodium

1. Chicken Enchiladas, page 222
2. Trendy Tacos, page 200
3. Fajitas, page 223
4. Breakfast Burrito, page 91
5. Chicken Burritos, page 219
6. Mexican Chicken Bundles, page 220
7. Empanadas, page 22

Mushroom Chicken Sauce

This delicious sauce cooks while you're out and about. Put some pasta on when you get home and dinner's on the table in minutes!

Bacon slices, diced	6	6
Cooking oil	1 tbsp.	15 mL
Chopped onion	1 cup	250 mL
Sliced fresh white mushrooms	3 cups	750 mL
Paprika	1 tsp.	5 mL
Garlic cloves, minced (or 1/2 tsp., 2 mL, powder)	2	2
All-purpose flour	3 tbsp.	45 mL
Salt	1/4 tsp.	1 mL
Pepper	1/4 tsp.	1 mL
Boneless, skinless chicken thighs, cut into 3/4 inch (2 cm) cubes	1 1/2 lbs.	680 g
Dry (or alcohol-free) white wine	1/2 cup	125 mL
Prepared chicken broth	1/2 cup	125 mL
Frozen peas	1/2 cup	125 mL
Chopped fresh parsley (or 1 tbsp., 15 mL, flakes)	1/4 cup	60 mL
Sour cream	1/4 cup	60 mL

Cook bacon in large frying pan on medium for about 5 minutes, stirring occasionally, until almost crisp. Transfer with slotted spoon to paper towels to drain. Drain and discard drippings from pan.

Heat cooking oil in same frying pan on medium. Add onion. Cook for 5 to 10 minutes, stirring often, until softened.

Add next 3 ingredients. Cook for about 5 minutes, stirring occasionally, until mushrooms are softened. Add bacon. Stir. Spread evenly in 3 1/2 to 4 quart (3.5 to 4 L) slow cooker.

Combine next 3 ingredients in large resealable freezer bag. Add chicken. Seal bag. Toss until coated. Arrange chicken over mushroom mixture. Discard any remaining flour mixture.

Pour wine and broth over chicken. Cook, covered, on Low for 8 to 9 hours or on High for 4 to 4 1/2 hours.

Add remaining 3 ingredients. Stir. Cook, covered, on High for about 10 minutes until heated through. Makes about 5 1/4 cups (1.3 L).

1 cup (250 mL): 344 Calories; 17.7 g Total Fat (6.7 g Mono, 3.5 g Poly, 5.3 g Sat); 100 mg Cholesterol; 11 g Carbohydrate; 2 g Fibre; 30 g Protein; 413 mg Sodium

Pictured on page 107.

Chicken Fricassee

Any fine French chef will tell you that fricassee is meat stewed in a white cream sauce. But never worry that this dish will pale by comparison—the carrot, red pepper and peas add nice shots of colour.

Chopped carrot	2 cups	500 mL
Chopped celery	1 1/2 cups	375 mL
Chopped red pepper	1 1/2 cups	375 mL
Boneless, skinless chicken breast halves, halved	1 lb.	454 g
Boneless, skinless chicken thighs	1 lb.	454 g
Sliced leek (white part only)	3 1/2 cups	875 mL
Butter (or hard margarine)	3 tbsp.	45 mL
Garlic cloves, minced (or 1/2 tsp., 2 mL, powder), optional	2	2
All-purpose flour	1/4 cup	60 mL
Prepared chicken broth	2 cups	500 mL
Dry (or alcohol-free) white wine	1/4 cup	60 mL
Can of artichoke hearts (14 oz., 398 mL), drained and halved	1	1
Dried thyme	1 tsp.	5 mL
Seasoned salt	1 tsp.	5 mL
Pepper	1/4 tsp.	1 mL
Frozen peas	2 cups	500 mL
Can of evaporated milk (5 1/2 oz., 160 mL)	1	1

Layer first 6 ingredients, in order given, in 4 to 5 quart (4 to 5 L) slow cooker.

Melt butter in medium saucepan on medium. Add garlic. Heat and stir for about 1 minute until fragrant.

Add flour. Heat and stir for 1 minute.

Slowly add broth and wine, stirring constantly, until smooth. Heat and stir for about 7 minutes until boiling and thickened. Remove from heat.

Add next 4 ingredients. Stir. Pour over chicken mixture in slow cooker. Cook, covered, on Low for 8 to 9 hours or on High for 4 to 4 1/2 hours.

Add peas and evaporated milk. Stir. Cook, covered, on High for about 15 minutes until peas are tender. Serves 8.

1 serving: 342 Calories; 11.9 g Total Fat (3.6 g Mono, 1.7 g Poly, 5.3 g Sat); 87 mg Cholesterol; 27 g Carbohydrate; 7 g Fibre; 31 g Protein; 622 mg Sodium

Cranberry Chicken

Take it slow with this cranberry-sauced chicken. Just let the flavours spend the day mingling in your slow cooker and you'll have a dinner that's worth the wait.

Chopped carrot	3/4 cup	175 mL
Chopped onion	3/4 cup	175 mL
Can of whole cranberry sauce (14 oz., 398 mL)	1	1
Hickory barbecue sauce	1/2 cup	125 mL
Ketchup	1/2 cup	125 mL
Brown sugar, packed	1/3 cup	75 mL
Dijon mustard	2 tbsp.	30 mL
Lemon juice	1 tbsp.	15 mL
Dried crushed chilies	1/2 tsp.	2 mL
Chicken legs, back attached (about 11 oz., 310 g, each), skin removed	6	6
Dried sage	1 tsp.	5 mL
Garlic powder	1/2 tsp.	2 mL
Pepper	1/2 tsp.	2 mL

Chopped fresh parsley, for garnish

Put carrot and onion into 4 to 5 quart (4 to 5 L) slow cooker.

Combine next 7 ingredients in medium bowl.

Sprinkle both sides of chicken with next 3 ingredients. Arrange 3 chicken legs over vegetables. Spoon half of cranberry mixture over chicken. Repeat with remaining chicken and cranberry mixture. Cook, covered, on Low for 6 to 7 hours or on High for 3 to 3 1/2 hours. Transfer chicken with slotted spoon to serving dish. Spoon vegetables around chicken. Skim and discard fat from sauce. Serve sauce on the side.

Garnish chicken and vegetables with parsley. Serves 6.

1 serving: 620 Calories; 15.4 g Total Fat (4.7 g Mono, 3.8 g Poly, 3.9 g Sat); 250 mg Cholesterol; 57 g Carbohydrate; 2 g Fibre; 63 g Protein; 844 mg Sodium

Pictured on page 107.

Chicken Rice Casserole

Get the classic flavour of a cheesy Parmesan and garlic risotto—without all that stirring! Your nearest and dearest will never suspect that your slow cooker did all the work.

Long grain brown rice	1 1/2 cups	375 mL
Chopped onion	1 cup	250 mL
Chopped red pepper	1 cup	250 mL
Sliced carrot (1/4 inch, 6 mm, thick slices)	1 cup	250 mL
Fresh (or frozen) whole green beans	4 cups	1 L
All-purpose flour	1/4 cup	60 mL
Grated Parmesan cheese	1/4 cup	60 mL
Paprika	1 1/2 tsp.	7 mL
Garlic powder	1/2 tsp.	2 mL
Pepper	1/2 tsp.	2 mL
Boneless, skinless chicken breast halves, halved	1 lb.	454 g
Boneless, skinless chicken thighs	1 lb.	454 g
Cooking oil	1 tbsp.	15 mL
Prepared chicken broth	1 1/2 cups	375 mL
Can of condensed cream of mushroom soup (10 oz., 284 mL)	1	1
Dry (or alcohol-free) white wine	1/3 cup	75 mL

Combine first 4 ingredients in greased 5 to 7 quart (5 to 7 L) slow cooker.

Layer green beans over rice mixture.

Combine next 5 ingredients in large resealable freezer bag. Add chicken. Seal bag. Toss until coated. Remove chicken. Reserve any remaining flour mixture.

Heat cooking oil in large frying pan on medium. Add chicken. Cook for 2 to 3 minutes per side until browned. Arrange chicken over green beans. Sprinkle with reserved flour mixture.

Combine remaining 3 ingredients in same frying pan. Cook on medium for about 5 minutes, stirring occasionally and scraping any brown bits from bottom of pan, until smooth. Pour over chicken. Cook, covered, on Low for 7 to 8 hours or on High for 3 1/2 to 4 hours. Serves 8.

1 serving: 400 Calories; 11.5 g Total Fat (4.0 g Mono, 2.8 g Poly, 3.0 g Sat); 73 mg Cholesterol; 41 g Carbohydrate; 5 g Fibre; 31 g Protein; 519 mg Sodium

Recipe Index

C

Q

R

Index   **301**

Measurement Tables

Throughout this book measurements are given in Conventional and Metric measure. To compensate for differences between the two measurements due to rounding, a full metric measure is not always used. The cup used is the standard 8 fluid ounce. Temperature is given in degrees Fahrenheit and Celsius. Baking pan measurements are in inches and centimetres as well as quarts and litres. An exact metric conversion is given below as well as the working equivalent (Metric Standard Measure).

Spoons

Conventional Measure	Metric Exact Conversion Millilitre (mL)	Metric Standard Measure Millilitre (mL)
1/8 teaspoon (tsp.)	0.6 mL	0.5 mL
1/4 teaspoon (tsp.)	1.2 mL	1 mL
1/2 teaspoon (tsp.)	2.4 mL	2 mL
1 teaspoon (tsp.)	4.7 mL	5 mL
2 teaspoons (tsp.)	9.4 mL	10 mL
1 tablespoon (tbsp.)	14.2 mL	15 mL

Cups

Conventional Measure	Metric Exact Conversion Millilitre (mL)	Metric Standard Measure Millilitre (mL)
1/4 cup (4 tbsp.)	56.8 mL	60 mL
1/3 cup (5 1/3 tbsp.)	75.6 mL	75 mL
1/2 cup (8 tbsp.)	113.7 mL	125 mL
2/3 cup (10 2/3 tbsp.)	151.2 mL	150 mL
3/4 cup (12 tbsp.)	170.5 mL	175 mL
1 cup (16 tbsp.)	227.3 mL	250 mL
4 1/2 cups	1022.9 mL	1000 mL (1 L)

Dry Measurements

Conventional Measure Ounces (oz.)	Metric Exact Conversion Grams (g)	Metric Standard Measure Grams (g)
1 oz.	28.3 g	28 g
2 oz.	56.7 g	57 g
3 oz.	85.0 g	85 g
4 oz.	113.4 g	125 g
5 oz.	141.7 g	140 g
6 oz.	170.1 g	170 g
7 oz.	198.4 g	200 g
8 oz.	226.8 g	250 g
16 oz.	453.6 g	500 g
32 oz.	907.2 g	1000 g (1 kg)

Oven Temperatures

Fahrenheit (°F)	Celsius (°C)
175°	80°
200°	95°
225°	110°
250°	120°
275°	140°
300°	150°
325°	160°
350°	175°
375°	190°
400°	200°
425°	220°
450°	230°
475°	240°
500°	260°

Pans

Conventional Inches	Metric Centimetres
8x8 inch	20x20 cm
9x9 inch	23x23 cm
9x13 inch	23x33 cm
10x15 inch	25x38 cm
11x17 inch	28x43 cm
8x2 inch round	20x5 cm
9x2 inch round	23x5 cm
10x4 1/2 inch tube	25x11 cm
8x4x3 inch loaf	20x10x7.5 cm
9x5x3 inch loaf	23x12.5x7.5 cm

Casseroles

CANADA & BRITAIN		UNITED STATES	
Standard Size Casserole	Exact Metric Measure	Standard Size Casserole	Exact Metric Measure
1 qt. (5 cups)	1.13 L	1 qt. (4 cups)	900 mL
1 1/2 qts. (7 1/2 cups)	1.69 L	1 1/2 qts. (6 cups)	1.35 L
2 qts. (10 cups)	2.25 L	2 qts. (8 cups)	1.8 L
2 1/2 qts. (12 1/2 cups)	2.81 L	2 1/2 qts. (10 cups)	2.25 L
3 qts. (15 cups)	3.38 L	3 qts. (12 cups)	2.7 L
4 qts. (20 cups)	4.5 L	4 qts. (16 cups)	3.6 L
5 qts. (25 cups)	5.63 L	5 qts. (20 cups)	4.5 L

Original Series

The original, most-trusted cookbooks in Canada!

Entertaining for the Holidays

Ring in the Christmas season with *Entertaining for the Holidays*! Whether you're planning a festive Christmas dinner, a New Year's Eve cocktail party or that yearly cookie exchange, these new and delicious recipes will help you entertain family and friends with ease and flair throughout the holidays.

Delicious Desserts

There's no better way to end a great meal than with a truly fabulous dessert. From cheesecakes and custards to pies and pastries, from fruit-filled treats to tasty drinks, there's a delectable dessert for every occasion in *Delicious Desserts*.

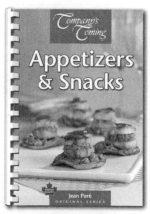

Appetizers & Snacks

Whether you're looking for a few hors d'oeuvres before a sit-down meal or a variety of tapas ideas for an impromptu cocktail party or backyard barbecue, we'll help you entertain with flair! *Appetizers & Snacks* features a great range of delicious and imaginative starters, including dips, spreads, canapés, wraps and skewers.

Easy Home Preserving

In times past, Grandma carefully canned each year's fruits and vegetables to feed her family over the winter. As commercially preserved food became available, canning became a lost art. Until now. Here are delicious, updated recipes to fill your pantry shelves with tasty colours and your heart with pride.

For a complete listing of our cookbooks, visit our website: **www.companyscoming.com**